'An investment in life is an investment in change . . .
When you are changing all the time, you've got to continue
to keep adjusting to change, which means that you are going
to be constantly facing new obstacles. That's the joy of living.
And once you are involved in the process of becoming,
there is no stopping. You're doomed! You're gone!
But what a fantastic journey!'

Leo Buscaglia

Leo Buscaglia was a native of California and an acclaimed professor of education at the University of Southern California. Beloved by millions for his influential message of the limitless power of human love, Buscaglia was the author of fifteen books, including the 4-million-copy bestseller *Loving Each Other*, He died in 1998.

LIVING, LOVING AND LEARNING

The art of being fully human

LEO BUSCAGLIA

PRELUDE

This edition published in 2017 by Prelude,
an imprint of Prelude Books Ltd
13 Carrington Road, Richmond, TW10 5AA, United Kingdom

www.preludebooks.co.uk

First published by Slack in 1982

ISBN: 978-1-911440-38-3

7 9 10 8 6

Publisher's Note

Living, Loving and Learning is a delightful collection of Leo Buscaglia's informative and amusing lectures, which were delivered worldwide between 1970 and 1981. This inspirational treasure is for all those eager to accept the challenge of life and to profit from the wonder of love.

Contents

Foreword

Nikos Kazantzakis suggests that ideal teachers are those who use themselves as bridges over which they invite their students to cross, then having facilitated their crossing, joyfully collapse, encouraging them to create bridges of their own.

The various presentations included in this volume represent such bridges. They are simply ideas, concepts and feelings which I shared in joy. They were delivered with the full understanding that they could be accepted, celebrated over, ignored, or rejected. It didn't matter.

They are restated here for those who may have missed them the first time, or for those who may desire to experience them a second time.

I am pleased that I shared these ideas. I am still rather awed that there were thousands who cared enough to listen. For me they represent ten exciting years of growth and sharing. In retrospect, I have no regrets, and I know, for better or worse, there will be more to come for I am determined to continue building bridges.

Leo Buscaglia

Introduction

Abundant thanks to Mr. Webster, who defines "introduction" as "preparing the way for a speech or a book." How very nice that I have been so often privileged to "prepare the way" for Leo Buscaglia—in print and in person.

On an earlier occasion, I wrote, "He is a man of many splendid facets—teacher, student, writer, reader, speaker, listener." Of all these, he seems most to exemplify his chosen profession—teaching. Leo teaches with enormous enthusiasm and sincerity and, best of all, he teaches by example. "If you will but listen," his message implies, "I will show you how rich and honorable life can be!"

A huge auditorium—or the space by his living room fire—or a stretch of beach—all are classrooms to Leo as he strives to educate—to *lead*—his students of all ages from all walks of life. At the University of Southern California he has more than once been voted "Outstanding Teacher of the Year" by the young people there; and, of course, young people *know*.

A friend and I met Leo's plane on one occasion, and as he moved away to claim his baggage, an elderly gentleman stepped up to me and asked, "Who is that man? I sat next to him on the airplane. Who is he?" After my brief sketch, he sighed and said, "I knew he was someone special. He seemed to be grading papers during the trip, and on each one he wrote something like 'Beautiful!'—'Fantastic!'—'Marvelous!' No one ever wrote anything like that on one of my papers. I wish they had." What that lovely old man was seeing was the ultimate professional in action, one who brings honor to the art of teaching; and, who is, in turn, honored by his colleagues and his students.

The same commitment and passion are found in the body of his written work. His definitive book on counseling, *The Disabled and their Parents: A Counseling Challenge*, moved one student to remark, "It's the only textbook that ever made me cry." Beginning with *Love* in 1972 and including the most recent *Personhood* in 1978, his books are carefully crafted marvels of scholarship generously laced with warmth and exuberance—and, yes, impatience at the wasted landscapes of lives lived in "quiet desperation."

More than once during the years that I have known Leo someone has come up to me and asked, "Is he really 'like that' all the time?" The question is genuine—and complex. And I find that my initial response has changed. Once an unequivocal and resounding "Yes!" is now, more accurately, "yes—and no."

Yes—he does not need to be in front of an audience, large or small, to be exuberant and thoughtful and funny and wise. Yes—the concern for human potential which audiences sense is profound and genuine. Yes—he is enjoying himself as much as anyone in the crowded room or auditorium. Yes—he is always impatient with bodies, minds, and purposes grown dormant. Yes—he believes with all his heart that "We are so much more than what we are." And, yes, one of the favorite words in his vocabulary is—YES! (I have a letter in my files to prove the point. It reads: Dear Betty Lou, yes, yes, *yes*! Love, Leo)

But, no, he is not "like that" all the time, for if he were, he would be no more than a delightful performer—in demand, popular, and hugely entertaining, but with a single message. Nothing could be more contrary to the facts. Leo's message, while based on universal truths, constantly changes, enlarges, takes on new dimension and depth, offers new challenge to us all.

From whence does this continual growth emerge? What is the wellspring? From people—old friends and new. From books—and the enchanters and enchantresses who write them. From nature—the prime example of change and growth and beauty. From his teachers: great mystics from Eastern cultures—and students—and children. From the music of the spheres! I think of Leo as a vast chunk of blotting paper, and nothing escapes imprinting itself on his quick eye, awesome intellect, and generous heart.

So convinced is he of the glory of a life that embraces change, he makes jolly well sure that others are rattled out of their comfortable complacency. I remember an encounter in Atlantic City, one of those late afternoon gatherings that seem to be a way of life at conferences. I was proudly and, I suspect, somewhat pompously regaling Leo with all I had been doing since last we met. He listened patiently, fixed me with a beady eye, and said, "Betty Lou, you must stop doing all the things you know you can do so well and try something new." I forthwith returned home and resigned from everything in sight, almost immediately embraced a number of new (and somewhat frightening) endeavors, and had the time of my life! Do I listen to Leo? You bet, and it has been my mission through the period of our friendship to urge others to listen carefully, too. With their minds and with their hearts.

And, no, he is not "like that" all the time—or one might assume that he requires constant reinforcement from the crowds who seem to gather wherever he goes. No one that I know can vanish quite so fast nor quite so far as Leo when he feels the need to replenish his energy, his awareness, his life forces. It may be for an evening in the solitude of his home; it may be a summer in a remote cabin on an Oregon river; it may be a year on an island with only his own reflections and those of the wise men from whom he is eager to learn. He is a very private person, but this privacy seems not so much an escape, a going away from, as a going *towards*—a time for rewakening and refreshing the senses, a getting ready for spiritual and cerebral growth and soaring.

Finally, the question, "Is he really 'like that' all the time?" has a man or myth connotation. No myth he—but very much a man, very much a human, who occasionally stumbles and bumbles about like the rest of us, who suffers through the complexities of bureaucratic twentieth century life like the rest of us, who has moments of private anguish like the rest of us, who is capable of anger at large and small inhumanities like the rest of us. *Unlike* the rest of us, he seems to glory in his own humanity and the weaknesses and imperfections and comedy that being human implies.

I have spoken of the man and not of the contents of this significant book even though I know the latter more intimately than the former. Of course, to know one is to know the other, at least in part. I will let the superb quality of the contents speak for themselves and will "prepare the way" only by saying—get ready to embark on a lovely adventure as you rejoice with Leo in a feast of life.

Betty Lou Kratoville

Love as a Behavior Modifier

I'm overwhelmed at the pleasure of being introduced by someone who knows how to pronounce my name. I love to talk about my name because it's one of those beautiful Italian names that has every letter in the alphabet. It's spelled B-u-s-c-a-g-l-i-a, and it's pronounced like everything. The best thing, I think, that has ever happened with it in terms of introductions was when I was making a long distance telephone call. The line was busy and the operator said she'd call me back as soon as the line was free. When she called back I picked up the phone and she said, "Would you please tell Dr. Box Car that his telephone call is ready?" I said, "Could that be Buscaglia?" She said, "Sir, it could be damned near anything."

Today I'm here to talk to you about love and I call this "Love In The Classroom." You're really very brave to allow me to come here and talk about love in the classroom. Usually I'm asked to disguise it or at least add something. You know, "Love, comma, As A Behavior Modifier." Then it sounds very scientific and it doesn't frighten anybody. It's the same way that, when I teach my love class on campus, all the faculty members giggle and poke me as I walk down the campus and say, "Hey, do you have a lab on Saturday?" I assure them that I don't.

I'd like to give you a little background about how I got started with this idea of love in the classroom. About five years ago I was interviewed by our Dean at the School of Education. He's a very official man, sitting behind a great big desk. I had just left the job as Director of Special Education in a large school district in California, having decided that I just wasn't an administrator, I was a teacher and that I wanted to get back to the classroom. I sat down and he said, "Buscaglia, what do you want to be doing in five years?" I immediately, without hesitation, said, "I'd like to be teaching a class in love." There was a pause, a silence, just like you are doing right now. Then he cleared his throat, and said, "And what else?"

Two years later I *was* teaching such a class. I had twenty students. I now have 200 students with a waiting list of 600. The last time we opened the class, it was full within the first twenty minutes of the registration period. It shows you what kind of enthusiasm and excitement there is for a class in love.

It always amazes me that every time the Educational Policy's Commission meets to decide the goals of American education, the first goal is always self-realization or self-actualization. But I have yet to find a class from elementary school right on up through graduate school on, for instance, "Who Am I?, 1A;" or, "What Am I Here For?, 1A;" or "What Is My Responsibility To Man, 1A;" or, if you will, "Love, 1A." As far as I know, we are the only school in the country, and possibly the world, which has a listing called, "*Love, 1A*," and I am the only professor crazy enough to teach it.

I don't teach this class. I learn in it. We get together on a great big rug and sit down and rap for two hours. It usually goes on into the night but we get involved for at least the formal two hours and share our knowledge, the thesis being that love is learned. Psychologists, sociologists and anthropologists have told us for years that love is learned. It isn't something that just happens spontaneously. I think we believe it is, and that's why we have so many hangups when it comes to human relationships. Yet, who teaches us to love? For one, the society in which we live, and that certainly varies. Our parents have taught us how to love. They are our first teachers, but they aren't always the best teachers. We may expect our parents to be perfect. Children always grow up expecting their parents to be perfect and then are very disappointed and disillusioned and really *angered* when they find out that these poor human beings are not. Maybe the point of arriving at adulthood is facing these two people, this man and this woman, and seeing them as ordinary human beings like ourselves, with hangups, with misconceptions, with tenderness, with joy, with sorrow, and with tears, accepting that they are just human beings. And the big thing is that if we *have* learned love from these people and from this society, we can unlearn it and relearn it; therefore, there is tremendous hope. There is tremendous hope for all of us, but somewhere along the line you've got to learn to love. I think many of these things are inside of us, and nothing that I'm going to say to you is going to be startlingly new. What you are going to find is that somebody is going to have nerve enough to stand up and say it, and maybe, therefore, release it in you so *you* can say, "That's the way I feel, too, and is it so wrong to feel this way?"

It's very interesting, but five years ago when I started talking of love, I was very lonely, indeed. I remember, and there are some people in this audience who were in that audience, when I stood up with a colleague from another university at a discussion about behavior modification versus affect. After I had been there screaming and crying about love, this gentleman turned to me and said, "Buscaglia, you are totally irrelevant." I think I have this singular distinction of being the only human being I know who is irrelevant. And it's groovy! But it's not so lonely now because more people are turning toward affect and studying it.

One of the most crucial developments for me was finding Leonard Silberman's book, *Crisis in the Classroom.* If you haven't read it, do, it's fantastic. It probably will be one of the most significant books in education. It's already on the bestseller list. Anyone who's interested in children must read Silberman's book, including parents. It should be available for everybody. This book is the result of a three-year Carnegie Grant given to Leonard Silberman, a great sociologist and a great psychologist, to find out what the state of American education is today. He concludes that considering that in America education is for all, we're doing a pretty damned good job when it comes to reading and writing, arithmetic and spelling. We're pretty good at that. But we fail miserably in teaching individuals how to be human beings. All we have to do is look around us and we can see this. The accent is definitely on the wrong syllable.

In my first year at USC I was teaching a class. It's an amazing thing—I imagine you feel the same thing I do—but you pick up vibrations from your audience. Things happen between you and your audience if you are talking *to* them and not *at* them. It would be marvelous if we could ever have a small group to sit down and really talk and relate instead of always these massive things. But nevertheless, you know that there are certain faces in an audience that come out, certain bodies that vibrate. They reach you and you reach them. Every once in a while, when you need support, you focus on them and receive a smile that says, "Go on man, you're doing fine." Then you can do all kinds of things. Well, I had such a person in this class, a beautiful young girl. She was always about the sixth row back and she'd sit there nodding. When I'd say something, she'd say, "Oh, yes!" You could hear her say "Wow," and then she'd write things down, and I'd think, "Oh, I'm really communicating with her—something beautiful is happening between us; it's going to be good; she's learning," etc. Then one day she stopped coming. I couldn't imagine what had happened and I kept looking for her but she wasn't there. Finally, I checked with the Dean of Women and she said, "Haven't you heard?" . . . this young lady whose papers were absolutely brilliant, whose mind was exciting, who had a creativity like you never dreamed . . . had gone to Pacific Palisades, an area where sheer cliffs fall into the sea. She parked her car, walked out, jumped off that cliff and splattered herself on the rocks below. It bothers me still and I thought to myself—what are we doing stuffing facts at people and forgetting that they are people, that they are human beings?

Carl Rogers recently said this very thing about missing the boat. He said,

> You know that I don't believe that anyone has ever taught anything to anyone. I question the efficacy of teaching. The only thing that I know is that anyone who wants to learn will learn. And maybe a teacher is a facilitator, a person who puts things down and shows people how exciting and wonderful it is and asks them to eat.

That's all you can do—you can't force anybody to eat, no matter what. No teacher has taught anything to anyone. People learn themselves. If we look at the word "educator," it comes from the Latin "educare," meaning to lead, to guide. That's what it means, to guide, to be enthusiastic yourself, to understand yourself and to put this stuff before others and to say, "Look how wonderful it is. Come on and join me in eating of it." Remember the line from Auntie Mame, "Life is a banquet and most damned fools are starving to death." So I begin to wonder, and it's become easier because more people like Silberman are making this statement and I don't sound so weird anymore.

Sorokin, a great sociologist, in the introduction to his book, *The Ways And Power Of Love*, makes this statement,

> The sensate minds, our minds, emphatically disbelieve in the power of love. It appears to us something illusionary—we call it self-deception, the opiate of a people's mind, idealistic thoughts and unscientific illusion. We are biased against all theories that try to prove the power of love in other positive forces in determining human behavior and personality, in influencing the course of biological, social, moral, and mental evolution, in affecting the direction of historical events, in shaping social institutions and cultures.

Then he proceeds to show us with scientific studies that it *is* so.

What a shame if all you believe exists is what can be shown statistically. I feel very sorry for you indeed if you are ruled only by what you can measure, because I'm intrigued by the unmeasurable. I'm intrigued by the dreams, not only by what is here. I don't give a damn what is here. I can see it. That's fine, measure it if you want to spend your life measuring it, but I am concerned with what is *out there*. There is so much that we don't see, we don't touch, we don't feel, we don't understand.

We assume that reality is the box we've been put in, and it's not, I assure you. Open the door sometime and look outside and see how much there is. The dream of today will be the reality of tomorrow. Yet, we've forgotten how to dream.

Buckminster Fuller was on our campus recently and this marvelous old man stood before us with just a little microphone—no notes, no blackboard, no audio-visual aids—and talked to us, enthralled an audience of three or four thousand for three hours and fifteen minutes nonstop. He said wonderful things about hope and about the future, and his last line was, "I have great hope for tomorrow. And my hope lies in the following three things—Truth, Youth, and Love." And he took off his little mike and walked off the stage. Truth, Youth, and Love. That will be our hope for tomorrow.

I think that people are beginning to look at this thing called love. And they are doing it unabashedly now. They are saying, "Maybe we have to return to this." Silberman says, "Affect is what is lacking. Schools are joyless and mindless places that are strangling children and destroying creativity and joy." They should be the most joyful places in the world because, you know, learning is the greatest joy. To learn something is fantastic because every time you learn something you become something new. You can't learn anything without having to readjust everything that you are around the new things that you've learned. So I'd like to talk to you for a little while about what I believe to be the loving human being. I could say the loving teacher, but I don't like that. You know, you are not only a teacher, you are a human being. Children can identify with people, with human beings. They have great difficulty identifying with teachers. When you start behaving like a teacher in a role, you find yourself saying all kinds of things you wish you hadn't said.

We prepare teachers. We prepare teachers all the time, and we send them out as beautiful human beings. Then we put them in a classroom, and you know what they come back saying? "I find myself saying all the horrible things that I hated the other teachers for saying, such as, 'We're waiting for Mary.' 'Johnny, we're waiting for you.' 'Oh, I love the way Johnny is sitting.' " You know? And you can just see Mary saying, "Wait, you old bag." We're waiting for Mary, indeed. Yet this is the role we find ourselves in. We find ourselves walking in front of the classroom and doing most of the talking because we are the teachers. And we still believe in the fallacy that we are teaching something. Kids will learn. All you have to do is guide them; that's your major function.

We are failing in schools of education because we're not helping teachers to shed the role of teachers and become human beings and to realize that they are guides. To the extent to which they recognize this, so will they be successful in the classroom because a kid can recognize a guide. I'll be tossing out some ideas about who is a loving person and then, if you want to attach it to who is a loving teacher, you know, that's up to you. But I'm more interested in who is a loving person.

First of all, I believe that probably the most important thing is that this loving person is a person who loves himself. Now people are going to sit up and say, "Oh, oh, what does he mean by that?" I'm not talking about the ego trip. I'm not talking about standing before a mirror and saying, "Mirror, mirror, on the wall, who's the fairest one of all? You're so right, mirror." You know that isn't what I'm talking about when I say a person who loves himself. I'm talking about a person who loves himself as being someone who realizes that you can only give away what you have, and so you damned well better work at getting something. You want to be the most educated, the most brilliant, the most exciting, the most versatile, the most creative individual in the world, because then you can give it away; and the only reason you have anything is to give it away.

"I can't teach you anything I don't know," is such an easy, silly, stupid thing to say. And yet, we have to say it. If I'm going to stand in front of a group, I had better know something or have something to say to them. If I'm going to be teaching a class in learning disabilities, I had better know something about learning disabilities. And I can only teach to my class what I know. Therefore, if I'm going to be a great teacher of learning disabilities, then I'm going to have to know every possible thing I can find in learning disabilities. And the wonderful thing about it is that I could teach everybody in this room everything I know, and yet I will not have lost anything—I will still know everything I know. So it isn't a matter of giving it away, it's a matter of sharing it. Fuller said the other night, "To teach you everything I know, I would need only fifteen hours." Imagine, this keen, fantastic mind—this great scientist, philosopher. "Fifteen hours and I can teach you everything I know." Yet if he does, he will not have lost what he knows; he still knows it.

It's the same thing with love. I could love everybody in this room if I had an opportunity to know you, with equal intensity, and I still would have the same amount of love and the same potential to love that I have right at this moment. I will have lost nothing. But I first must have it. If my love is neurotic, if it's possessive, if it's sick, all that I could teach you is neurotic, possessive, sick love. If my knowledge about anything is vast and endless, I can give that to you. And so my responsibility to me is to make myself enormous, full of knowledge, full of love, full of understanding, full of experience, full of everything so that I can give it to you and then you can take it and build from there.

No one ever takes my love class longer than one year. It's a year's course. You take what I have to give you. You put it together with what you have and you go out and you do something beautiful. I see personality, for instance, not only as what the psychologist or sociologist or anthropologist sees, but also as something that we have been missing for a long time. That something is uniqueness. I see everyone as being a unique individual, having within himself an X factor, for want of a better name. Something within the you of you that is only yours, that is different from everybody else, that causes you to see differently, to feel differently, to react differently. I believe that each of us has this and I only hope that you've been fortunate to have met someone along the line who's helped you to develop it. Because maybe the essence of education is not to stuff you with facts but to help you to discover your uniqueness, to teach you how to develop it, and then to show you how to give it away.

Imagine what this world would be like if everyone in this room had the opportunity to be encouraged to be a unique human being. But you know how it seems to me? That the essence of our educational system is to make everybody like everybody else. And when we've done that, we consider ourselves very lucky, indeed. You see it happening all the time! "I'm not interested in your uniqueness. I'm interested in knowing if I have succeeded in giving you me, and to the extent to which you can parrot me, I have been a successful teacher."

I always tell the story of the animal school, a fabulous story that educators have had around for years. We laugh about it but we never do anything about it. A rabbit, bird, fish, squirrel, duck, and so on, all decided to start a school. Everybody sat down to write a curriculum. The rabbit insisted that running had to be in the curriculum. The bird insisted that flying be in the curriculum. The fish insisted that swimming be in the curriculum. The squirrel insisted perpendicular tree climbing be in the curriculum. All the other animals wanted their specialty to be in the curriculum, too, so they put everything in and then made the glorious mistake of insisting that all the animals take all of the courses. The rabbit was magnificent in running; nobody could run like the rabbit. But they insisted that it was good intellectual and emotional discipline to teach the rabbit flying. So they insisted that the rabbit learn to fly and they put him on this branch and said, "Fly, rabbit!" And the poor old thing jumped off, broke a leg and fractured his skull. He became brain damaged and then he couldn't run very well, either. So instead of an A in running, he got a C in running. And he got a D in flying because he was trying. And the curriculum committee was happy. The same way with the bird—he could fly like a freak all over the place, do loops and loops, and he was making an A. But they insisted that this bird burrow holes in the ground like a gopher. Of course he broke his wings and his beak and everything else and then he couldn't fly. But they were perfectly happy to give him a C in flying, and so on. And you know who the Valedictorian of that graduating class was? A mentally retarded eel, because he could do almost everything fairly well. The owl dropped out and now votes "no" on all tax elections that have to do with schools.

We know this is wrong, yet nobody does anything about it. You may be a genius. You may be one of the greatest writers in the world but you can't get into a university unless you can pass trigonometry. For what! You can't get out of high school without passing this and this and this and this! You can't get out of elementary school without doing this and this! It isn't a matter of who you are. Look at the list of dropouts: William Faulkner, John F. Kennedy, Thomas Edison. They couldn't face school. It was a bummer. "I don't want to learn perpendicular tree climbing. I'm never going to climb a tree perpendicularly. I'm a bird. I can fly to the top of the tree without having to do that." "Never mind, it's good intellectual discipline."

As individuals we must not be satisfied with just becoming like everybody else. We must fight the system. For example, art supervisors. (I have nothing against art supervisors. I feel very sorry for them, poor old things.) I can remember when they used to come to my classroom in elementary school, and I'm sure you can remember it, too. You were given paper and the teacher would put up the drawing in front of you and you were really excited. It was going to be art time. You had all the Crayolas in front of you and you folded your hands and you waited. And soon this poor, haggard woman would come running in, because she had been to fourteen other classrooms that day teaching art. She ran in, her hat askew, and she'd huff and puff and she'd say, "Good morning, boys and girls. Today we are going to draw a tree." And all the kids would say, "Groovy, we're going to draw a tree!" And then she'd get up there with a green Crayola and she'd draw this great big green thing. And then she put a brown base on it and a few blades of grass. And she'd say, "There is the tree." And all the kids would look at it and they'd say, "That isn't a tree. That's a lollipop." But she said that was a tree and then she'd pass out these papers and say, "Now draw a tree." She didn't really say, "Draw a tree;" she said, "Draw *my* tree." And the sooner you found out that's what she meant and could reproduce this lollipop and hand it to her, the sooner you would get an A.

But here was little Junior who knew that wasn't a tree because he'd seen a tree such as this art teacher had never experienced! He'd fallen out of a tree, chewed a tree, smelled a tree, sat in the branches of a tree, listened to the wind blow through the leaves of a tree, and he knew that her tree was a lollipop. So he got magenta, and orange, and blue, and purple, and green, and he scribbled it all over his page and happily brought it up and gave it to her. She looked at it and she said, "Oh my God, brain damaged—Special Class."

How long does it take somebody to realize that what they're really saying is, "To pass, I want you to reproduce my tree." And so it goes through the first grade, second, third, fourth, fifth, and right on into seminars in graduate school. I teach seminars in graduate school. It's amazing how people have learned to parrot by then. Think? Don't be ridiculous. They can give you the facts, verbatum, just as you've given it to them. And you can't blame those students because that's what they've been taught. You say to them, "Be creative," and they're fearful. "He doesn't really mean that, does he?" And so what happens to our uniqueness, what happens to our tree? All this beautiful uniqueness has gone right down the drain. Everybody is like everybody else and everybody is happy. R.D. Laing says, "We are satisfied when we've made people like ourselves out of our children: frustrated, sick, blind, deaf, but with high I.Q.'s."

The loving person is not satisfied only to be unique, to develop his uniqueness, and to fight to maintain his uniqueness. He wants to be the greatest, because he realizes that this is something he can give away. I don't know how many of you know R.D. Laing's writing. *The Politics of Experience* is one of the most beautiful gifts I could give you. It's a little paperback, and is unbelievable. In this book he talks of human potential and the development of human potential. He makes a statement, which I think is one of the most beautiful I have ever read. And it isn't italicized or underlined. It's just part of the way he writes. He says,

> We think much less than what we know. We know much less than what we love. We love much less than what there is. And to this precise extent, we are much less than what we are.

How do you like that?

Exciting things are happening all over the country. There are institutes for the development of the human person. Herbert Otto, Fitzgerald, and Carl Rogers are all doing it and receiving no pay. They are setting up institutes and are living off royalties of their own books to find ways to help people develop their potential again because otherwise we're going to be lost. This is what Fuller is screaming. "Let's go back to us." We have potential to see, and to feel, and to touch, and to smell, that we've never dreamed of. But we've forgotten how to do it. These are the things we want to be doing, if we care about ourselves and if we love ourselves.

I had a very unique experience about seven years ago. I sold everything. I did something that everyone said was absolute madness. I sold everything that our culture says has value . . . the hi-fi set, the records, the books, the insurance policy, the car, and I collected a little bit of money and I spent two years going around the world. I spent most of that time in Asia because I knew less about Asia than any other place in the world. Two thirds of the world is not the Western World. These people think differently, and feel differently, and understand differently, and you learn a lot about yourself and about the human condition when you get out of our Western environment and find out that there are people and areas where even Jesus is unknown. There are places that have no idea what our Western culture is thinking about, doing, feeling; and yet these are the people that we're meeting head on in conflict. Their words are not our words. Their feelings are not our feelings. But nevertheless, I learned a lot by traveling these countries.

I learned something really unique when I was in Cambodia. I was in Angkor Wat looking at the wonderful Buddhist ruins. They're fantastic—great tremendous Buddha heads being devoured by Banyan trees, and monkeys swinging in the air, everything wild and open and beautiful, ruins such as you never dreamed of—a completely new world for us. There I met a French woman who stayed on after the French had left Cambodia. She said, "You know, Leo, if you really want to experience Cambodia, don't sit here in the ruins. This is all well and good, but get out and see the people. Find out what they're doing. And you've come just at a good time because the Monsoons are coming and the way of life changes." And she said, "Go down to the Tonle Sap," (If you remember in your geography, it's a great lake that makes up most of Cambodia) "because the people are now involved in a very interesting thing. When the Monsoons come, the great rains wash away all their houses and take away everything they have. Then these people get on communal rafts, several families together. The rains come, the rafts rise, and they go right on living, but now communally." I thought, wouldn't that be beautiful, if six months out of every year some of us could live together? I can see you thinking—Who the hell wants to live with my neighbor? But maybe it would be a beautiful thing to live with a neighbor and to find out what it is again to be dependent upon people and how beautiful it is to be able to say to someone, "I need you." We think to be a grownup we must be independent and not need anyone *And that's why we're all dying of loneliness.* How wonderful to be needed! And how great to need and to be able to say to someone, "I need." I have no hangup about saying I need all of you, every single one of you. The bummer is that our lives only pass occasionally. But the greatest experiences in my life are when lives intersect and two human beings are able to communicate.

But the Cambodians learn this early, and nature teaches it to them. Nature is a great teacher. All we have to do is to read *Walden* again. Thoreau's marvelous line, "Oh God, to reach the point of death only to find that you have never lived at all." Think about that. Anyway, I went down there on a bicycle, and there they were. And I thought I'd like to help these people move in order to become a part of their community. The French woman that I was talking to laughed and said, "Yes, help them move." What do they have to move? Nature has taught them that the only thing they have is from the top of their head to the bottom of their feet . . . themselves. Not things. They can't collect things because every year the Monsoon comes and there is no place to bring these things. And I couldn't help thinking to myself, "What would you do, Buscaglia, if a Monsoon were to come to Los Angeles next week? What would you take? Your color TV set? Your automobile? The spittoon that Aunt

Matilda left you?" The only thing you've got to take is you. In Los Angeles we have earthquakes of which you've undoubtedly heard. It's a very unique sensation, I guarantee you, to find that you have no control over where you're going to go or where the house is going to go.

Just recently, we had a severe earthquake in Los Angeles and it very much affected my home. The ceiling in the living room fell in and the fireplace collapsed on itself. We didn't have water, and so on. Suddenly it taught us the value of things; it showed us again that *things* were stupid, that all we had was us. I walked out of the house with everything falling around me. It was just dawn and there was a streak of light coming over the sky. I have a great big flowering peach in the back yard. Well there it was, flowering its head off. And all of a sudden, in a split second it occurred to me, "You know, the beautiful world is going to go on, with or without you, man." And for me, it was worth the price of the earthquake to be reminded again.

Philosophers and psychologists have told us this for years. "You are all you have. Therefore, make yourself the most beautiful, tender, wonderful, fantastic person in the world. And then you will always survive." Remember Medea in the Greek tragedy? Remember the line of that beautiful play, when everything is gone and the oracle comes to her and says, "Medea, what is left? Everything is destroyed, everything is gone." She says, "What is left? There is me." *There's* a woman for you! "What do you mean what is left? Everything is left. *I* am left!" When we recognize this importance of you again returning to a respect for you, a love for you, and realizing that all things come from you, then you can give to others. Then you have arrived at a very important place because if you don't like you, you can always learn again to like you. You can create a new you. You can do it. If you don't like the set you're involved with, strike it and put up a new one. If you don't like the cast of characters you're involved with, get rid of them and start a new bunch. But *you've* got to do it. And it's all yours. Okay, so that's number one. And if we've got nothing else said but that, I would believe with all my heart that I'd left something with you anyway. A return to you.

Saint-Exupéry, the French philosopher, makes a magnificent statement in one of his books, and he's written some lovely ones. He said, "Perhaps love," (and you can substitute education if you want to,) "is the process of my leading you gently back to yourself." I have no definition of love, but that comes the closest to being the healthiest one I've heard. "Perhaps love is the process of my leading you gently back to yourself." Not to whom I want you to be, but to who you are.

I don't know how many of you know the City Lights Book Store in San Francisco but it's an incredible place, and if you ever visit there, you must go. It's three floors of paperbacks. You've never imagined there were so many paperbacks in the world but it has one section that's uniquely its own. It's a section that publishes manuscripts from people like you and me, who are frustrated poets and frustrated writers. In one section they offer poetry. All you have to do is mimeograph it on a piece of paper and staple it together, put it on the shelf, and you can put in one corner "five cents please" to cover the cost of paper. And then people buy them and really read them.

I was wandering by and I saw a book, the title of which really threw me. There were only five hundred copies of it printed, and I'll explain how it happened later. But the name of the book was, *I Am Neither A Sacrilege Or A Privilege. I May Not Be Competent or Excellent, But I Am Present.* That just came right off the shelf and smacked me across the face. And I thought—well good for you! I opened up the book and I found out that it was written by a young lady who signed her name only as Michelle. She did the drawings and she did the poems, and I slipped through it in my usual way, skipping the preface and everything and diving right into the heart of it. And I found a poem that attracted my eye and I read it! This is what it said:

My happiness is me, not you.
Not only because you may be temporary,
But also because you want me to be what I am not.

Think of this in terms of the educator.

I cannot be happy when I change
Merely to satisfy your selfishness.
Nor can I feel content when you criticise me for not thinking your thoughts,
Or for seeing like you do.
You call me a rebel.
And yet each time I have rejected your beliefs
You have rebelled against mine.
I do not try to mold your mind.
I know you are trying hard enough to be just you.
And I cannot allow you to tell me what to be—for I am concentrating on being me.

And then listen to this line:

You said that I was transparent
And easily forgotten.
But why then did you try to use my lifetime,
To prove to yourself who you are?

Think about that as teachers. Think about that as lovers. Think about that as citizens. Think about that as fathers and mothers. Applicable to all. "You said that I was transparent and easily forgotten. But why then did you try to use my lifetime to prove to yourself who you are."

Then I went back to find out, who is Michelle? And I found this line in the introduction. It says:

> Michelle! You were with us for such a short time before choosing that fog-swept beach to continue on your way. It was July 1967, and you were only 20.

She left us twenty five poems. She found it too hard to be "just me."
We hope these poems are presented as you wish, Michelle. You are present, we love you, and we need you, and we promise we will remember, until we meet again . . . . San Francisco, July 1969.

I think the second big thing about a loving individual is that he frees himself from labels. You know, man is an incredible creature, really incredible. He does wonderful things. He has a marvelous creative mind. He created time but then was ruled by time. I have to keep watching the clock because at a certain time coffee will be out there, and at a certain time you're supposed to come in here, and at a certain time we're supposed to be going to lunch. And it's twelve o'clock and you're not hungry but you eat, because it's twelve. And you're sitting down in a classroom—you have this in elementary schools and secondary schools—you're really grooving on a lesson and something fantastic is happening. Then the bell rings and everybody runs out. "It's seven o'clock. Oh, I'm sorry, I've got to leave now." If a mother is sitting in your office weeping and gnashing her teeth but you've got someone else waiting outside, you've got to tell this mother, "I'm sorry, you've got to stop in the middle of your story. I'll see you tomorrow at 8:04."

We have classrooms that are ruled by this—education ruled by the clock. Nine o'clock to 9:05 we will have Share and Tell; 9:05 to 9:30 we will have Reading Group One. From 9:30 to 9:45 we will have Reading Group Two. And Reading Group One may really be excited about something and the teacher says, "Oh my goodness, it's half past. All right, Reading Group Two." Nobody learns by the clock. No one learns in blocks. This is not arithmetic time. This is not spelling time. You learn everything together. But we still go on. Now you must turn your mind onto spelling and then go onto the Westward Movement.

Up the Westward Movement! But we still do that kind of thing! We create time and then we become the slaves of time.

We also create words and words are supposed to free us. Words are supposed to make us able to communicate. But words became boxes and bags in which we became trapped. It was a wonderful thing to hear Buckminster Fuller say that, "I was being so involved in words as other people had taught me them that I went away into a ghetto in Chicago, away from family and friends, for two years to clear my mind of words and to find the words that were right for me. So that when I spoke them I knew they were mine and not somebody else's." What a fantastic statement. And now he worships words but we're trapped with words.

When Timothy Leary was doing fantastic work at Harvard in psycholinguistics, he made a statement that I will never forget. He said, "Words are the freezing of reality." We teach children the meaning of words before they are able to truly understand them and rebel. And in words we teach fear, we teach prejudice, we teach all kinds of things. And all somebody has to do now, talking about words being a distancing phenomena, is to poke you and to say, "Watch out for this Buscaglia cat, because he's on the list; he's a Communist." Pow, off I would go. And everything I said would be filtered through this word Communism. And yet, an Eastern University did a study in the United States on what Communism means. They went around talking to the common man and saying, "Would you define Communism?" And some people were really frightened to death. You should read that study—it's hilarious. One woman said, "Well, I don't really know what it means, but there hadn't better be any in Washington." Now there's a good definition of Communism. And they were all about that caliber. All you have to do is be a Communist and you'll be run out of town. And you don't even know what it means. And so it is, with "Black man," with "Chicano," with "Protestants," with "Catholics," with "Jews." All you have to do is hear a label and you think you know everything about them.

No one ever bothers to say, "Does he cry? Does he feel? Does he understand? Does he have hopes? Does he love his kids?" *Words.*

You, if you are a loving person, will rule words and not allow words to rule you. You will tell yourself what this word means only after you find out by experience what it means; not by believing what people have told you it means.

When I was growing up I had a very interesting experience. I was born in Los Angeles of immigrant parents, Italians of course, and we lived in the city, right in the ghetto area with all the other Italians. It was really kind of beautiful. When I was a year old my parents had to return to Italy and so they took me with them. They went back to their little home city which is at the base of the Swiss Italian Alps, a little whistle stop called Aosta. Many trains pass through on their way to Milano and Torino but they don't stop at Aosta. Only one stops at Aosta. I remember as kids we used to go there and watch the trains zooming through. But everybody in that little village knew everybody else. Wine was the main thing in that village and so everybody was stoned out of their minds all the time. It was beautiful. The fantastic thing is how everybody cared about everybody. The closeness. If Maria was sick, everybody in the city knew it and brought her chickens and squash and took care of her kids, and so on, because it was a community of people, of human beings. Then after I was five, my parents decided to return to Los Angeles. And so they did. Talk about a cultural shock! Here I was all of a sudden dumped in the city where no one cared if I lived or died. An interesting thing about labels is that at that time the Mafia was running rampant and every Italian was considered to be a member of the Mafia. I was called a "dago" and a "wop." You know, kids would say, "Get away, you smelly wop." I remember going to my father and saying, "Papa, what's a wop? What's a dago?" He said, "Never mind, Felice. Don't let it bother you. People have names. They call you names but it doesn't mean anything."

But it *did* bother me because it was a distancing phenomena and they never learned anything about me by calling me "wop" and "dago." They didn't know, for instance, that Mama was an opera singer in the old country and that Papa was a waiter. We had an enormous family, enough to cast any opera. She'd sit at the piano and play the complete operas and we'd all take the roles. We'd all sing and it was beautiful. By the time I was eight, I knew five operas. I could take any role. But they didn't know that by calling me a "dago" and a "wop."

And they didn't know, also, that Mama believed that garlic was the cure-all for any disease. Every morning she'd line us all up and she'd rub garlic on a little hankie and tie it around our necks. We'd say, "Mama, don't do that." She'd say, "Shut up." (She was a very loving woman.) She'd send us off to school with this garlic around our necks and we stunk to high heaven. But I want to tell you a secret; I was never sick a day. My theory about it is that no one ever got close enough to me to pass the germs. It was incredible, because I remember getting an award at the end of elementary school for never having missed a day. Now I've become very sophisticated and I don't have garlic on and I get a cold every year. They didn't know that when they called me a "wop" and a "dago."

They also didn't know that Papa was a great patriarch. On Sundays, when he was home, we would sit around a big table that he'd never let us leave without telling him something new we had learned that day. So, beforehand we'd be washing our hands and I'd say to my sisters, "What did you learn today?" and they'd say, "Nothing." And I'd say, "Well, we better learn something!" So we'd go over and get the encyclopedia and we'd flip to something, like, the population of Nepal is one million, and then we'd sit there and think about it while eating. And boy, talk about the meals! Mama never in her life prepared a TV dinner. I remember string beans piled so high that I couldn't see my sister across the table. We'd eat and when finally it was over, Papa would push this dish away and turn to me and say "Felice, what did you learn today?" And I'd say, "The population of Nepal is one . . ." And nothing was ever insignificant to this man! He would turn to my mother and he'd say, "Mama, did you know . . ." And we'd look at them and we'd say, "Freaks!" And we'd ask our friends, "Do you have to tell your parents about Nepal?" They'd say, "Our parents don't care if we know anything or not." But I want to tell you a secret. Even now, when Felice goes to bed, maybe he's worked twenty-nine hours that day and he's exhausted, but when he crawls into the sheets, that gorgeous moment before you go off, he says to himself, "Felice, what did you learn today?" And if I can't answer that question, I have to get up and get the encyclopedia and flip to something and learn something new.

Maybe that's what education is all about. Who knows? But they didn't know that by calling me a "dago" and a "wop." If you want to know about me, you've got to get into my head, and if I want to know about you, I can't say, "She is fat. She is thin. She is a Jew. She is a Catholic." She is more than that. And those of us who are interested in Special Education know these damned labels. We call children mentally retarded. What does that tell us? I have never seen a mentally retarded child. I've only seen children, all different. We call them students and, therefore, we think we can stand in front of a classroom and teach them all in the same way. *Labels*. The loving individual frees himself from labels. He says, "No more."

I also think this loving individual is one who abhors waste and will not stand for hypocrisy. Rosten says, "It is the weak who are cruel. Gentleness can only be expected from the strong." It is true. We need strong people in education who are willing to stand up and say, "This is hypocritical, and we won't do it anymore." People who are willing to get on the line and say, "No, we've got to have changes or we are going to destroy ourselves." It's like walking into doom. We are teaching for today and we're already in tomorrow. No wonder we're participating in self-destruction.

I want to tell you a little story about hypocrisy. At a time when I was training student teachers, I was working with a young woman who was not only a teacher, but the most beautiful human being I ever saw, so enthusiastic about getting in a classroom she couldn't stand it. Finally she got her own classroom, that dreamy day that we can all go back and remember. She walked into her first grade classroom and flipped to this beautiful thing called The Curriculum Guide. You know, to me, books are holy, but I wouldn't hesitate one moment having the biggest book burning of Curriculum Guides in the world. But anyway, she looked in this damned Curriculum Guide and she saw that in the first grade in this school district in California, (and this was only a couple of years ago,) you teach the store. The s-t-o-r-e. She said, "That is impossible. I don't believe it. I can't believe they teach the store." These kids were raised in a store. They were wheeled around in carts when they were two and three years old. They knocked over Campbell's soup cans. They did all kinds of crazy things in stores. They go there every day with Mama. And the grand culminating unit has you go to the supermarket.

Well, she said, "This is impossible." But there it was in black and white. It said you do all kinds of things. You make a store and you make little clay bananas. The kids have been eating real bananas all their lives and slipping on banana peels, but you spend six weeks making clay bananas. A waste of human potential. Anyway, she sat down because she was a good teacher and she sided with her kids, and she said, "Kids." She thought she'd get up their enthusiasm. She said, "How would you like to study the store?" And they said, "Rotten." And you know, the moral of that is that little kids are not as stupid now as we used to be. McLuhan has shown us that on the average, children have five thousand hours of TV before reaching kindergarten. They have seen people die in technicolor. They have seen disasters. They have seen wars and massacres. And then we bring them in and we try to interest them and get their motivation by reading, "Spot said, 'Oh, Oh.' "

So she said a beautiful thing. She said, "Okay then, what would you like to do?" And one kid said, "Oh, my father works for Jet Propulsion and he could bring us a rocket ship and we could set it up in the classroom and we could get it working and we could all fly to the moon." And all the kids said, "Groovy!" So she thought for a minute and said, "Okay, you tell your dad to bring it." And the next day he brought in a little miniature rocket ship and set it up. He explained to them what this rocket ship was all about, what they were trying to do, what the parts of it were. And he wrote the vocabulary on the board. This was the first grade! You're not supposed to study rocket ships until you're in the university. What on earth are they going to study when they get to the university if they can do this in the first grade? Well, we can't allow this to happen! This is terrible. They've got to go to the Supermarket! But you should have seen what was going on. They were learning mathematical concepts you couldn't believe. They went on a Saturday field trip to Jet Propulsion and they were shown real rocket ships. They were put through them; their minds were freaking.

I also feel very sorry for supervisors who have to protect this Curriculum Guide because that's their job, poor things. They want to do something better but, here it is, and your job is to teach this stuff, and their job is to carry the book around and abide by it. So the supervisor walked in and looked around this room. Here was a rocket ship, things on the wall you never saw, a spelling list that even she didn't know half of, formulas on the walls, all kinds of weird things which the kids understood and were really happy doing. And she asked Mrs. W., "Where is your store?" And then Mrs. W. said, "Well, you know, the kids wanted to fly to the moon, so we set up a . . . .". The supervisor said, "Nevertheless, Mrs. W., did you read your Curriculum Guide? It states that the first unit in this school district is the store." Then she smiled broadly because she was a sweet little creature and she said, "You *will* have one, won't you dear?"

So Mrs. W. said to the kids, "Do you want Mrs. W. to be here next year?" And they said, "Oh, yes." "Okay, then we've got to have a store." And you know, the kids were beautiful (as they always are when you're a human being). They said, "Great. But let's do it fast." So they did a six-week unit in two days! They knocked together those damned boxes and they made the clay bananas and then, hypocrisy on hypocrisy, every time the supervisor came, they would walk over to the cash register and say, "Would you like to buy some clay bananas?" And after she left satisfied, they went on flying to the moon. We can't afford to allow these things to go on anymore. Some teacher has got to stand up and say, "I will not take them to another store. If you want to take them, *you* take them."

I also think that a loving individual is spontaneous. The one thing that I would like to see more than anything else in the world is your returning again to your initial spontaneity, the spontaneity of a kid who said what he felt and what he thought and was easily adjustable to what other people were thinking and feeling. Getting back to looking at each other again. We are so ruled by what people tell us we must be that we have forgotten who we are.

Emily Post tells us, "A young lady does not laugh out loud boisterously, she titters." Well if you want to laugh and fall on the floor and beat the rug, you do it; it's good. "You do not get angry: human beings do not get angry." You keep it all in and then you go to a mental institution! It's far better to go into a classroom if you're not feeling good, and rather than spend the entire day with your neck all tied up in knots and your eyes bulging, saying, "Children, sit down," to state right at the beginning, "Look kids, take it easy today because teacher's hung." If you do, you're going to find out that kids can understand this and they'll creep around the room quietly because they can identify with a human being. And they'll poke each other when someone makes a noise and say, "Stop it. Teacher's hung." But teacher has got to reveal herself as a human being. If you feel like laughing at a kid's joke, laugh. It always amazes me when I would be in schools and the teachers would die laughing in the teachers' room over something that Johnny said. But they didn't let Johnny see them die laughing. They'd say, "Johnny, that's enough now!" Why couldn't they laugh to Johnny? It's funny. "Johnny, you're a clown. Now sit down and shut up." Why can't you just be yourself? Be spontaneous. But we have to ask permission for everything because we can't trust our own feelings anymore.

It always amuses me when I speak to formal groups. Before I walk in, I can always tell what's going to happen. I have a big thing about touching people. Spontaneity, you know, I believe in it. When you touch someone you know they are. The existentialist movement had reached its zenith when it said, "In order to become you, you must kill someone or kill yourself because then you know you were being." If you could jump off a building, you must have lived. Because we're so alienated that no one looks at you, no one touches you, no one recognizes you in the environment. You are the invisible man. You don't have to go to that extent. Just touch someone. It's good. You know, in Europe everybody hugs each other and kisses each other. In my family at Christmas time and all the holidays, everyone walks in the door and everybody kisses everybody. That's the first thing that's done from the little bambinos to grandpa. We exchange diseases and it's beautiful. But Emily has told us that a lady extends her hand to a gentleman if she so desires. *Distancing phenomena!*

If you want to see how alienated we've become, watch when a door of an elevator opens. Everyone's standing like zombies, facing straight forward, hands to the sides. "Don't you dare reach this way because you may touch someone." Heaven forbid! So we all stand at attention and the door opens and then one gets out and another goes in and turns around immediately and faces forward. Who told you you had to face forward? You know, I love to walk in an elevator and turn around with my back to the door! And I look at everybody and I say, "Hi! Wouldn't it be marvelous if the elevator got stuck and we could all get to know each other?" And then an incredible thing happens. The door opens on the next floor and everybody gets off! "There's a crazy man in the elevator. He wants to know us!"

Return to being human again and to liking the human state. Returning to saying you are human and I am human, we do crazy things. But we're beautiful. We're the most beautiful creatures on earth. Being human is good. When I go to formal groups there's always Mrs. So and So who meets me at the door. And she says, "Oh, Dr. Buscaglia. How nice." That's our introduction, with her hands to her sides. So I reach for her hand. And she thinks, "What's he doing?" I reach around and I grab her hand and I put my hand over it and very nervously she takes me into the living room where all the other ladies are sitting in a semi-circle. And they're all in Position #1—one knee over the other knee, hands gently folded on the lap, and a smile on the face. They learn that, you see. It would have been much more comfortable if they could have flopped on the floor, leaning on an elbow. But I never saw that; I would freak if I did. Position #1. *Everybody.*

What's happening to us, what's happening to our spontaneity? You feel happy, you tell people you're happy. You walk into your classroom and you say, "I feel so joyous today we're all going to freak all day long." Why not let them know? Laugh! Cry! Another thing; men don't cry. *Who* said? I cry at everything. My students always know I've read their papers because when I find something that moves me, they see little tear drops there. I very much identify with Don Quixote de la Mancha. This beautiful cat used to charge windmills! Of course you can't beat a windmill, but he didn't know that. He'd charge the windmill and it would knock him on his hoopy-doopy. But he'd get up again and he'd charge again and he'd get knocked on his hoopy-doopy. My feeling as I put that book away was that he may have had a calloused hoopy-doopy but, boy, he lived a wonderful life. He knew that he was alive. "Oh God, to have reached the point of death, only to find that you have never lived at all." That wasn't true of Don Quixote. He knew it! And when they did the beautiful musical, "The Man of La Mancha," at the ending when he died, all the people he loved were around him and they were all weeping for his death. *He* wasn't weeping for his death, for he had lived. Finally he rose up and from the back of the stage came a great staircase with its ray of light shining down. He picked up his lance and looked at everybody he loved and he smiled and walked up into this light. And the orchestra and chorus were all blaring away "The Impossible Dream." I was sitting there in the audience and tears were streaming down my cheeks. And a woman next to me poked her husband. She said, "Look honey. That man is crying." And I thought, "You silly . . . . I'll give you something to really go home and tell your friends about." So I took out my hankie and really wailed. That blew her mind! She may forget Don Quixote, but she'll never forget me!

I think the loving person must return to spontaneity—return to touching each other, to holding each other, to smiling at each other, to thinking of each other, to caring about each other. You know, anybody in this audience who wants to hug me, they're free to, and I won't disintegrate. I'll stand here all day if it means getting back to us, getting us together again. Hugs are good, they feel nice, and if you don't believe it, try it.

Then I think, lastly, the loving individual is one who hasn't forgotten his own needs. That's an amazing thing to say. But we do have needs. We don't really need too much physically, even though we believe we do, but we spend all of our time satisfying our physical needs and those of our children. We eat well, we usually have nice houses to live in. We take care of all those things. We go to the doctor if we're feeling bad. But the most important needs of all are what we need in ourselves—a need to be seen, a need to be known, a need to be recognized, a need for achievement, a need to enjoy our world, a need to see the continual wonder of life, a need to be able to see how wonderful it is to be alive. But we've forgotten how to look at each other anymore. We don't look at each other; we don't listen to each other; we don't touch each other, heaven forbid. Not even our kids. You know in our culture when a kid is three years old we take him off our lap and we say, "you don't do that kind of thing; it's mushy stuff. You don't do it with your father. Get off my lap, what are you doing kissing your father at three years old? You ought to be a man. Men don't kiss men." You may not know this, but in Los Angeles there is a city ordinance that makes it a misdemeanor for two men to embrace. How do you like that? That's where we've gone. One of these days you are going to read in the newspaper that I've been jailed because I embraced everybody. I hug our Dean. It freaks his mind. Nobody ever gets across the desk to him; it's two miles long. I see him in an elevator and I say, "Hi, Dean," and I put my arms around him.

It's understandable how out of this generation, how out of our time, a philosophy like early existentialism developed, and that is our tremendous alienation. Am I Real? Do I Exist? Because nobody looks at me. Nobody touches me. I speak to people and they don't hear me. They're looking over my shoulder to see who else is there. Nobody looks in my eyes anymore, I'm alone and I'm dying of loneliness. As Schweitzer says, "We are all so much together and yet we are all dying of loneliness."

Many years ago Thornton Wilder wrote a beautiful play called "Our Town." And in his play he said an incredible thing. Remember the scene where little Emily dies? She goes to the graveyard and is told "Emily, you can return for one day in your life. Which day would you like?" and she said, "Oh, I remember how happy I was on my twelfth birthday. I'd like to come back on my twelfth birthday." And all the people in the graveyard say, "Emily, don't do it. Don't do it Emily." But she wants to. She wants to see Mama again and Papa again. So the scene switches, and there she is, twelve years old, and she's gone back in time to that wonderful day she remembers. She comes down the stairs in a pretty dress with her curls bouncing. But her mother is so busy making the cake for her birthday that she cannot stop long enough to look at her. She says, "Mama, look at me. I'm the birthday girl." And Mama says, "Fine, birthday girl. Sit down and have your breakfast." And Emily stands there and says, "Mama, look at me." But Mama doesn't. Papa comes in and he's so busy making money for her that he's never looked at her either and neither does brother because he's so involved in his own bag, he can't stop to look at her. The scene ends with her standing in the middle of the stage saying, "Please somebody, just look at me. I don't need the cake or the money. Please look at me." And nobody does and when they don't, she turns to her mother once more and says, "Please Mama?" so then she turns and says, "Take me away. I've forgotten what it was like to be human. Nobody looks at anybody. Nobody cares anymore, do they?"

It's come to that! Your kids grow so fast you don't see them. All of a sudden you look up and there's an adolescent or someone ready to be married. And you've missed the joy of looking in their faces because you've been so busy, running around making things for them, that you've missed the joy. You know, we are a culture of goal seekers. I have news for you—it's not the goal, it's the *trip* that's life. Life is the trip; life is the process; life is getting there. Well you've gotten there and what have you got? People to look up to you. You have a Cadillac. A Cadillac is a cold bedfellow . . . The doors and the steering wheel get in the way. But we've forgotten what it's like to look at each other, to touch each other, to relate to each other, to care about each other. It's no wonder we're all dying of loneliness.

I always use the little thing of share and tell time which could be one of the most beautiful ways of seeing kids in your classroom. But it's so abused. The teacher's doing her enrollment because the principal says that her enrollment must be in by 9:15 and this is the time she chooses to have share and tell. Little Sally comes in with a rock and she says, "I found a rock on the way to school." The teacher says, "Fine. Put it on the science table." But we could take the rock and look at it and we could say, "What is a rock? Sally, where does a rock come from? Who made a rock?" We could stop everything for the day and everything would revolve around that rock because all things that are, are in all things. You don't have to create artificial nonsense. It's all here, not outside. It's all there. All that there is to know is in a tree. All that there is to know is in a human being. The little kid stands in front of the classroom and says, "Yesterday my daddy hit my mommy with a hammer and they called the ambulance and they took her away and she's in the hospital." And the teacher says, "All right, next." It's time to see kids, and you know how little it takes? All you have to do is to look down and say, "yes," or "What a beautiful dress." Little Sally will wear that dress every day for the rest of the year because you have seen it.

Ellis Page did a wonderful study in affect where he took his class and he divided it up into three groups, A, B, and C. On every Group A paper, he put only a grade. Remember writing those wonderful papers that were a bit of you and then finding that you got it back with only a grade on it? An A, a B, or a C, a D, an F? Meaningless. You look somewhere for a little spot of spaghetti or maybe a place where some coffee has been spilled on it so you can see that maybe the guy had read it. Group B, he gave them a grade and a word, like: good, fine, excellent, nice work. With Group C he stopped and wrote each of them a letter and he said, "Dear Johnny: Your syntax is atrocious. Your grammar is not to be believed. Your spelling is nonexistent. And your punctuation is like James Joyce. But you know, as I was sitting in bed last night talking to my wife, I said, 'Sally, he has the most beautiful ideas in this paper. And I'm really going to try and help him develop it.' Sincerely yours, Teacher." And if somebody did something really beautiful, he wrote down, "Thank you. You continually blow my mind. Such a good paper with so many good ideas. Keep it up. I can't wait to hear what you're going to say next." And then he did a statistical study. Group A remained the same. Group B were stationary and Group C grew and became.

Look at the study "Pygmalion in the Classroom." It's another paperback. Every educator should read it. Talk about expectation! These people from Harvard came in and said to all the teachers like yourselves, "Now we are going to go in your classroom and we are going to give (and this isn't the exact statement, this is the essence), we're going to be giving a test to be called the Harvard Test of Intellectual Spurts. And what this test is going to measure is which kids in your classroom are going to grow intellectually during the year that they're in your class. And it will pick them out. It never fails. We'll be able to tell you, and think of what a help this will be." So they went in and they gave some old obsolete I.Q. tests. After they finished giving it, they threw it in the garbage can. Then they just took five names at random from roll books and sat down at an interview. They said to a teacher, "Now these are the kids that are going to spurt this semester: Juanita Rodriquez." "Juanita Rodriquez couldn't spurt if you put her in a cannon," said her teacher. "Nevertheless, the Harvard Tests of Intellectual Spurts never fail," said the bigwigs. And do you know what happened? Every name that they had put on that list spurted all over the walls. Which shows you, you get what you expect. You walk into a class and you say, "These dumb kids. They'll never learn anything." You walk in saying, "These kids will and can learn; it's my challenge to bring them to that table and to show them how fantastic it is." We all have a need for achievement and recognition. We've got to be able to do something and the greatest thing is joy in the work.

It's too bad when you go to work and you don't love it, especially in our profession. If you don't get excited every morning about getting into that room with all those little kids with their bright eyes waiting for you to help them to get to that table, then *get the hell out of education!* Do something where you're not going to be coming into contact with little kids and killing them at an early age. There are other things you can do . . . . . but let children alone. We all need to be recognized for what we're doing, for our work. Every once in a while we need someone to come up to us and say, "You're beautiful, kid. That was well done. That's nice." And don't forget, if *you* need it, so do your kids. How about giving up this nonsense about twenty-seven wrong. Wrong. Wrong. Wrong. Wrong. Wrong. Getting back papers with all of the things marked wrong. What about marking those things that are right? "You've got two right, Johnny. Good for you. Wow!" How about letting them know they can do something well and building from that instead of always counting on what is wrong? Accentuating what is right and what is good is just as simple. In fact, you have less wrist movements.

We all have a need for freedom, too. One thing that Thoreau says is that: "Birds never sing in caves." And neither do we. In order to learn, you've got to be free. You've got to be free to experiment, to try, free to make mistakes. That's the way you learn. I can understand your mistakes and I profit greatly from mine. The secret is not to make the same one twice. But I need to be free to experiment and to *try*. Give me that chance. Allow me the freedom to be and to be myself and to find the joy in need. Don't give me your hangups! Let me find and overcome my own!

I'd like to close with a quote from Leo Rosten which, in his very special way, says it all:

> In some way, however, small and secret, each of us is a little mad . . . Everyone is lonely at bottom and cries to be understood; but we can never entirely understand someone else, and each of us remains part stranger even to those who love us . . . It is the weak who are cruel; gentleness is to be expected only from the strong . . . Those who do not know fear are not

really brave, for courage is the capacity to confront what can be imagined . . . You can understand people better if you look at them—no matter how old or impressive they may be—as if they are children. For most of us never mature; we simply grow taller . . . Happiness comes only when we push our brains and hearts to the farthest reaches of which we are capable . . . The purpose of life is to matter—to count, to stand for something, to have it make some difference that we lived at all.

On Becoming You

Tonight I'm going to talk to you about some of my ideas on counseling, and we might call the talk "On Becoming You." One of my big frustrations is that there was a time when the group was small; I could get near you, we could share ideas, and I could get some feedback from you. I've asked to have the lights on because I like to see your eyeballs! This way, with such a large audience, I have to count on your vibrations—so will you shake a little bit every now and then?

Now let's "become."

How I see counseling can be summed up briefly in a simple statement. I don't know how many of you have read Saint Exupéry's book called *Wind, Sand & Stars*. If you haven't, may I, with all my heart, give you this book? It's beautiful, and it gets more fantastic with years. There's one chapter in *Wind, Sand & Stars* in which, without defining it, Saint Exupéry talks about love as love has never been talked about before—in simple childlike terms. He says, "Perhaps love is the process of my leading you gently back to yourself." I have always hesitated to define love because I see love as limitless, and as you become bigger and more beautiful and more expansive, so does love. And so to limit it by a definition seemed really bad. But I like Saint Exupéry's definition, and I believe that maybe this is what teaching is and certainly this is what counseling is—a process not of my wanting to make you over in my image as I would desire you but my wanting to lead you back to yourself, to what you are, to your uniqueness, to your original beauty.

So many people are trying to make us what they want us to be, and after a while we just give up and decide that maybe this is what is called "adjustment." *Heaven forbid!* Occasionally, someone will rebel and say, "No! I will not become what you want me to be. I am, and I will remain. I want to become who I am."

I wonder sometimes: no matter how we rebel, are we really what we are or are we only what we are told we are? We know as teachers and psychologists that we *learn* to be human—and who are our teachers? First of all, our teachers are our parents, our family. We can't any more, unless we are still children, blame our parents and family, because parents and family are only human beings like everybody else. They have their own problems. They have their own frailties. They have their own strengths and their own weaknesses. They taught us only what they know. You will finally grow up when you can walk up to the man who is your father or woman who is your mother and say, "You know, with all your hang-ups, I love you."

A father came to me once after a love class, and he said, "I want to see you." He took me out in the back parking lot, put his arms around me, hugged me, and began to cry. He said, "The other day my son, after twenty-one years said, 'You know, Dad, I really love you,' and I know he meant it. I knew it was there, but you taught him how to say it." So we can no longer have any regrets about the fact that we were not taught, or that perhaps we were not always taught adequately. We can always learn!

I feel very strongly about change. As teachers we must believe in change, must know it is possible, or we wouldn't be teaching—because education is a constant process of change. Every single time you "teach" something to someone, it is ingested, something is done with it, and a new human being emerges. I can't understand why people aren't just dying to learn, why it isn't the greatest adventure in the world—because it's the process of becoming. Every time we learn something new, we become something new. I'm different tonight for having been here today. I'm overwhelmed with Texas hospitality, and I'm not just tossing off compliments, because that's not for me. This afternoon I was rewriting my whole speech. I had thrown the other one in the wastebasket and started all over again pounding out a new speech for you because the other one wasn't right. While I was doing this, the phone kept ringing, people kept saying, "We're going to get together tonight—be with us." "We're over here in such and such a place—will you come over and see us? We'd like to talk with you." Little notes under the door. This is fantastic! Human beings are relating with human beings, and that's what it's all about.

And so I have changed. I am no longer the person who walked in this morning. I'm something new because I experienced something new with you. This is why learning is such an exciting thing, why it shouldn't be a drag. Every book leads you to new books. Every time you hear a piece of music, there are ten thousand new pieces it introduces you to—you listen to one Beethoven sonata, and you're lost! You read one book of poetry, really hear it, and you're lost! And then there are thousands of things to read, to see, to do, to touch, to feel. And each one of them makes you a different human being. So are you really what you are or are you what you are learning and what people have told you through time that you are?

Saint Exupéry's statement about leading you back to yourself is a beautiful thing but in order to be led back to yourself, you must decide, to some extent, who you feel comfortable becoming. I promise you that if you dedicate yourself to the process of finding out who you are, it will be the most exciting trip you've ever taken in your life. You're not so bad. You're not evil. You're pretty good. Think about this morning's talk—what did I say that was new? Come on, face it, I said nothing that was new. I simply suggested what was already inside of you, and the reaction from doing such a thing is that people open up and say, "It's true. Why have I been keeping it caged up? I'm gonna go over and hug 'em." That's all it is. It's a release of what is there. It says it's all right for you to be you. It's giving yourself permission to be and grow. Isn't it incredible that we have to wait to have somebody say that it's all right for you to be you?

We know it's true that with words we can tell little children what they are and who they are. Wendell Johnson has suggested that with words we can make children stutterers. From nonverbal speech, for instance, when a little kid comes in, excited, and says, "Oh, M-M-Mom, there's an ice c-c-cream man outside." The mother stops him and says, "Now you stop and say it over again slowly—you're stuttering." If he hears this enough times, he's going to believe that he really does stutter, and pretty soon he's going to internalize stuttering and say, "I am a stutterer." We have created a stutterer. We can also do this by continually saying to someone, "You are beautiful, you are beautiful, you are beautiful." If enough people tell you that, you will begin to behave as beautiful. You'll stand up straighter, you'll be prouder of yourself. But "You are ugly, you are ugly, you are ugly," will make you bend, become smaller and smaller, until you will become ugly. "You're wrong! You're stupid!" will make you wrong and stupid.

This morning I said, "Love is learned," and it is. Love is learned, fear is learned, prejudice is learned, hate is learned, concern is learned, responsibility is learned, commitment is learned, respect is learned, kindness and gentility are learned. All of these are learned in a society, in the home, in a relationship. You start language processes at the age of one and two when words begin to appear and take on emotional and intellectual content. And those are the words with which you will structure your environment and with which you will live for the rest of your life and which will either cage you or free you. This is tremendously important.

Also, self-concept—who we are—we learn mostly from our family. This is why the family has an enormous responsibility. No one ever teaches people how to be parents. All of a sudden you have a baby, and there you are. While you may feel the responsibility, you can only filter this through who you are. That's why I said this morning the most important thing in the world is that you make yourself the greatest, grandest, most wonderful, loving person in the world because this is what you are going to be giving to your children—to all those you meet.

I believe that you control your destiny, that you can be what you want to be. You can also stop and say, "No, I won't do it. I won't behave this way any more. I'm lonely, and I need people around me. Maybe I have to change my methods of behaving." And then you do it—volitionally. You try it out. I did an interesting experiment with a bunch of students in a psycholinguistics class. I had them make two lists of words. On one side we made a list we called "bummer words." They were words we were never going to use again—words like "hate," "despair," "no." We made a dictionary of bummer words, all the really bad words. On the other side we had another dictionary, and we wrote positive words like love. We decided these were the words we were going to use to talk about people and to talk and think about ourselves and to talk about the world. We began this process, and fantastic things happened—to the way we felt, to the way we made other people feel, and the interaction among us. All this simply by using positive words!

No family is free of hang-ups. No family is free of fear. No family is free of prejudice. Let's take a look at the so-called normal family with all of its problems and let's see what happens when a child arrives who is different, who is impaired, who is handicapped. Strange things happen, and happen right from the beginning. There's a fantastic study going on now, and I'm dying to see the final results. At UCLA Medical Center, when an impaired child is born, a counselor is sent immediately to the bedside—not next week, not next New Year's, but the next moment—to talk with the parents, to tell them not to fear, to tell them that there are educational possibilities, to give them hope, to spark again the candle that is flickering, that delicate balance that occurs when something like this happens.

We are in a culture that stresses perfection. We're from the Doris Day-Rock Hudson school. MGM has taught us our concept of what is beautiful and what is good, and this scares me to death because MGM has also taught us our concept of what is love. They really have, and people go around believing that love is a process of chasing some female for six reels. You've all seen it—Rock is always chasing Doris, and Doris is always running around screechingly protecting something—I've never figured out just what. Finally, at the last reel he wins her over, and he takes her up in his arms, and he carries her across the threshold. And it says, "The End." And, boy, is it! What I would like to see is what happens after it said, "The End," for I'm positive that anyone who runs for six reels is frigid, and anyone crazy enough to chase her must be impotent.

In this study at UCLA, they are counting time, they are counting minutes. How long does it take, for instance, when a "normal" child is born to bring this child to the mother. They are finding that there is a significantly longer gap of time with the imperfect child. None of the nurses want to take the child in. When it's a perfect little child, they skip in and say, "Look, Mrs. Jones, what you've got here," and everyone's happy. But when a handicapped child is born, a sort of gloom settles over the hospital. What does this tell mama right away, even before she sees the child? It tells her that she's rejected, that something's wrong. There isn't a woman in the world who, when she got her little bundle of joy alone, didn't open up the blanket and count the toes and the fingers. Mothers have expressed very strongly that birth is a gift—"I give something to the world, I give something to my husband, to my family." So right away there is fear. "What's wrong with this kid?" There is guilt. "Is it something I've done?" We're human.

This idea of perfection frightens me. We're almost afraid to do anything anymore because we can't do it perfectly. Maslow says there are marvelous peak experiences that we all should be experiencing, like creating a pot in ceramics or painting a picture and putting it over here and saying, "That's an extension of me." There's another existentialist theory that says, "I must be because I have done something. I have created something—therefore, I am." Yet we don't want to do this because we're afraid it isn't going to be good, it isn't going to be approved of. If you feel like smearing ink on a wall, you do it! It's you, and that's where you are at this moment, and be proud of it. Say, "That came out of me, it's my creation, I did it, and it is good." But we're afraid because we want things to be perfect. We want our children to be perfect.

Drawing from my own personal experiences, which is all I can do, I remember P.E. class in junior and senior high school. If there are any P.E. teachers here, I hope you hear me loud and clear. I will not deny anything I say because I mean it. I remember the striving for perfection. P.E. should be a place where we all should have an opportunity. If we can't throw a ball, then we learn to throw a ball the best we can. But that wasn't it—we were striving for perfection. There were always these big guys standing up there, and they were the stars. And there I was, skin and bones with my little bag of garlic around my neck and shorts that didn't fit and little skinny legs. I'd stand there in line waiting to be chosen, and I used to die every single day of my life. You remember, you all lined up, and there were the big guys standing there with their chests out, and they'd say, "I choose you," and "I choose you," and you saw the line going away, and you were still standing there. Finally it got down to two people, one other little guy and you. And then they'd say, "Okay, I'll take Buscaglia," or "I'll take the old Wop," and you'd step out of line dying because you were not the image of the athlete, you were not the image of perfection they were striving for. That goes with you all along the line. At school now there is a student who is a gymnast. He was almost in the Olympic games last year. He has a clubfoot. In every other way in this world he is as perfect as you can imagine, a body that would be the envy of anyone, a beautiful mind, fantastic crop of hair, sparkling, alert eyes. But he isn't a beautiful boy in his perception—he's a clubfoot. Somewhere along the line somebody missed the boat, and all he hears when he walks down the street is the clump of a foot even though almost no one else sees it. But if *he* sees it, then that's what he is. So this idea of perfection really turns me off.

As soon as this imperfect child is delivered or as soon as the family finds out they have an imperfect child, all kinds of things are brought to the fore. The loss of the ideal image, the fears of the future. What's in store for this kid? Will he get a job, will he ever learn, will he learn to read? These are real fears. Guilt: "What did I do—what did I have to do with it—was it diet—did I not take care of myself?" Confusion—and this is a big one—"*What do I do?*"

I spent six years counseling parents of exceptional children, and all I heard again and again and again from these confused people was how many professionals they had been to see. They went to this one, and they went to this one, and they went to this one, and they still had no information about their own kid. That's frightening. No one in the world will have more contact with the child than the parents. They are the ones who should know the most. But somehow there's some sort of guarded secret among professionals—"We mustn't let them know. I know about Johnny but let's not tell Mama." Well, Mama is going to be doing for Johnny, and she might as well be doing right for Johnny as wrong. It's about time that we recognized this and let parents know. My theory of counseling is let's keep our mouths shut but let's *show* them. Let's have a one-way mirror where a mama can sit and watch what a teacher is doing with a kid and then the teacher comes out and walks around and says, "Look, this is what I was doing, this is how I was reinforcing; maybe you can continue this at home." A team approach—that's the only way it's going to happen. No more mystery. We're working together for Johnny's benefit. Johnny needs every person he can get, so let's do it together. Not this feeling of confusion every single time. Doctor A told me this, Neurologist B told me this, Teacher C told me this.

I know many mothers who were actually told "Leave him alone, he'll get over it, he'll be all right, you're over-concerned, Mrs. Jones." Good God, nobody sees him like Mrs. Jones sees him! "He's falling, he's uncoordinated, he's not behaving like the other children, something's wrong, somebody help me." And so the parents go from pillar to post.

I don't know how many of you have read Pearl Buck's book about her little girl but it is a very, very important book that every educator should read. This is an educated, sensitive woman who took her child to a hundred different people. She travelled all over the world looking for help until finally someone leveled with her and said, "Look, Pearlie, old girl, your child is severely retarded, but let's do everything we can for her. Let's try to help her learn everything she can, but stop thinking she's going to be a genius. Now knock it off and let's get to work and do the best job we can for this kid. Let's not put any limits on her. Let's not say she can't learn—that's a lot of nonsense. But let's put all our energies toward doing everything we can and stop running all over the world." And she said, "Okay," and from that moment on it happened. But somebody's got to level with parents.

In addition to all of the hang-ups and the problems of the regular "normal" family, the family with a handicapped child has to cope with so many other things. Last year this was drawn to my attention dramatically when a mother said to me, "I have a severely cerebral-palsied child, and do you know I've never been out of the house for five minutes since that child was born? Every place we go I have to take him with us. I can't get a babysitter to sit with him; they're scared of him." What kind of life is this? Parents are people, too, and they need to get out; sometimes we forget about this. I told this story to my students, and I was mad. I beat on the blackboard, and I screamed about this, and one of the students said, "Why don't we start a babysitting set-up?" And so they started free babysitting for parents who had impaired children. The students weren't scared of these kids, and so they went in and sat and released the parents to go for an occasional snazzy dinner so that they would remember what it is like to be human and to be away and alone together. This is so important because the day is going to come when all the kids are gone, and Mama is going to sit across from Papa, and they're going to look at each other, and I'm afraid she's going to have to say, "Who the hell are you?" So busy has she been, so busy has he been.

It is no wonder, then, that parents are crying for help. Now anyone who is going to help anyone else—and it doesn't matter who you are—has to remember certain essential things. First of all, we must always remember that man is not a thing and stop dealing with people as if they are objects. We are frail, we are vulnerable, we are tender, we're easily spooked. It is so easy, because we are so frail, to put a hole in someone and make him suffer. But it's almost as easy to cover up the hole with the same finger that made it. It just depends on what side of the person you're on.

Man is so incredible. The defense mechanisms that we build to protect ourselves, the psychoanalytic theory of a symptom that says to the busy business man who feels his ulcers acting up, "Slow down, buddy." The symptom that says when you find yourself so anxious you can't talk to people, "Watch it, man, you're going too far. Sit down under an apple tree." I've heard of incredible defense mechanisms that people use, and woe be it to you, if you want to help somebody, if you say, "Oh, wise up. You know that isn't so." I remember a mother who sat across from me and in all honesty she said, "I understand at last. I have insight at last why I have an exceptional child and why I am tied to the home and why my husband and I can't do things together and why all these other things, and that is because God chose me out of all the people in the world because he knew that I could take care of this child." Talk about a defense mechanism! And you would be a pretty poor human being if you said, "Now, Mrs. Jones, wise up."

Sometimes we are supported—Albee calls it the delicate balance, and I like that—sometimes we are just balancing delicately and far be it from anybody to think he is so great that he can shake that balance, take away a defense mechanism. I remember once a counselor saying to a parent, "You must accept your exceptional child. You must." And she said, "Why the hell must I?" And that's the best answer I ever heard. What do you mean, "I must?" So man is not a thing, he is a wonder, and must be treated gently.

Secondly, man is capable of change, and if you don't believe this, you are in the wrong profession. Every day you should be seeing the world in a new personal way. The tree outside your house is never the same—so *look* at it! There have never been two sunsets exactly the same since the beginning of time—so *look* at it! Everything is in a process of change, including you. The other day I was on a beach with some of my students, and one of them picked up an old, dried-out starfish, and with great care he put it back in the water. He said, "Oh, it's just dried out but when it gets moisture again, it's going to come back to life." And then he thought for a minute, and he turned to me, and he said, "You know, Leo, maybe that's the whole process of becoming, maybe we get to the point where we sort of dry out, and all we need is a little more moisture to get us started again." When I picked myself off the sand, I said, "Wow!" Maybe this is what it's all about.

An investment in life is an investment in change, and I can't be concerned with dying because I'm too damned busy living!

Let dying take care of itself. Don't ever believe that you are going to be peaceful—life is not like that. When you are changing all the time, you've got to continue to keep adjusting to change, which means that you are going to be constantly facing new obstacles. That's the joy of living. And once you are involved in the process of becoming, there is no stopping. You're doomed! You're gone! But what a fantastic journey! Every day is new. Every flower is new. Every face is new. Everything in the world is new, every morning of your life. Stop seeing it as a drag! In Japan, the running of water is a ceremony. We used to sit in a little hut when the tea ceremony took place, and our host would pick up a scoop of water and pour it into the teapot, and everybody would listen. The sound of the falling water would be almost overpoweringly exciting. I think of how many people run showers and water in the sinks every single day and never hear it. When was the last time you listened to water? It's beautiful! Go home tonight and open the faucet and listen.

Herbert Otto says, "Change and growth take place when a person has risked himself and dares to become involved with experimenting with his own life." Isn't that fantastic? A person has risked himself and dared to become involved with experimenting with his own life, trusting himself. To do this, to experiment with your own life, is very exhilarating, full of joy, full of happiness, full of wonder, and yet it's also spooky. It's also frightening because you are dealing with the unknown, and you are sharing complacency. You can sit back and say, "Everything's all right with me, got a good job, got a car," but then you decide you might change, this may no longer be your value—and so you're shaking complacency.

I have a very strong feeling that the opposite of love is not hate—it's apathy. It's not giving a damn. If somebody hates, they must feel something about me or they couldn't possibly hate. Therefore, there's some way in which I can communicate. But if they don't even see me, I'm finished—there's no way in which I can get to them. If you don't like the scene you're in, if you're unhappy, if you're lonely, if you don't feel that things are happening, change your scene. Paint a new backdrop. Surround yourself with new actors. Write a new play—and if it's not a good play, get the hell off the stage and write another one. There are millions of plays—as many as there are people.

And then man needs a guide. A teacher—and that includes parents—is a guide. I like to be called an educator. I hate to be called a professor. A professor professes, and there's too damn much professing going on. Education is from the Latin "educare" which means to lead, to guide, and that's what it should be. There's a table full of wonder. Education is the process of leading people to it. You can decorate the table, you can put all the food in the world on it but you can't make anybody eat. Carl Rogers says, "No one has ever taught anything to anybody," and it's true—you only teach yourself. The teacher who thinks that he or she has all the answers is the biggest bummer in the world! How marvelous when Junior asks a question that's brilliant, and the teacher says, "Wow! I don't know the answer but let's go together and find it." Maybe this is saying to somebody, "it's exciting to learn. You don't have to *know* everything. We will guide each other."

I have another theory. Our mental institutions are getting more and more full. I was on Suicide Prevention in Los Angeles, and my phone rang day and night, so something's wrong somewhere. We're missing the boat, and I think one of the reasons is this idea of, "I will love you, *if*." If everyone had just one single person in his life who says, "I will love you *no matter what.* I will love you if you are stupid, if you slip and fall on your face, if you do the wrong thing, if you make mistakes, if you behave like a human being—I will love you no matter," then we'll never end up in mental institutions. And this is what marriages should be. But are they? And this is what a family should be. But is it? Certainly society can never say that—it has too great a responsibility to too many. But just one person in your life that you can call. I love Robert Frost's definition of a family: "Home is a place that when you go there, they have to take you in." That's what a home should be—like "Come on in. Okay, you've been dumb, but I'm not going to say it; I love you, and I'll take you as you are." This is the kind of guide I'm talking about.

Man needs someone who cares about him. Again, just *one person*, but someone who really cares, and I'm not talking about a great big scene. I'm talking about little things, little ways of showing that you care. I've told you how easily satisfied we are—one finger mends the dike.

And man needs a feeling of achievement. We all do. We've got to be able to be recognized for doing something well. And somebody's got to point it out to us. Somebody has got to come up occasionally and pat us on the shoulder and say, "That's good. I really like that."

Then to learn and to change and to become, man also needs freedom. You've got to be free in order to learn. You've got to have people who are interested in your tree, not the lollipop tree, and you've got to be interested in their tree. "Show me your tree Johnny. Show me who you are, Johnny, and then I'll know where I can begin." We need to be free to *create*.

I had an incredible experience recently. I talked to a bunch of gifted kids in a California school district, and I ranted and raved in my usual fashion, and they sat there just sort of glued—the vibrations between us were incredible. After the morning session, the faculty took me to lunch. When I came back, the kids met me and said, "Oh, Dr. B., a terrible thing has happened. Remember the guy who was sitting right in front of you there?" And I said, "Oh yes, I'll never forget him, he was so with it." "Well, he's been thrown out of school for two weeks." I asked "Why?" It seems that in my lecture I had been talking about the way that you know something, really know it, is to experience it. And I said, "If you really want to know a tree, you've got to climb in the tree, you've got to feel the tree, sit in the branches, listen to the wind blow through the leaves. They you'll be able to say, 'I know that tree.' " And the boy had said, "Yeah, I'll remember that, there's where it's at." So during lunch time this little guy saw a tree and climbed up in it. The boys' vice principal passed by, saw him up there, dragged him down, and kicked him out of school.

I said, "Oh, there must be a mistake; there was a misunderstanding. I'll go talk to the boys' vice principal." I don't know why it is, but boys' vice principals are always ex-P.E. teachers. I went to the office where he was sitting with his bulging muscles, and I said, "I'm Dr. Buscaglia." He looked up at me, and he was furious. He said, "You're the man who comes onto this campus and tells kids to climb trees? You're a menace!" And I said, "Well, you don't understand. I think there was a little mis-" He shouted, "You're a menace! Telling kids to climb trees. They're revolting enough!" Well, I never got through to him, it was impossible, I couldn't deal with him. So I went to the house of this boy who now had two free weeks to climb trees. He said, "I think the thing I've learned from this is when to climb trees and when not to climb trees. Because this is a society that tells us, that puts up signs about when to do it and when not to do it. Man, I know that's true. I guess I just used bad judgment, didn't I?" He had listened, and he's going to have to adjust to the man in the office—but he's still climbing trees! There are ways to meet the needs of society, and there are ways to do your own thing.

And then I think that people need nurturing. I mean that in all honesty. We need to be loved. We need to be felt, we need to be touched, we need some sort of manifestation of love. Those of us in special education certainly know the studies that Skeels did, the wonderful work when he went into an orphanage for abandoned children. He had noticed that kids left alone in an orphanage got progressively more and more apathetic until they just ended up sitting. I.Q.-wise they were normal kids when they entered but after about a year and a half, their I.Q.'s dropped right down into the severely retarded range. He wondered, "What's happening?" So he took twelve kids—after much ado because they didn't want him to do it—and he left the rest of the kids there. He took these twelve across town to a home for retarded adolescent girls and gave each one of these kids to a little girl. These girls were no great shakes intellectually but they really cared. You know a lot of kids that are tremendously intelligent but will go nowhere—they have nothing else. And I know lots of other kids that are good, solid, average kids who have fabulous affect, and can turn people on, and they are going to fly! Skeels gave one of these abandoned kids to each of the girls who loved them to pieces and who cried when they put the little kids on the bus at the end of the day because they had to give them up. The only variable was the affect, nothing else was changed, just the fact that these kids were taken and loved and played with and independently seen. He has just written a paper which all of you should read called "Head Start on Head Start." In the paper he does a follow-up study on these twelve kids. Every one of the control group left in the orphanage is in a psychotic state in an institution or severely mentally retarded in a state hospital. But in the group that was cared for by the retarded girls, all but one graduated from high school, all of them are married, there is only one divorce, none of them is on welfare, every one is self-supporting. The independent variable was that *somebody saw me, somebody touched me, somebody felt me, somebody cared a damn about me!*

The next point is that everybody has his own path. There are a thousand paths to discovering yourself, to becoming. Every one of you will find your own way. Don't let anybody impose theirs on you. There's a wonderful book called *Teachings According to Don Juan* written by an anthropologist named Castaneda. It's all about the Yaqui Indians whom he studied. In it there is a man called Don Juan, who says,

> Each path is only one of a million paths. Therefore, you must always keep in mind that a path is only a path. If you feel that you must now follow it, you need not stay with it under any circumstances. Any path is only a path. There is no affront to yourself or others in dropping it if that is what your heart tells you to do. But your decision to keep on the path or to leave it must be free of fear and ambition. I warn you: look at every path closely and deliberately. Try it as many times as you think necessary. Then ask yourself and yourself alone one question. It is this: Does this path have a heart? All paths are the same. They lead nowhere. They are paths going through the brush or into the brush or under the brush. Does this path have a heart is the only question. If it does, then the path is good. If it doesn't, it is of no use.

If you are going to start helping people, you're going to have to start doing the following things. First, you've got to stop imposing yourself on others, and your value systems upon them, you've got to be real, and you've got to learn to listen. There are all kinds of symbols. Verbal language is only one. Sometimes by opening our mouths, we make dreadful errors. It's often so much nicer just to look at somebody and vibrate. I'm determined that one of these days I'm going to free myself of all responsibility and study human vibrations because I am sure they exist even as much as the vibrations that are sending this sound to you. When we find that secret, we may find some means of communication that is a little more adequate than words. I think that listening is tremendously important, and yet we abhor and are frightened of silence. The most beautiful things could go on if we were silent. If you are a counselor, if you ever want people to talk, just be still. After a minute they'll say anything.

You've got to be real. Don't be a phony. Come on as yourself. The hardest thing in the world is to be something you're not. As you get closer and closer and closer to what you are, be that, and come on all the time that way. You'll find it's an easy way to live. The easiest thing to be in the world is you. The most difficult thing to be is what other people want you to be. Don't let them put you in that position. Find "you," who you are, come on as you are. Then you can live simply. You can use all of this energy that it takes to "hold back the spooks," as Richard Alpert calls it. You won't have any spooks to hold back any more. You won't be playing games any more. Just clear them all away and say, "Here's me. Take me for what I am with all my frailties, all my stupidity, and so on. And if you can't, leave me alone."

Another thing, don't order anyone to do anything. You are not God. You do not know what is in someone else's head. You can guide but you can't order. And try to communicate, try to understand. So often the professional sits across the desk from a little mama, who is obviously scared to death and clutching her purse. The professional will say, "Now we've done a complete diagnostic study of your child, and we have decided that he has developmental dyslexia due to minimal brain dysfunction. Do you understand?" What can this mother say? She smiles and she says, "Mmm." I can just see her going home, and her husband says, "Well, what did the professional say, Honey? You know we paid a hundred and ninety bucks." "Well, he has some kind of lexia, and it's due to something wrong with his head." And he says, "That we paid a hundred and ninety bucks for?" You know it's a wonder more parents of exceptional children don't crack up. So we've got to communicate.

Finally, remember that you are a team. Your dealings with people are only going to be as successful as you are together. You are going to want to plan together what you are going to do because there are greater resources and strengths in two than there are in one. Sometimes it takes a very, very little thing to bring you together. But you have to do several things if you are going to make a team: you've got to give parents the straight dope, at least the way you see it right now, not hide anything, let them know. This is where Johnny is, this is where we'd like to bring him, these are our aspirations for him. Then plan a program step-by-step to accomplish these.

First of all, you determine where Johnny is right now. That's what we have to work with. It won't help you to know that he has minimal brain dysfunction. You can't do anything about his brain—you're a parent or a teacher. It's irreparable anyway. Next, determine the immediate next step, not what he's going to be doing ten thousand years from now, but the next immediate step we want him to be able to take. Is it sit? Is it attend? Is it move a pencil? Is it read a word? Then, thirdly, plan how to get there. "This is your job as a parent, and this is my job as a teacher or counselor, and we'll work together. You do your part, and I'll do mine." Then together look at your success and say, "Did we get there? Yes, we did. He's doing it all the time. Okay, what do we want to do next?" And on and on. That's what educational counseling is all about, not getting into somebody's psyche and trying to find out what kind of a sexual hang-up they have. It's a step-by-step-by-step process. If you do these things and you do them together, you are not going to hear parents saying, "Help me." They are going to be helped.

I have one more thing to share. It's written by a wonderful man named Zinker, who is at the Gestalt Institute in Cleveland. He wrote this as the end of a paper which he calls *On Public Knowledge and Personal Revelation*. He says:

> If a man in the street were to pursue his self, what kind of guiding thoughts would he come up with about changing his existence? He would perhaps discover that his brain is not yet dead, that his body is not dried up, and that no matter where he is right now, he is still the creator of his own destiny. He can change this destiny by taking his one decision to change seriously, by fighting his petty resistances against change and fear, by learning more

about his mind, by trying out behavior which fills his real need, by carrying out concrete acts rather than conceptualizing about them—

I feel strongly about that. Let's stop talking and start doing—

by practicing to see and hear and touch and feel as he has never before used these senses, by creating something with his own hands without demanding perfection, by thinking out ways in which he behaves in a self-defeating manner, by listening to the words that he utters to his wife, his kids, and his friends, by listening to himself, by listening to the words and looking into the eyes of those who speak to him, by learning to respect the process of his own creative encounters and by having faith that they will get him somewhere soon.

We must remind ourselves, however, that no change takes place without working hard and without getting your hands dirty. There are no formulae and no books to memorize on becoming. I only know this: I exist, I am, I am here, I am becoming, I make my life and no one else makes it for me. I must face my own shortcomings, mistakes, transgressions. No one can suffer my non-being as I do, but tomorrow is another day, and I must decide to leave my bed and live again. And if I fail, I don't have the comfort of blaming you or life or God.

That’s Where the Light Is

There's something that I don't want to have happen tonight and I'd like to explain what that is, then we can start right in. There are many ways of learning, and I learned one way when I was in a Zen Monastery in Asia for a year. I had a marvelous Japanese teacher. He was so gentle and so wondrous and so full of beautiful things to share—his entire life was a sharing, as I would like my entire life to be, and as I hope you would like your entire life to be—and that's why I'm very concerned that I become more and more, so that each time I'm with you I have more and more to share.

I remember, on this particular day, that we were walking in a garden of giant bamboo. Some of you who have been to Japan know how beautiful that can be. We were wandering through this garden, and I was verbally carrying on for some reason. I was running off at the mouth about all the wondrous things that I knew, all of the great wisdom that I had, and I was really trying to impress this man, trying to tell him, "this is what I know,"—when all in a sudden this very nonviolent person turned around and slapped me right on the mouth! Talk about a good learning technique! And I looked at him, holding my bloody lip, and I said, "Why did you do that?" And with all the vehemence—more vehemence than I had ever seen in this man, he said to me, "Don't walk in my head with your dirty feet!" And I promise you that before I came here tonight I washed my feet clean. I have no intention of walking in anybody's head. All that I want to have happen between us tonight is a very gentle sharing. You take from what I share what is right for *you*. And what isn't, you let go. I have no axe to grind. I have nothing to sell. But I have a lot to share, and I'm excited about sharing.

And what I hope is that we can share together, and maybe we'll have that opportunity in some way or another before we part.

I guess most of you know through tapes or books of mine that I am very heavy into the study of love as a learned phenomenon. I truly believe that each of us have this great incredible potential to love, but it is only a potential, and like all potentials, unless it is realized, unless you do something about it, it's not going to happen. I was one of the weird ones, years ago, who started a class that I called "Love"—a love class. In the beginning there were only 15 or 20 in the class. Now if we'd allow 400 or 500, it would be so. But I try to limit it to about 50 so that we can really get together. I don't *teach* that class. I facilitate it. I make it possible to happen. I sit down with people and I learn from them. We learn together. Since love *is* learned, each of you has learned it differently, and you have as much to teach *me* as I have to teach *you*. That's why really, at heart, love is a sharing.

I thought maybe somehow people who needed could come and tell us that they need—and it wasn't psychotherapy! I'm an educator, I'm not a psychotherapist. I believe that wherever you are in life, and however you learned it, that if you want to learn it *differently*, anything that can be learned, can be unlearned, and relearned. So there's always hope and there's always wonder, and you don't have to sit and cry about the fact that somebody mistreated you in the past, or that you learned love incorrectly or that you're dying of loneliness.

Recently I had an interesting experience. I go around the country a lot, and when I do, I take mounds and mounds and mounds of work because it's the only really peaceful time I have. You see, my rule is always, "People first, and things second." So when I'm in my office, there is no peace. And when I'm at home there's the telephone ringing and there are people around—it's what I ask for and what I want and what I love. But when I'm on an airplane—it's like having your own private office: you disappear into the clouds and nobody knows who you are. So I say, "Could I have the seat next to me free? I have a lot of work to do." And they say yes if the plane isn't very crowded, so most of the time I get it, and I spread out my things and I work and I think. And when I'm finished I look out at the clouds and I think of the wonder and the magic of the universe.

On this particular day there was an empty seat between me and a very attractive middle-aged lady who was all jeweled and beautifully attired. She watched as I spread out all my things, but I could feel from her vibrations that she *wanted to talk*. I thought, "Oh my God! I love her but I have exams to grade and papers to read!"

She said, "I bet I can guess what *you* are!"

I said, "What am I?"

She said, "I'll bet you're a lawyer."

I said no, I wasn't a lawyer.

She said, "Then you're a teacher."

I said, "Yes, that's what I am. I'm a teacher."

So she said, "Oh, how nice," and I went back to my work. But she started to talk, and all in a sudden I realized: "Where are you going? You're always talking about people first. If you really mean it, this lady *needs* you. She obviously wants to talk—talk to her awhile, then maybe you can explain your need to get to work."

Well, it didn't work that way . . . but it was magical because like an *avalanche*, she began to tell me all kinds of things! Sometimes you'll tell a stranger what you won't tell the closest person in your life. She knew when we arrived in Los Angeles we'd just split. There was no danger, perhaps, of my ever seeing her again. So she started to tell me she had four children, and that she had just come from the Bahamas. I said, "Did you have a good time?" She said, "No, it was terrible."

I said, "Were you alone?"

She said, "Yes."

I just said, "Oh." I thought that was rather interesting, but I wasn't going to pursue it. But she immediately told me. She was on a holiday by herself: "I'm trying to get myself together."

"Oh, really?"

"Yes!" she said. "Two months ago my husband left me."

"Oh, I'm sorry."

And then she started. And she told me the story of her life!

"Imagine. I gave *him*," she said, "the best"—[really!]—"the best years of my life!"

I didn't think people said that any more! "I gave him the best years of my life. I gave him beautiful children! I gave him a magnificent house, and I always kept it clean. There was no dust anywhere!"

I was sure of that.

"My children were always on time to school"—she went on and on—"I was a magnificent cook, I always entertained *his* friends. I was always ready to go every place *he* wanted to. "I"—and she went *on* and *on* and *on* and *on*! I really felt sorry for this lady! Because all of the things she had considered *essential* were things that he could have paid for.

She had *lost* her *self*! She had not given her husband what was essential about *her* . . . the magic, the wonder . . . the undiscovered self. She'd given him good food—he could have gone to a restaurant. She cleaned his sheets—he could have gone to a laundramat! That's frightening!

I asked her, "What did you do for *you*?"

She said, "What do you mean—what do you mean for *me*?"

"I mean what did you do for *yourself*?"

"There wasn't any *time* to do anything for myself!"

There was a pause, then I said, "What would you *like* to have done?"

"Oh, I've always had a dream of throwing pots."

How wonderful, if she had thrown some pots . . . She didn't know it was essential. I felt sorry for her because what she did was what she *believed* was essential. This is what the culture had *told* her was essential! She was fulfilling a role! And she had lost herself in her role! Then the story unfolds, "Husband Meets

Interesting Young Lady In Office," who isn't interested in dust and doesn't care a damn about clean sheets.

We talked a long time that day about what is essential. She cried a little bit, I cried a little bit. We hugged each other, and she went her way and I went mine. But you know, she had never bothered to ask herself, "What is essential about *me*?" "What is *my* worth?" "What are *my* needs?"

And if you don't know this yet as a lover, think about it a little. If you are truly a lover, you want to give the best *you* there is. And that means developing all the wonder of you—as a unique human being. And, indeed, even though you've been taught differently, everybody in this place is unique. That's the wonder of it. There are no two of us alike. Everyone is different. How marvelous it would have been if somehow we had taught this woman her uniqueness early, or taught her how to develop it. And taught her the *wonder* of sharing it with everybody else.

Because there is no limit to you, you will always be exciting. You will always have something to share. But she didn't bother to look for herself, and she took on the role of what people had told her was essential, and, in the process she had lost her self.

But, the wonderful thing is, you never really lose yourself. Only temporarily. If you want to find yourself, you're still there! You don't lose anything you ever had. And if sometimes you feel a vast emptiness in you, a gnawing in your gut, something screaming to get out, it's that *wonderful* uniqueness saying, "I'm still there! I'm still there! Inside! Find me! Develop me! Share me! And then you begin to find a little bit of what is essential. But we're certain that what is essential must be "out there." It *can't* be "in here!"

I don't know how many of you are familiar with the little Sufi books, but they're magnificent little books that have come out of the Sufi religious sect. They're fabulous little parables that are delightful to read. The stories are the adventures that happen to a crazy little man that they called "Mullah." There's one story that's very poignant. It tells of the day Mullah was out in the street on his hands and knees, looking for something and a friend came up and said, "Mullah, what are you looking for?"

And Mullah said, "I lost my key."

"Oh, Mullah, that's terrible, I'll help you find it." So he got on his hands and knees, then said, "Mullah, about where did you lose it?"

Mullah said, "I lost it in my house."

"Then what are you looking out *here* for?"

He said, "Because there's more light here."

You know, that's hilarious, but that's what we do with our lives! We believe that everything there is to find is out there in the light where it's easy to find, when the only answers for *you* are *in you!* Go ahead and look and look and look, but you're not going to find them out there! Nobody has your answers—only *you* have your answers. And if you think you can pack up your bag and escape *you*, you're in for a mighty big surprise. Run to a mountaintop in Nepal, and when you get over the wonder of being in Nepal, who are you faced with in the mirror? You! With all your hangups, with all your fears, with all your confusion, with all your loneliness, with all the things that *you are*. So it's time to begin looking where it makes sense to look. What is essential is not out there. What is essential is indeed in you. But it's frightening inside and dark and it's not easy to search in the dark. And nobody teaches us how. How many classes did you ever have in your entire educational career that taught you about you? They taught you mathematics, and I'm not saying that that is not essential, but you can *live* without it. Did you know that? It's nice to have! It's nice to be able to read, but you can also live very joyously without being able to read. I'm not encouraging you not to learn how to read, even though many of you spent years learning how, and now you don't read anyway. Statistics show that the average university graduate—and this is going to shock you—reads maybe one book a year after graduation.

There are no classes in life, there are no classes in love, there are no classes in "I Am Lonely. What Can I Do? 1A" And when you try to teach these classes, I swear to you, you are treated like you are some sort of a fool. I've been labeled by the media, "The Love Doctor." Good grief! And supposedly one of the greatest honors came to me when I received a letter asking me to appear on "What's My Line?" I mean it! I swear! "What's My Line." And the person said "They'll never guess you!"

Go into a library and gather up all the holy books and sit down and read them for commonalities. How marvelous! There are so many commonalities! Jesus said, "If you want to find life you've got to look inside you. Buddha said it. The Hebraic Holy Books say it. The Koran. The Gita, The Tibetan Book of the Dead, the Tao—they all remind you of this. Trips outside of you are worthless. They are what lead off into the forest where you are going to be lost. If you want answers for you, the answers are inside, not outside.

But what do we think is essential? Well, first of all, one of the things we think to be essential—and we work most of our lives for it—is *this body*. We think this is essential. We spend so much time with this that we keep Madison Avenue rich! My God, the thousands of varieties of tooth paste. And the millions of kinds of hair shampoos. I remember when I was a kid, we used to wash with plain old ordinary Ivory soap. And now there is something for soft hair, for thick hair, for thin hair, for falling hair, for rinsing hair, for no hair! There is a hair tonic for children, and babies, and adults and senior citizens! We can't even share each other's hair tonics! It's really a distancing phenomenon when you think about it.

Don't you really get tired of all this nonsense? You do this, and this, and this, and this, and this. Then you put your clothes on and go out ready for your day. Then you return home and do everything in reverse. You take it all off, then you go to bed. In the morning you put it all on again! But we do it, because we're afraid the people around us are going to leave us on the dock if we don't use a certain kind of deodorant. And the boat will come back for us if we use it. So we use it!

The body is only a vehicle. It's a magnificent vehicle because it carries what is essential, but in itself, is not *essential.*

So what *is* essential? We think our learning is essential, and we've become addicted to our learning. We forget that facts are not wisdom. We learn facts, and spend our lives filling our minds with facts that we consider to be essential. But these facts are mostly useless static. And we become addicted to this static! Then anything that tries to get in, that's new, has to be screened through this static, through this old outdated, useless learning. And that's why it's so hard for some of us to change.

I often ask people, "Are you truly the *you* of you? Or are you the you that other people have told you you are?" People do spend their entire lives telling us who we are. Some make a profession of it and with others it's done in unconscious ways! The mama, for instance, standing in the market with her child in her hand, telling her friend, "This one's the dumb one. His brother is smart. But you have to have some dumb ones, and after all, he's not a bad kid. He doesn't give me any trouble." What is she telling this kid!? Does she think he's deaf? Everybody teaches everybody, all of the time, what they are, and who they are. That's why everybody is a teacher. As a lover, you had better be very, very cautious indeed about the labels you put on others.

I don't care where you are in your learning, you are still nowhere. We're very impressed with people who have impressive labels. We believe that an M.D. or a Ph.D. makes one wise indeed. I have news for you! Some of the most stupid people I know have Ph.D.s! Some of the wisest people I know don't even know what a Ph.D. is!

Remember that your learning can hamper you if you believe that what you know is reality and therefore, you are screening out all things that are coming in. Through that kind of static you will never grow, you will never change. I know people who are still teaching classes they taught 20 years ago, in exactly the same way. I've seen teachers who have taught fourth grade classes for nine years. Every time it's time to teach, say, The Westward Movement—that's very important—they go to their file, and open the drawer, and pull out this old decaying Westward Movement File, and you can see they have taught it nine years because there are nine pinholes in the pictures.

Knowledge is not wisdom! Learning alone is not wisdom. Wisdom is the *application* of knowledge and facts. Wisdom is realizing you know nothing. Wisdom is saying, "My mind is open. Wherever I am, I'm just beginning. There is more to be realized by a *hundred-fold* than what I know." That's the beginning of wisdom.

We're certainly not our learning. We often consider, in our culture, that constant *joy* is essential. I don't know of any other culture so bent on pleasure. We are lost in the continual pursuit of pleasure, so much so that we forget there are other things. The minute we feel we are slightly unhappy, we drop a pill or drink some joy juice. Who wants to suffer? We're a culture that abhors and fears suffering. Now I'm not saying, for goodness sake, "let's groove on suffering." Don't misquote me! I would much rather teach and learn in joy. Joy is a great teacher. But so is despair. Wonder is a great teacher, but so is confusion! Hope is a great teacher, but so is disillusionment. And life is a great teacher, but so is death. To deny yourself any of those—any aspect—is not experiencing life totally. I don't know any other culture in the world where so many of us go through life without experiencing life. So many of us don't know the value of money, the value of things, the value of hunger. We don't understand pain—and heaven forbid!—we don't understand death. Goodness, a child isn't even allowed to be around death.

Many of you know that I was born in a very simple and beautiful immigrant family. They had lived in the northern part of Italy where the vineyards grow, and they brought us up in a very simple way. But they didn't protect us against life. We were always a part of everything. The joy in the house, the music in the house, the wonder in the house. But the pain and despair in the house was ours, too. We were not sheltered from anything.

Our family was a very strange one because sometimes we were flying high, and we had *everything* we wanted—ravioli, and gnocchi, and spaghetti, and sausages, everything we wanted—and other times there was practically nothing. We'd make a great polenta. You know polenta? It's a northern Italian dish that's a big cake made of corn meal, and it's very filling. Six bites and you're dragging! But at least your stomach doesn't hurt! But we were never protected against pain, because every time Papa walked in, and we'd see on my father's face a long, long, long expression, he'd say something like "We don't have any more money." Then he would add, "What are *we* going to do about it?" Oh, it was so nice to see everybody get together as a "we." My sister would say, "I'll go to the market and collect the leftover leaves for the rabbits." And I became a vendor of magazines. Remember when we used to sell magazines from door to door? Boy what an education that was. And everybody did something. We experienced the togetherness.

Mama used to do a wonderful thing. She knew how to deal with Papa's long faces. She had a little thing she called a survival bottle. She used to put a little bit of money in a bottle and bury it in the backyard for the day when we were starving. Then she used to do something *outrageous* with that money! All of a sudden she'd bring in a chicken!

But we learned a lot from despair. We learned a lot from hunger. We learned a lot by being taken in as a "we" and made a part of a family.

Sometimes we think *possessions* are essential. Big homes, lots of money. Other people. Goals, big important goals are essential. We spend our lives insuring ourselves against impending doom, which we're sure is just outside the door. And by doing all of this, we cease to live in the moment. If there is something a lover is, it's a person who realizes that the only reality is the "*now*." Yesterday is gone, and there's nothing you can do about it. It's good, because it brought you to where you are right now. And in spite of what people have told you, this is a good place to be! But there's nothing you can do about *yesterday*, it isn't *real* anymore. And tomorrow? Tomorrow is a wonderful thing to dream about. It's marvelous to dream about tomorrow, but it isn't *real*. And if you spend your time dreaming about yesterday and tomorrow, you're going to miss what's happening to you and me *right now*. And that's the *real* reality, to be in touch. Tomorrow is too nebulous.

Recently two students were murdered on our campus. They were leaving a party where they had had a wonderful time, and they were walking across our campus when *senselessly* they were both shot in their heads! We still don't know why, or who did it. Both of those students were my students at one time—a beautiful young lady and a handsome fantastic boy. All I could think about when I read about it, and it was a real trauma, was, I hope I taught them at least in the time that they had, to *live it!* I hope they weren't waiting for *tomorrow* to live. It's sad to think of how many people have invested so much in tomorrow. We don't know what might happen in the very next moment, and that moment may be lost forever.

There was a girl who gave me a poem, and she gave me permission to share it with you, and I want to do that because it explains about putting off and putting off and putting off—especially putting off caring about people we really love. She wants to remain anonymous, but she calls the poem, "Things You Didn't Do" and She says this:

Remember the day I borrowed your brand new car and I dented it?
I thought you'd kill me, but you didn't.
And remember the time I dragged you to the beach, and you said it would rain, and it did?
I thought you'd say, "I told you so." But you didn't.
Do you remember the time I flirted with all the guys to make you jealous, and you were?
I thought you'd leave me, but you didn't.
Do you remember the time I spilled strawberry pie all over your car rug?
I thought you'd hit me, but you didn't.
And remember the time I forgot to tell you the dance was formal and you showed up in jeans?
I thought you'd drop me, but you didn't.
Yes, there were lots of things you didn't do.
But you put up with me, and you loved me, and you protected me.
There were lots of things I wanted to make up to you when you returned from Viet Nam.
But you didn't.

O.K. I don't know about you, but *I* don't feel that it's my vehicle that is essential. I don't know about you, but *I* don't think it's my education that is essential. I don't think what is essential about me is my *house* or my *car* or my *clothes*. What is essential about me? Well, I think what is essential is that I live and embrace life *right now*, wherever I am. I grab it in my arms! Don't spend time crying about yesterday—yesterday is over with! I forgive my past. I forgive the people who've hurt me. I don't want to spend the rest of my life blaming and pointing a finger. I get so sick and tired of hearing people gripe about what their parents did to them. You know what your parents did to you? The best thing they *could* do. The best thing they knew how, the *only* thing in many cases that they knew how. Nobody has set out maliciously to hurt their child, unless they were psychotic.

Can you forgive? Can you forget? Can you say it's "OK?" Can you say, "They are people, too?" and you take them in your arms and embrace them? Then take your *self* in your arms. Find out again that you *are* special, that you *are* unique, that you are wondrous, that in all the world there is only *one* of you! *Hug yourself*, you sweet old thing! Sure you're screwed up, and sometimes you do dumb things and you forget that you are a human being, but the most wonderful thing about you is that, no matter where you are, you have potential to grow. You are just *starting*. There is only this much of you now, and there is an infinite amount to discover and to find! Don't spend your time crying! Forgive *others*! Forgive *yourself*. Forgive yourself for not being perfect. And accept the responsibility for your own life.

Nikos Kazantzakis says, "You have your brush, you have your colors, *you* paint paradise, then in you go." Do it!! Take orange and magenta and blue and purple . . . and green, and *yellow*—and paint your paradise. You can *do* that! You can do it right now. It's your life that is essential.

I don't know how many of you are acquainted with Arthur Miller's wonderful play called "After the Fall." It's probably one of the most underrated works of American literature. He wrote it right after the suicide of Marilyn Monroe, who had been his wife, and he tried to ask the question I tried to ask myself earlier, and that maybe many of you have asked yourselves: What could I have done to have saved someone in my life? This was a play that said, "I have to learn to forgive. Others and myself. In it he has a beautiful thing that I'd like to share with you. One of the healthier characters says this:

> I think it is a mistake to ever look for hope outside of yourself. One day the house smells of fresh bread, and the next, smoke and blood. One day you faint because the gardener cut his finger. Within a week you're climbing over corpses of children bombed in subways. What hope can there be if that is so?
> I tried to die near the end of the war. The same dream returned to me each night until I dared not go to sleep, and I grew ill. I

dreamed I had a child. And even in the dream I felt that the child was my life, and it was an idiot, and I ran away from it. But it always kept climbing into my lap, and clutching at my clothes, until I thought, if I could kiss it, whatever was in it that was my own, perhaps I could sleep again. And I bent to its broken face, and it was horrible. But I kissed it. *I think, Quentin, one must finally take one's life into one's own arms, and kiss it.*

Fantastic statement. It doesn't matter who you have hurt, if you've learned not to hurt again. It doesn't matter what mistakes you've made as long as you don't make them again. As long as you learn, as long as you're willing to take your life in your hands, and kiss it and go on from there. Then there is growth. Then there is life!

Then, what is essential, is that we accept our death. I don't want to be gruesome, but I think the only way you can accept *life* is to accept *death*. Death will teach us that there is a *limit*. I give an assignment in my class—if you had only five days to live, how would you spend those five days? And with whom? Oftentimes the answers are so simple. I always write notes—long, long letters on all my students' papers—"Why don't you do these things *now*?"

"If I had only five days to live I would tell so-and-so I love them." I say do it *now*! "If I had five days left I would walk on the beach and watch a sunset." *What are you waiting for?*

But we're protected from death, as we're protected from life. Most of us don't know how to handle death and we carry that albatross around our necks for the rest of our lives, always on the verge of tears. We've got to learn that death is just another aspect of life. It's a parting with the vehicle, it's a going on. Death teaches us to *go on*.

You know, my mama died just about two years ago, and she taught me wondrous things, right up to the end. We didn't believe the doctor when he said to us that she was in a coma, "Don't worry about her, she doesn't know whether you're there or not. Don't bother to hang around the hospital. You'll just get in the way." *How does he know!? He never died!*

So the family took shifts and spent many hours, day and night, with her while she was alive. We held onto her hand! No one should die alone!

I had one of the late shifts, and we were sitting there alone in the room, Mama and me. All in a sudden she opened her eyes. She had big, big brown, wonderful eyes. Just before that I had thought, "I'm going to miss her. She was a great lady, we always had fun together, and she always had laughter, and chocolates to give me. And she always came up with something outrageous. And I'll miss her garlic." Did you notice that everything I said was "me?" "*I'll* do this, and *I'll* miss that, and don't leave *me*!"

Do you know what the last words she spoke to me were? She opened her great big, wondrous Italian eyes, and saw me with tears running down my cheeks and she said—imagine this!—"Felice, what are you holding on to?"

What am I holding on to? You see what death can teach you? Death isn't a spooky thing. Death teaches us the value of time. We realize how precious it is. We realize we don't have forever! Death teaches us to look and to see . . . and that the people we love aren't going to be the same all the time. We don't look at each other any more! We're so busy doing things that we don't stop to look at each other. You won't be here forever. You know you won't be the same in the morning. How many of you have children old enough to get married, and you realize that when they leave you never had time to see them grow up or you were so busy doing things *for* them that you never took the time to look at *them*!

I said that once at a conference, and two ladies looked at each other with tears in their eyes, and one said, "You know, I haven't looked at my kid in so long that I wouldn't be able to reproduce him." The other one said "That's true with me. Let's split." So they left the conference, drove to their homes, about 40 miles away, burst in in the middle of the night, went in and shook the kids awake! The kids said, "What are you doing—what's the matter?" The mothers said, "Shut up, I want to look at you!" My God! Don't miss it!

The faces of the people you love are not going to be the same in the morning, and neither is yours. Don't miss them. The trees outside are doing wondrous things. Watch them step by step—it's magic. I said to someone today, "Oh, your trees!" They said, "What trees?" We have a Governor in California who said, "Once you've seen a redwood, you've seen them all!" I'd like to send him to Wisconsin! Heaven forbid! Really the saddest phrase to me is hearing someone say, "I only wish I had—". Well, you know, you can! Is he sitting next to you now? *Look* at him. Is *she* sitting next to you now? *Look* at her, touch her hand. It isn't going to feel the same. What are you afraid of?

"Oh God, to have reached the point of death," said Thoreau, "without ever having lived at all." Death teaches us this. Death is a good thing to know. In Asia, death is in every street. Children grow up with death. They're not fearful of it, it's nothing to be frightened of. There's an insurance against *everything*, you know? But no one has made an insurance that you won't be sad. No one has insurance that you won't die. It's the most inevitable thing, it will happen to everyone and to all of us. It teaches us what *love* is—it's open arms. It's freedom. Keep your arms open and people will come and go—as they will anyway. You have no control! "I refuse to allow you to die"—what are you holding onto? Experience life; agonize, scream, cry. And then let it go.

Then what is essential, I think, is to live life in wonder. All this magic that's around us, but we let it go by! In Asia they say life is a great river, and it will flow, no matter what you do or don't do. We can decide to flow with the river, and live in peace and joy and love, or we can decide to battle it, and live in agony and despair. But the river doesn't care. Life doesn't care. In either case, all of our streams run into the same sea. It's up to *you*.

Finally, what is essential is not only to take from life, but it is essential that you put something back into it.

We've forgotten our responsibility to give. I have several charities to which I give but, because I send it to "other lands," I can't deduct from my income tax. People say, "You're crazy!" How sad. We've really forgotten how to give. I give love because I love you, not because I expect you to love back. If I give expecting something in return, I'm sure to be unhappy. When you say good morning to someone, it's because you volitionally want to say it, not because you expect something back. If you expect something back and they don't say it, then you're bummed out, "I knew I shouldn't have said good morning."

I go out sometimes—and really, we've reached this point—and say good morning and somebody turns to me and says, "Do I know you?" And I say, "No, but wouldn't it be nice?" Sometimes they say no. That's their privilege. But I did *my* thing. I said hello. They did their thing, saying hello back or not.

If we don't expect, we have all things, says Buddha. Love because you *will* to love. Give because you *will* to give. Flowers bloom because they must, not because there are people fawning over them! You *live* and *love* because you will. Because you must.

I had a girl come into my office this week who sat there for almost an hour talking about "me, me, me!" This is a quote: "I'm not sure what *I* want from life." Finally, this good old nondirective counselor shouted out, "What the hell are you *giving* to Life!?" Every day you take from the ground, you take from the air, you take from the beauty—what are you giving back?" We never think about what we're putting back, do we?

While writing a book on counseling, I spent three months alone in northern California in a little cabin. Every day I would go for long, long walks along the Smith River into the redwoods, and spend hours. One day I got into a grove of giant redwoods and saw a sign against one of those enormous redwoods that some ranger had scribbled out explaining the life cycle of a redwood, probably without realizing how really beautiful it was. It showed that when the redwood was this big, Buddha was born, when it was this tall, Jesus was born, when it was so big, Hannibal crossed the Alps, and on and on. In the last paragraph he said, "Even when a tree dies and lies on the earth's surface, all is not over. Decomposers begin their job of breaking the tree down slowly. As the years go by the tree blends into the soil, returning all it took so that others may live." Isn't that outrageous? And immediately I thought this could be applied to human beings. At least in the end we will have to give something! That wonderful, continuous cycle. Maybe Leo Rosten was right when he said the purpose of life is simply to count, to matter, to have it make some difference that you lived at all. Maybe *that's* essential.

Lastly, I have a wonderful time with words. I love to play with words. I wrote a list of words that I feel are a guide to what is essential:

1. *Right Knowledge*, to supply you with the tools necessary for your voyage.

2. *Wisdom*, to assure you that you are using the accumulated knowledge of the past in a manner that will best serve the discovery of your presence, your "now."

3. *Compassion*, to help you accept others whose ways may be different from yours, with gentleness and understanding, as you move with them or through them or around them on your own way.

4. *Harmony*, to be able to accept the natural flow of life.

5. *Creativity*, to help you to realize and recognize new alternatives and unchartered paths along the way.

6. *Strength*, to stand up against fear and move forward in spite of uncertainty, without guarantee or payment.

7. *Peace*, to keep you centered.

8. *Joy*, to keep you songful, and laughing and dancing all along the way.

9. *Love*, to be your continual guide towards the highest level of consciousness of which man is capable.

10. *Unity*, which brings us back to where we started—the place where we are at one with ourselves and with all things.

So the study of love has brought me to the study of life. To live in love is to live in life, and to live in life is to live in love.

To me, life is God's gift to you. The way you live your life is your gift to God. Make it a *fantastic* one.

What Is Essential Is Invisible to the Eye

I have asked to keep the lights turned up because those of you with whom I've talked before know I need your eyeballs, and, for some reason, tonight I need them as never before. This is an enormous group, and I feel such a tremendous sense of responsibility that I want to give you all that I am.

I always like to start by telling you new stories about my name, and those of you who know me know that I always have a new one. This time it is so outrageous, you won't believe it! I was in Asia again. I had to have my visa renewed, and in order to do so, I had to cross over from Thailand to Cambodia. This was a very tense time because, for some reason I never quite understood, we were dropping bombs on Cambodia (it's very weird to be on the back side of a bomb, you know!). Anyway, I crossed over at the border, and the border official was quite upset because usually tourists don't go to this little town called Poi Pet. To get there you must take a six-hour train ride from Bangkok, and it's a tiny village right smack on the border, I showed the official my passport, and he looked at me as if I were really a strange person, turned to the wrong page,—and then he listed me on this very official book as Mr. Scar-Above-Right-Eye!

I'm really a lucky human person because I have been able to go to so many places all over the world, and I come into contact with fantastically interesting things. I'm going to share with you one thing that I'm finding all over our country. It's something that seems to be happening to us in our minds. I'm finding that too many of us have become lost on the "external trip." This "outer" trip involves the collecting of things and being the wealthiest, the biggest and the best. Now we have most of the things we need for "comfort," and they haven't gotten us very far. We're basically still fairly lonely, many of us are lost, and most of us are confused.

There does seem to be a trend to go in another direction, and that is the *inner* trip. And I am really excited about it because I realize, having worked with children all of my life, that the only thing of value we can give these kids is what we *are* not what we have. Too often we give only the external things. But we have learned in our wisdom, as we get older, that those aren't the most important things. In dealing with children the most essential thing we have to give them is *who and what we are*. It delights me when I see people really interested in finding out just what that is. That's why, when I was asked to speak tonight, I decided I would like to talk on the subject of "What Is Essential Is Invisible to the Eye."

Many of you lit up when I spoke that statement because you recognized it. It's a quote from a beautiful book called *The Little Prince*, by Saint Exupéry. The story concerns a small boy who lives on a star. He has nobody or nothing on the star except a great boabab tree and a couple of volcanoes. He's a very delicate, sensitive, wondrous little boy. For instance, he loves sunsets because they're both beautiful and a little sad. Because the planet is so tiny, every time he moves his chair, he can see another sunset, and so he can see as many as forty-four sunsets a day. Spectacular!

One day a little seed comes, and he watches it grow into a rose. He watches intently as it blossoms and becomes a gorgeous flower. He has never seen a rose, and along with becoming beautiful, the flower becomes very vain (as sometimes beautiful things are). She preens herself, and she says, "Protect me from the sun," and "Protect me from the wind," and she is literally driving him mad until finally he decides that he doesn't understand her at all. He leaves her and flies down to other planets to gain wisdom by finding out about love, life and about people. He encounters some pretty strange things.

On earth among others, he meets a very wise individual, a fox, and the little fox says to the little prince, "Tame me." The little prince says, "Well, I don't know what that means. What does it mean 'to be tamed?' " And the fox tells him how to form relationships with people, how to get into people, how to care. It's this great section of wisdom which I wish we had time to go into, but you can read it on your own. The little prince says, "If I tame you, remember that I can't stay with you very long. I've got to go away." And the fox replies, "Indeed, when you do, I'm going to be very sad, I'm going to cry." The prince asks, "Why on earth would you want me to tame you if it is going to cause you pain?" And the fox says, "It's because of the color of the wheat fields." And the prince says, "I don't understand."

> . . . . I do not eat bread. Wheat is of no use to me. The wheat fields have nothing to say to me. And that is sad. But you have hair that is the color of gold. Think how wonderful that will be when you have tamed me! The grain, which is also golden, will bring me back the thought of you. And I shall love to listen to the wind in the wheat. . . .

And so they began the ritual of taming, which is the beautiful ritual of getting into each other. I'd like to read to you a little section about what the fox finally says to the little prince after the little prince has been his friend for a long time and finally must go away. . . .

> So the little prince tamed the fox. And when the hour of his departure drew near—
>
> 'Ah,' said the fox, 'I shall cry.'
>
> 'It is your own fault,' said the little prince. 'I never wished you any sort of harm; but you wanted me to tame you . . . .'
>
> 'Yes, that is so,' said the fox.
>
> 'But now you are going to cry!' said the little prince.
>
> 'Yes, that is so,' said the fox.
>
> 'Then it has done you no good at all!'
>
> 'It has done me good,' said the fox, 'because of the color of the wheat fields.' And, then he added:

'Go and look again at the roses. You will understand now that yours is unique in all the world. Then come back to say goodbye to me, and I will make you a present of a secret.'

The little prince went away, to look again at the roses.

'You are not at all like my rose,' he said.

'As yet you are nothing. No one has tamed you, and you have tamed no one. You are like my fox when I first knew him. He was only a fox like a hundred thousand other foxes. But I have made him my friend, and now he is unique in all the world.'

And the roses were very much embarrassed.

'You are beautiful, but you are empty,' he went on. 'One could not die for you. To be sure, an ordinary passerby would think that my rose looked just like you—the rose that belongs to me. But in herself alone she is more important than all the hundreds of you other roses: because it is she that I have watered; because it is she that I have put under the glass globe; because it is she that I have sheltered behind the screen; because it is for her that I have killed the caterpillars (except the two or three that we saved to become butterflies); because it is she that I had listened to, when she grumbled or boasted, or even sometimes when she said nothing. Because she is *my* rose.'

And he went back to meet the fox.

'Goodbye,' he said.

'Goodbye,' said the fox. 'And now here is my secret, a very simple secret. It is only with the heart that one can see rightly; what is essential is invisible to the eye.'

'What is essential is invisible to the eye,' the little prince repeated, so that he would be sure to remember.

"What is essential is invisible to the eye . . ."

Several years ago I went away to Cornwall, and I bought all of the holy books that I could get my hands on to take with me. I spent months reading them all to try to find commonalities, and this was the commonality of them all: if you look only at the externals of life and man, you are missing what is essential.

Again, let me define: when I am talking about a teacher, I'm not just talking about somebody who has a diploma that says he has taken so many boring courses. I'm talking about parents, I'm talking about custodians, I'm talking about the person who sells ice cream on the corner. Everybody teaches all of the time, and, therefore, it is imperative that we all know as teachers what is essential because only when we know collectively what is essential, can we know what is possible. And the wonder of it all is that what is essential is so vast and so marvelous and what is visible to the eye is so limited and so small.

One of my heroes is Buckminster Fuller, and this little old man was at our university recently. He's just spectacular! He wears big, heavy lenses, and he has hearing aids behind each ear, but he is so vital that with a piece of chalk and a blackboard, he can keep everybody mesmerized for three solid hours. You wonder how he can do it. Just recently he, too, was asking the question along with so many other great individuals: what is essential about the human person? Is it our body? Is it our mind? Is it our arms? Our legs? Our fingers? What is truly essential. Who am I? Who is the "I of I"?

He wrote a wonderful article that appeared in the *Saturday Review/World*. It is so typical of Buckminster Fuller, who even at seventy-eight is still so vitally interested in what makes the human being unique and wondrous. He wonders why we are all so magical, why it is that when we really begin to know man, we can't help but love him because he is so unique and so different. If you deny even one man entrance in your life, you'll never get his uniqueness from anyone else. I, for instance, want you in my life because without you, my life will never be complete. But only when you find the you of you, will you have anything to give me, just as I must find the me of me. Why do I read? Why do I travel? Why do I listen? Why do I care? So that I can get more and more and more and share it with you—that's the only purpose for having it.

In this article, Buckminster Fuller, his eyes still dancing (seventy-eight years of dancing eyes, what a wonder!) wrote something in his own little whimsical way. He wrote,

> I am seventy-eight—and at my age I find that I have now taken in more than 1,000 tons of water, food, and air, the chemistry of which is temporarily employed for different lengths of time as hair, skin, flesh, bone, blood, etc., then progressively discarded. I weighed in at 7 pounds, and I went on to 70, then 170, and even 207 pounds. Then I lost seventy pounds, and I said, 'Who was that seventy pounds?—because here I am.' The seventy pounds I got rid of was ten times the flesh-and-bone inventory at which I had weighed in, in 1895.
>
> I am certain that I am not the avoirdupois of the most recent meals I have eaten, some of which will become my hair, only to be cut off twice a month. This lost seventy pounds of organic chemistry obviously wasn't 'me,' nor are any of the remaining presently associated atoms 'me.' We have been making a great error in identifying 'me' and 'you' as these truly transient and, ergo, sensorially detectable chemistries . . . There have been quite a number of weighings of people as they died. Many cancer-doomed paupers have been willing to have their beds placed on scales. The only difference manifest between weight before and after death is that caused by air exhaled from the lungs or urine that has been passed. Whatever life is, it doesn't weigh anything.

And then he goes on to talk about our minds. He says our ideas are constantly changing. The mind of a child is not the mind of an adult. The mind you have tonight won't be the mind you have next week or the week following, so obviously it isn't your changing mind that is essential. What is the you of you? What is this wondrous, nebulous something that he calls eternal?

He ends the article this way:

> . . . humanity has an essential function in the universe—in the macro-micro ranges of the great design scenario and its realization in time. An intuition is dawning in us of the integrity and immortality of the individual. Awareness is terminable, but knowledge is eternal. The brain is temporal; the mind, eternal. Being aware and apprehending are temporal and terminable. Comprehending and knowing are eternal. Little children know this is fact intuitively.

Those of us who work with children should be bound and determined that we're not only going to find in ourselves the "I of I" so that we can share it with these kids, but we're also going to help them and set them free so they can find the "I of I" in themselves, develop it, revel in the wonder of it, and then share it with others.

When you have come to grips, for instance, with what is essential about yourself, only then will you be able to decide what is essential about your children. And the truth of it is that so often we professionals tend to see children as their externally manifested bits and pieces. We tend to divide them up. We tend to see each other, also, as *our* bits and pieces, instead of our external whole.

It always interests me how we look at kids. I've been in the educational scene all my life as far back as I can remember, and I've seen the following: the language pathologist sees the child as a lisp or a stutter or a language problem; the occupational therapist sees him as a motoric problem; the school psychologist sees him as a learning or emotional problem; the physical therapist sees him as a muscle problem; the neurologist sees him as a central nervous system disorder; the behaviorist sees him as a behavioral response; the reading consultant sees him as a perceptual problem; the school administrator sees him as an organizational problem; and the teacher sees him as an enigma and often even as a pain in the neck! And here's Mama and Papa trying to see him as an integrated whole, but pretty soon we convince them that this is not so. Then they lose sight of his potential total wonder so that he becomes, even to them, a "problem child." This, to me, is really not seeing what is essential.

All of these people are using only their eyes to see what is essential, and the eye is really the most inaccurate, the most inconsistent, and the most prejudicial organ we have in the body. They are looking at him, but they are missing him. He is certainly, perhaps, all of the things they see, but he's a hell of a lot more! What is truly essential about him is invisible to the eye.

Unless we are careful, we're going to do what Maslov says, which I just love, "If the only tool you have is a hammer, you tend to treat everything as if it were a nail." And so if we're going to see him, we're going to have to see him as the many things—visible and invisible—that he is, and we're going to have to have an awful lot of tools with which to work. That's the excitement, the challenge, the *wonder* of working with human brings, as contrasted to working with machines.

What are some of the factors that keep us from seeing what is essential? First of all, I think, our learning—the things we've learned, our language, our perception, all the things that our central nervous system has done for us. Our fixed mind. Just recently I was reading an interesting group of books on perception, and I finally came to the realization on my own (and I'm sure it has been written in a thousand different places) that actually the purpose of the central nervous system is not to let things *in*, the way we have taught it, but actually to screen things *out*. It's called "selective perception." That's why we see only a small part of the things in our environment. Of course, we need the ability to screen out extraneous stimuli in order to attend. There are all kinds of things going on the room right now. You may volitionally select to focus on me. That is very nice of you, because it is important that the two of us are communicating. So you are not hearing the coughing, and you are not hearing people come in, and you are not hearing the person's stomach next to you growling and saying, "I'm hungry, and I wish he'd hurry up." You are not hearing all these things because you select volitionally to focus on me and to turn off everything else. If you didn't do this, then you could daydream, think about home and loved ones, or whatever you willed. Recent studies in LSD showed that people took LSD without any thought in mind about what harm might be done and were not ready for the kind of experience that opened up all their senses and let everything in at once, and they ended up in mental hospitals. But the central nervous system, as we have educated it, is there to screen out, to take out. And so our learning is, indeed, very limited.

More is going on between you and me right now than just the vibration of air producing these crazy words. I am certain that the day is going to come when many of us will be so heavy into vibrations that I or another speaker will be able to stand up here and send off vibrations which will cause you to rock in your chairs! Words will no longer be necessary, and what a happy day that will be. As you know, one of the greatest hangups we have in the world is the hangup of words. It is always amazing to me that we can communicate at all. If I used a word like "love" and if I said, "Please define it," we would have different definitions. So it is with "home," "caring," "fear," "wonder." Okay, so our minds are very limited and simply the receptacle of prescreened experience.

We truly believe that what we perceive as reality is all there is. My goodness, no matter where you are, you are only just beginning! You are only just beginning to find the universe and yourself. In small sensitivity groups, you can find, in minutes, that you have feelings you never dreamed you had; abilities to sense, abilities to smell, abilities to taste—wondrous kinds of things that were always there but never before discovered. But they have to be developed. It isn't any kind of magical thing; you've got to *learn* them; you've got to *develop* them. But in our ignorant, limited world, we think that's all there is.

I didn't realize that I was getting the best lesson in the world in perception from Papa. I always bring up Papa because he was a great man. He taught us as children how to savor wine—isn't that nice? And it always amuses me when we are sitting in a restaurant, especially in America, and the waiter comes up and asks, "Would you like to taste the wine, sir?" We become sort of embarrassed and say, "Thank you." So the waiter puts a little bit of wine in the glass, we pick it up, sip, put it down and say, "Marvelous!" And it could be vinegar!

Papa used to say, "Wine is a ceremony—it's almost a sacrament." Wine appeals to all the senses. First, hold it up to the light. Look at the color. Different wines have different colors. Freak the wine steward out! Say, "Oh, look at this color—isn't it beautiful?" then pass it around for everybody to see. Waiters are so accustomed to our drinking it down, they don't even wait to pour it any more. They are already half way round the table before you've checked it out. And then the bouquet—oh, my word, the smell! When you swirl it a bit and put it under your nose, and get the wonderful aroma of the grape. Then—just think you've swirled it, you've looked at it, you've smelled it—and then the moment of putting it on your tongue, just on the tip because the tongue is so sensitive that it has something to say—here, and then it goes further back, it has another thing to say—the message is different. You start on your tongue. You run it back in your mouth. Only then can you really tell if it is right or if it isn't right. It is such an outrageous multifaceted experience.

We also consider our ego as essential, this self that we have constructed! But let me tell you that *you* haven't constructed that self. Somebody has done it for you. People have told you whom you should be and whom you should not be, how you should move, how you should smell, and how you should do most of what you do. How wonderful to step back and do what the Asian says: "Leave your ego on the table." Step out of yourself and leave it there. Say, "You just wait a while." That is the only way that new messages are going to come in. The self constructs enormous walls around itself for "self" protection. It calls those walls reality. Anything that doesn't go along with what the caged self sees as real, the wall doesn't let through so that by the time the new perception comes in, it's back to what it wanted it to be. And so most of us continue through life seeing what we *will* to see, hearing what we *will* to hear, smelling what we *will* to smell, and everything else remains totally invisible. All things are there. All we have to do to see them is to let them in, touch them, taste them, chew them, hug them (that's the nicest), experience them as *they* are—not as *we* are.

And then we view our addictions as essential. I call them our "addictions" because we are literally addicted to weird ideas, and we don't know how to shake ourselves free of them. We have all kinds of strange notions. I sat alone on a beach near La Paz one day, and I wrote down all kinds of self-defeating addictions. I am human, and I am also addicted. I am far from perfect. I cry, I am lonely. I am overwhelmed that people should come to listen to me. That always amazes me. I was told there was somebody who was flying in from New Jersey who called and asked, "Is Leo there? Because I don't want to come if he's not." Good God—what a responsibility! What have I got to say? I guess that's why I rewrote this talk seventeen times!

While on the beach, I found seventy-three self-defeating addictions. I call them, as Paul Reps refers to them, "the paraphernalia of anti-self." Isn't that nice? The "self-defeating self," those crazy ideas that have been taught to us which we believe, and then we walk through life trying to let new things come through but these ideas won't let them.

And then the worst thing of all which keeps us from seeing what is essential is *apathy*. "I don't give a damn." "I'm fine just the way I am." "Who the hell wants to feel vibrations?" "Let Buscaglia feel vibrations!" "Who cares?" "A flower is a flower is a flower." "A tree's a tree." "Who wants to see forty-four sunsets?" As I said in my book *Love*, I really think that the opposite of love is not hate, it's apathy. I'll do anything—and that means *anything*—to wake people from an apathetic state, for that is worse than death. I can deal with hate, I can deal with anger, I can deal with despair, I can deal with anybody that is feeling anything, but I can't deal with *nothing*. I received a letter the other day that was really devastating. It said, "I heard a tape of yours and you quoted Faulkner's *Wild Palms*. You said, 'If I had to choose between pain and nothing, I would choose pain.' " The letter continued, "That sounds insane to me. I'd choose nothing over pain, any time."

R. D. Laing, the psychiatrist I mention so often, said, "From the moment of birth you are programmed to become a human being, but always as defined by your culture and your parents and your educators." And then the horror of it all is that we become hooked on this learning, and we begin to equate the learning with *us*. Here we are, ourselves, and then onto that self we pile thousands and thousands of things that may not indeed be ourselves, but rather belong to our families, our cultures, our friends and so on and so forth. We take them with us, and then they become us, and we will die to defend that "us" and become apathetic to avoid facing the challenge of a new self.

We also create models of perfection. We spend our lives trying to make the outside world fit our notion of what is perfect. We really do! And what is, for example, the idea of a perfect day for us? A day that meets all of our needs, that goes just as *we* want it. And what is a bummer day? A bummer day is one that doesn't quite come out the way we wanted it. Well, tough for us! That's *too bad* if the day doesn't turn out the way we want it. The day was perfect—it's *we* who were tampering with perfection.

These expectations reinforce themselves. They shut out all possibilities of anything new coming at us which doesn't meet our addictions. I've seen it happen a million times. Families work night and day to build a beautiful home for their children in which they do not allow the children to live: "Don't sit on the couch." "Don't play in the living room." "Take your shoes off." "Not in that room!" Addictions that say everybody must go to university and college; it's a disgrace unless you do. Then we force people through this mill, and if they aren't destroyed before, they will certainly be destroyed after.

I was working very closely with a family, and it was a devastating experience. Their sixteen-year-old-child had a severe learning disability and couldn't read, but was one of the most beautiful boys I have ever known. He used to work out every day. Physically he was beautiful, he liked people, he was in constant wonder at the world—not his parents' world—but his *own* wondrous world. He really tried. Educators couldn't teach him to read, but his parents insisted that he read. They insisted and insisted and insisted because they were addicted to the fact that *everybody's got to read.* They disregarded what was essential for him, and he is now in a mental hospital. The point is that our mind is really nothing more than an instrument of experience and even if this child were to satisfy twenty of our addictions every day, the one addiction that he doesn't satisfy will pry on our consciousness and will make us unhappy. *We really work this way!* People can tell us all day long that we are wondrous and marvelous, and we are worthy of all kinds of things. Then one person will tell us that he doesn't like us; and we are destroyed!

I was reading Orenstein's book on consciousness, and you should really read it. It's gorgeous. In it he says an interesting thing:

> Our senses limit, our central nervous system limits, our personal and cultural categories limit, our language limits, and beyond all these selections, then, the rules of science cause us to further select information which we consider to be true and it, too, limits.

Everywhere we turn, we are being limited. *Yet all this can change.* You can change your inside programming, and it's a very easy thing to do, but *you* make the decision to have it happen. All at once, right now, say to yourself: "I'm going to start experiencing. I'm going to start tasting my food! experiencing people! looking at the sky! smelling the air! feeling things! Not just popping into bed, but feeling the sheets, feeling my body, being aware of someone else's feelings, touching my neighbor, being aware of myself, my changes, my growth, my being." It's *outrageous* that there is so *much*, and we are satisfied with so little. We are aware of such a little space, and we are satisfied to believe that's all there is.

Then we consider our physical bodies to be essential. My God! We spend more time taking care of our physical self than anything else in the world! We get up in the morning, we shower it, we spray it, we comb it, we set it, we deodorize it, and we dress it. Once we do all this and we go through the day, we do it all over again in reverse. It's utter madness! There was a time before I went to Asia when I really got annoyed with this body because it took so much time. I have a seminar of beautiful students, and we sit around in my house and talk, and I told them one evening how annoyed I was with this body of mine. Some of them got very upset because they thought that what I was implying was that I was going to destroy it. Never! I like me! I had a yoga teacher then who was a very phenomenal lady, and she said, to me, "Hey, wait a minute! That body is your vehicle. If you want to get to the right place at the right time in the right way, you put it in tiptop shape. You respect it, because it is the vehicle that carries what is essential—at least for the time being." So all of a sudden I got a renewed feeling about my person. Now I even pet myself occasionally! Paul Reps has it all together when he says, "Man used to keep his mind on his work, and now he loses it in his mirror."

So it isn't our bodies which are essential. Certainly they are important, and certainly our thoughts and our programming are important. Wherever we are right now is important. I like the idea of wherever you are, love where you're at for it all starts there. You have got to start by saying, "Yes, I love me where I am with all my addictions and limitations, but that doesn't necessarily mean it's where I am going to be tomorrow. It just means that I like me where I am now. You can't go on until you make that statement. If I had a single wish in the world and had a magic wand, I would wave it over everybody and have you say, and have you *believe*, "I like me wherever I am right now, right this minute. I'm great."

In Asia I was very lucky to study with Dr. Wu, who is one of the leading scholars in the Tao of Lao Tzu. He taught me a marvelous thing that gave me even greater respect for human beings. This wonderful, wise, gentle scholar, Lao Tzu, said that everyone is the perfect "they." We are already perfect. The world is already perfect. We try to tamper with perfection, and therein lies all of our problems. How wondrous if we could accept the fact that we are our perfect self. That's so logical, isn't it? Who is a more perfect you than you? Your neighbor? And how can they tell you what is the perfect you? Only you can know what is the perfect you. But you are the perfect you, and you are the only perfect you who will pass this way *in the history of the world*! Maybe others try to make it imperfect, but we should do as e.e. cummings recommends—fight the battle of being "you" forever because it will always be the greatest battle you will ever have to fight, and it's the only battle worth fighting. So, as I said in the beginning, we are going through a time when people are starting to look at themselves, and they are commencing to do something about loving the perfection that is already there in their true selves.

We also think that what is essential are our ceaseless mental and physical activities. Do you know what I have started labeling this? Static! Really, most of us are just full of static. Paul Reps, in his book *Be*, says, "Thinking five to six thoughts at once, we train to keep chronically tense. Everywhere we find training in tenseness. Nowhere do we find training in ease and happiness. Poor man, created to befriend all creatures, does not even befriend himself."

We are constantly racing, analyzing. We are constantly thinking. We go to bed with our heads full of things, and we have no way of emptying them, so we can't sleep. That is why there's a rise now in people who are trying to decrease this static. Yet other people are standing on the sidelines saying, "Idiots!" You had better learn how to empty your minds or you're going to go mad with the static. You can't sit and worry about Junior twenty-four hours a day. Every once in a while you've got to let all things go. And a wonderful thing happens when you do. You don't find "nothing" but rather "everything," only now, unexpurgated, it is yours without effort. It's the most unique of feelings.

We're learning to let our minds go without fear of losing them. We're learning things like "suggestology." Do you know that in the Communist Bloc countries there is a new science (which soon we will find out about, but which they are guarding like a weapon) in which they are finding that by emptying the mind, a teacher then can put into that mind whole courses of study in two or three weeks?

When I was in Asia, I had a happy experience in a monastery. The first thing they did was teach me about Zen nomind. What is Zen no-mind? That is a situation you learn in which they may put you in a room that is totally free of all external stimuli, a dark room. There you sit by your "self." Food is brought to you, a bare minimum to keep you alive. You live in total darkness. You have no books to read, no television to watch, no one to talk to, just you. What a joy it is to be faced only with you for a change and to see what happens. And do you know what the first feelings were? I started to feel, "I've got to keep thinking. I've got to keep holding onto my static. I've got to say to myself. 'This is where it is.' " And so I kept talking to myself—literally!—sitting there saying things like "Mary had a little lamb" because I thought that if I let language go, I would literally lose my mind.

Several holy books say, and ponder this one, "In order to find your self, you must lose your self." And what a joy it was after a while when I let my mind go, said "to hell with it," and just sat back and let it happen. How wonderful it was to stay quiet, to get out of my head just for a while, to rest my tired mind, to know a moment of peace. Try it! There's a marvelous technique they taught me that you might like to play with some time. They say, "Meditate on the tip of your nose. Close your eyes. Get your mind and all your energies right on the tip of your nose. Clear your mind of everything else. Now, let the tip fall off! Isn't that magical? Try it some night before you go to bed, and you'll fall asleep instantaneously. But, anyway, this eternal static that you think is essential is nonsense! Let it go, and maybe you will be surprised how many new things will come at you.

I also discovered a wonderful book called *The Kabala*. This is a marvelous Hebraic, mystical holy book. It taught something that really excited me that I want to share with you. The book says,

> 'Man must see that nothing really is, but that everything is always becoming and changing. Nothing stands still. Everything is being born, growing and dying. The very instant a thing reaches its height, it begins to decline. The law of rhythm is in constant operation. There is no reality. There is no enduring quality, fixity or substantiality in anything. Nothing is permanent but change. Man must see all things evolving from other things and resolving him to other things, a constant action or reaction, inflow or outflow, building up or tearing down, creation or destruction, birth and growth and death. Nothing is real, and nothing endures but change.

In order to accept this, we've got to leave the static behind. You've got to lose yourself to find yourself. You've got to lose your mind to find your mind.

And then we consider security needs essential. Oh, this is a big thing in our culture—the many security needs we see as essential. We learn these addictions from other adults who are also addicted to security needs. We think accumulating things is necessary. Collecting people with influence is necessary. Having goals makes us feel secure. Money, lots of money, makes us feel secure.

I had a very interesting experience before I left for Asia. My house was robbed three times in two months. The first time it happened, I called to report it, and the officer came in and looked around. We checked a lot of things that were missing, and I said, "Well, maybe those guys needed it more than I do." He got furious with me and replied, "You're a menace—thinking like that!" So I didn't say it again. Then I came home two weeks later, and my house had been robbed again. Then, just three or four weeks after that, my house was robbed *again,* and I sat down in the middle of my living room floor, and thought, "Well, every time they come, they take something and I have less and less to steal. Maybe when they take everything, there will be nothing left to take, and I will have singlehandedly stopped crime."

And then money . . . The first time I went to Asia, when I produced *The Way of the Bull*, I lived on thirty-five cents a day. This last time I went to Asia, and lived on twenty dollars a day! And, you know, I didn't have any better time. I just got fatter. Money's not necessary. It's *nice*, but it's not *necessary.* The only security there is, is *you*. That's all. Each day money is losing its value. Everybody's grabbing for gold. But the Buddhist again says something interesting? "We wake up as angels, but we fall asleep as demons because all day long we rush for security." We push, we shove, because we think we must, because we fear or because we forget to pause and consider what is truly essential and what truly matters. Security lies in you. *You* are your only security.

Then you consider the satisfaction of your sensory needs as essential. The more you have, the more you must have. You never have enough of a good thing. You never have enough attention. You never have enough reinforcement. Seeking gratification for these things keeps you always busy. Yet no matter how much you receive, it is never enough until *you* are enough.

We are continually seeking highs. We don't want to suffer. Well, you know there is a great deal to be learned by suffering. Certainly I would rather learn and teach in joy but to deny that there is some value in suffering is a tremendous error. Don't cling to or wish for suffering. Experience it, take it in your hand, and then let it go. But do experience it because it can teach you all kinds of things. To suffer without learning from it is absolute stupidity. Life really, for most of us, is striving for a nice homeostatic state. It's wonderful for us to experience highs, and we should experience as many highs as we possibly can. Build upon your highs, experience more—and more—and more—and more—in terms of potential, and then even your lows become just low highs and are easier to accept and let go!

So what are we not? We are not our mental static. We are not our bodies. We are not our programming. We are not our education. We are not our present mind. We are not our physical selves. We are not our sensations. We are not our perceptions. We are not our power. We are not our present feelings. We are not our present responses. We are, in part, all of these things but we are a hell of a lot more! But if you are addicted to these things, you are going to remain with them forever. Realize that these things may be you *now* but they are only a small part of what you *can be*. There is more of you unrealized than realized. In fact, what is realized is infinitesimal to what is unrealized.

I have another hero, Dag Hammarskjold. He said something that really fits this all together:

> At every moment you choose yourself, but do you choose *your* self? Body and soul contain a thousand possibilities out of which you may build many 'Is.' But in only one of them is there congruence between the elector and the elected, only one which you will never find until you have excluded all those superficial feelings and possibilities of being and doing with which you toy out of curiosity or wonder or greed and which hinder you from casting anchor in the experience of the mystery of life and the consciousness of the talent entrusted in you and the wonder of you which is truly your 'I'."

That was in his magical book called *Markings*.

How, then, do we come into contact with ourselves? Number one, by becoming *aware*. Isn't that a nice word—aware? It kind of hits you right where it matters, doesn't it? To be aware. To be aware of everything. To be aware of life. To be aware of growth, to be aware of death, to be aware of beauty, to be aware of people, flowers, trees. Open your mind and begin to see and feel! Begin to experience, and don't be ashamed of it! Touch, feel, chew, as you never have before. Keep growing! Keep consistently growing. Every moment that you do, you change. Open your mind, open your heart, open your arms, take it all in. You can keep taking and taking and taking, and what is, never runs out. There's always more. The more that you see in a tree, the more that there is to see. You hear a Beethoven sonata, and it leads you to infinity. Pick up a book of poetry, and it leads you to beauty. You love one person, and that love leads you to hundreds. Keep growing.

Find alternatives. The patterns that you are in are only one possibility. There are thousands of possibilities for everything. I always use the example of the young lady who is waiting for a phone call from Buster. She's waiting. He said he was going to call at four o'clock, and her heart becomes ready to receive him at one o'clock, and she waits, and she tells all of her sorority sisters to stay away from the phone. She waits and waits, and finally four o'clock comes, and the phone doesn't ring. And she continues to wait, and at four thirty it doesn't ring, and at five it doesn't ring, and at six it doesn't ring, and by nine o'clock she is devastated. She goes to the bathroom, and she slits her wrists. Why? Because she thought that was the only alternative. I am beginning to believe that maybe the truly mentally healthy individual is the one who has the most alternatives, the most viable alternatives. A person who can say, "If this doesn't happen, what else and what else and what else, is possible?"

For instance, let's think about the girl. What else might she have done? Be creative—what could she have done other than slit her wrists? What? Yes! Call *him*! You bet your life! Say, "What the hell happened, Buster; did you break your finger?" What else could she have done? Come on! Healthier! And what *else*? Yes! She could have made a pizza, she could have taken a cold shower, she could have called me! How sad that she thinks she has only one alternative. There are not only a million alternatives, but some that haven't been dreamed of yet.

Dichotomies: good, bad, right, wrong—nonsense!—normal, abnormal—no such thing but gradations and possibilities and creativity. I have a blind girl in my class now who is far more normal than I. She sees—definitely. She says, "It is as normal for me to be blind as it is for you to see." What is normal? What is right? What is wrong? As long as you are free, you are free to select and to choose alternatives, provided that you are willing to accept the responsibility for being free. And after you've tried your alternatives, and they don't work as you would wish, don't blame me. Blame your choice. Try another alternative.

You make the decision, you take your paintbrush, you choose your colors, you paint your paradise, and then you live in it. Or paint hell if you want to, but don't blame me for it. Only you can be responsible for not being. Forget what *was*. Get hooked on what *is*! The moment will take care of that. Life isn't an isolated phenomenon but it is part of the general experience, constantly influencing and being influenced by every new moment. You don't like where you are? Then change it! Be someone *else*. Do *your* thing for a change, and learn from what happens.

And another thing—don't avoid negative states. Negative states can teach you a lot. Don't avoid people who create negative states in you. We have a tendency to turn around and walk away, but they are going to require you to reevaluate yourself and see yourself in a new light. Sally doesn't upset you. You upset you. She puts you in a negative state because she doesn't meet your expectations. Well, tough for you! The cause for your pain is not Sally—it's you. Learn from your negative states.

Another thing I learned in Asia that I'd like to give you, which may be pretty far out for some people, and if it is, discard it: Rid yourself of *expectations*. Buddha once said a magical thing. He had a way of saying a lot of magical things, very simply. He said, "When you cease expecting, you have all things." That is wondrous. "When you cease expecting, you have all things." If you go around doing your thing without expectation, then you already have everything you need. If they do give you something in return, you take it with open arms. It should always come as a surprise. But if you expect a response and it comes, it's a bore. Cease expecting, and you have all things. Take whatever people give you. If you appreciate it, hug it, kiss it, and take it in joy, but don't *expect* it. If you want pain, just go around with expectations. People are not here to meet your expectations.

Finally, all you really need is already in you. All that you have to do to realize it is to recognize it. You are the perfect you. And to tamper with perfection is to court pain. Grow into your perfection.

I want to end with a quote from Bynner's translation of Lao Tzu's *The Way*. This book sums up what I have been talking about but much more beautifully than I. Isn't it fantastic that all books of wisdom are always so small? It has taken me an hour and fifteen minutes to say what it takes Lao Tzu fifty words.

> Existence is beyond the power of words to define. Terms may be used but none of them are absolute. In the beginning of heaven and earth there were no words. Words come out of the womb of matter. And whether a man dispassionately sees to the core of life or passionately sees the surface, the core and the surface are the same, words making them seem different only to express appearance. If a name be needed, let the name be wonder, and then from wonder to wonder, existence opens.

If a name be needed, wonder names them both. From wonder into wonder existence opens.

The you of you is limitless. The children that we work with, no matter what label we put on them, the essential *they*, that which is immortal, is limitless. Those of you who have worked with children know that they have a limitless potential, no matter how much they've realized. All we have to do is make it possible for them to recognize it in *their* way and be there to help when they need help, support, encouragement. "And if the name be wonder," they are all going to succeed.

Bridges Not Barriers

I was tremendously excited—and I think you probably were, too—by the theme of this conference: "Bridges to Tomorrow." Since I was a child, I have been fascinated by bridges, so when I first learned of the theme, I immediately got out the dictionary, and this is what it said: "Something that fills a gap; a pathway over a depression or an obstacle." And I thought how marvelous, for I have really tried during the last four or five years to dedicate myself to filling gaps, to building paths over depressions, to surmounting obstacles, and to making life simpler for the people in my sphere.

I like to ask children about definitions. They give the most beautiful answers. If you want to experience a lot of joy, ask a child, "What does such and such mean?" My five-year-old niece is just beginning to braille the world. She's touching everything, she's tasting everything—it is a most beautiful thing to watch. And I asked her, "What is a bridge?" She thought for a long time, and then she said this: "A bridge is when the ground falls out under you, and you build something to connect the cracks."

Wouldn't it be marvelous if we could get into the spirit of bridging to tomorrow and could dedicate this conference to connecting cracks, to filling gaps, to building bridges, to surmounting obstacles? What a wondrous two or three days we would have! But that means you have really got to get into yourself—every one of you. The group can do it, but it all begins with the individual. Before we can do it as a group, we have to start with something, and my feeling is that the first bridge you have to build is the bridge to you.

It bothers me how little self-respect and belief in ourselves we have learned. Many of you know that for about eleven years I taught a class on love. Isn't that outrageous? Love 1A! Since the early years, I have taught B, C, D, and E. Maybe I will feel I am getting somewhere when I begin Love 1Z. In the love class, I asked my students if they could tell me whom they would choose if they could be anyone in the world and where they would choose to be if they could be anywhere in the world. Amazingly enough, in this group of beautiful, sensitive people, eighty percent or more said they would like to be somebody else and to be somewhere else. I asked, "Who?" They wanted to be Jackie Onassis! There is nothing wrong with Jackie Onassis, and, in fact, if we really wanted to sit back and get centered with Jackie Onassis, we would find that she is, indeed, the best Jackie Onassis. But if *you* try to be Jackie Onassis, you are going to fail. And it will serve you right!

And the fellows wanted to be Burt Reynolds! One Burt Reynolds is enough. It is delightful that Burt Reynolds is Burt Reynolds. I am glad he is around; I am glad Jackie Onassis is around; but I am also glad that *you* are around. It is essential that you reach the point where you can stand before a mirror and say, "Mirror, mirror, on the wall, who is the most incredible one of all?" and really believe it when the mirror replies, "You are, you sweet old thing!" You may not be as tall as you wish or your thighs may be a little bigger than you would like them to be, but you are the best damn thing you've got! And when you recognize that, you are on your way. No one can hold you back.

There aren't very many schools in self-respect. There aren't many models who can stand up and say, "I really like me. I like not only what I am, but I like the magic and potential of me." Because, you know, you are not only actuality; you are far more potentiality. There is so much more of you. Somehow we need to tell the children, "There's more than just a reader. There's more than just a simple perceiver. You are unlimited." We need people to teach this who believe it themselves. Otherwise it is phony, and it is not going to work.

One of the most incredible moments of my teaching career came when I first started at the University of Southern California. I had never been before a university class. I had taught elementary school and secondary school, and I had loved it, but then I went to Asia for two years. After I returned, I decided I would like to try my hand at the university class for the first time, I discovered that we had created a bunch of apathetic people, people who were so sick of learning that when you walked into the classroom enthusiastic about what you had to share, you found only the tops of their heads—or if not the tops of their heads, you found people who automatically wrote down everything you said. Fearing there might be a trick question on the exam. Sometimes I have to say, "Put down your damn pencils and listen!" (I am a real nondirective counselor, I've been known to throw oranges at my students. You've got to wake them up somehow!)

Many of you know I have this thing about eyeballs, and that is not very popular in our culture. You look someone in the eye, and immediately you see the expression, "What in hell does *he* want?" I don't want anything. I just want to make human contact. You don't ever have to be afraid of me. I caress, and I hug. Try me. When someone is frightened of appearing before an audience, I suggest, "Take a minute and look for what I call 'kind eyeballs.' " You will be surprised at how many kind eyeballs there are, and when you find a pair, latch onto them because if you are saying something stupid, if your syntax goes berserk, you can look at those eyeballs, and they will be saying, 'It's all right, man. Go on.' " The first thing I did in my university class was to look for kind eyeballs, and I didn't see too many. Tops of heads—yes. Pencils moving—yes. But eyeballs—no. I did find one pair of beautiful eyeballs in a young lady about five rows back, and I knew they were my kind of eyeballs because she responded to everything I said. I knew I was communicating with at least one person, and that was a start. I loved that girl.

I have a lot of things in my classes that I call "voluntarily mandatory." One of the things that is voluntarily mandatory is that every student come to see me in my office at least once. I cannot teach bodies. I can only relate to people. And so I say, "Come in, and we will sit across from one another. I don't want to talk about the texts or the class. We can do that another time. I just want to know the last time you saw a unicorn and do you still believe in primeval forests. And when you come, I am going to *touch* you—and if that bothers you, *take your tranquilizer*." It is amazing how many are intimidated by someone who says, "I want to touch you." I was raised in a large Italian family, as most of you know, and everybody hugs everybody all the time. On holidays everyone gets together, and it takes forty-five minutes just to say hello and forty-five minutes to say goodbye. Babies, parents, dogs—everybody's got to be loved! And so I have never suffered that existential feeling of not being. If someone can hug you and not go through you, you are. Try it some time.

About two years ago a young lady came into my office, and I knew immediately something was wrong. Her eyes were kind of glazed, and her head was nodding, and I asked, "What's the matter?" She replied, "Oh, Dr. Buscaglia, in order to get enough courage to come to see you, I had to drink a whole bottle of Ripple! And I think I am going to be sick!" Imagining having to drink a bottle of Ripple to summon up the courage to come to see *me*. All I do is put my hands out and say, "Hi." I cover their hands with mine and lead them into my office, and I can see a look of panic on their faces, "What's he going to do to me?" I am not going to do anything to you! I just want you to know that I cry, too, and I feel, too, and I care, too, and I don't know everything, too, and, therefore, we can start with a common frame of reference—human being to human being. If anybody tries to play the game of "follow the guru" with me, they will be lost, for they will learn that I am just as confused as they are. The difference may be that I *know* it. A Buddhist teacher once said to me, "Why do you keep moving? You are already there." And all of a sudden it occurred to me—my goodness, I am!

A wonderful realization will be the day you realize that you are unique in all the world. There is nothing that is an accident. You are a special combination for a purpose—and don't let them tell you otherwise, even if they tell you that purpose is an illusion. (Live an illusion if you have to.) You are that combination so that you can do what it is essential for you to do. Don't ever believe that you have nothing to contribute. The world is an incredible unfulfilled tapestry, and only you can fulfill that tiny space that is yours.

"Oh, God, to have reached the point of death," says Thoreau, "only to find that you have never lived." You've never done anything. You've never felt intensely. You've never laughed. You've never cried. You've never felt despair. You deny all these things and push them away and live in a Never-Never Land that doesn't exist, that is illusion. But you are the best you. You are the *only* you. You have something to give. Give it! One reason I love this Association is that there are so many parents in it who give a damn. But it frightens me when I hear a parent say, "I'm *just* a parent." What does that mean? As parents you make all things possible. That's what you are. Teach us because you know.

Celebrate your humanness. Celebrate your craziness. Celebrate your inadequacies. Celebrate your loneliness. But celebrate you. I don't want to be anything but what I am, and that is a human being. I really like being human. And that means forgetting; it means bumping into walls; it means going into the wrong rooms; it means getting out at the wrong stop in the elevator. The door opens, and I walk out and discover I am on the sixth floor instead of the third, and I say, "Oh!" And then I think, "You sweet old thing, you did it again!" It is just great to be human. Last night I went to a very elegant cocktail party, and someone handed me a glass of gorgeous ruby red wine. I am a wine freak, and I took it tenderly in my hand. Then someone dashed up and shouted, "Leo!" and grabbed me, and the wine flew into the air! Everyone within miles screeched although the wine landed only on me. And I exclaimed what the Italians say when you spill wine—"Allegria!," which means joy, but nobody thought so. No one saw that it added color to my evening.

Those of you who really care and who are truly teachers are always learning from kids. You are wide open to children. You are not the kind to stand in front of a classroom and snarl, "We are waiting for Sally." It is no wonder Sally says, "Wait, you old . . ." Imagine what a triumphant feeling it is to have a whole class waiting for you! Maybe the teacher should wonder what it is that Sally finds so essential to say—and should listen. It is amazing to me how adults always talk "at" children. Listen to what you say. Ninety percent of what you say is talking at them, never with them. You don't have conversations with children. You constantly feed things into them.

On one of my visits with the Sioux Indians in South Dakota, I was picked up at the airport, and we traveled across the Badlands in a great big truck with all of the Indian family. In the front were little David and Mama and Papa and I. As Mama and Papa and I were talking about all of the significant things we do, I suddenly realized that we were talking right through little David. I turned to him (inspiration!) and I asked, "David, what can you do?" And he replied, "Lots of things!" I said, "Like what?" And he said, "I can spit." Top that! Many of you who have worked with exceptional children all of your lives, as I have, know that when the orbicularis oris isn't working, it can take many years to teach someone to pucker his lips for the miracle of being able to spit voluntarily. Yet we take it for granted. "What else can you do, David?" "I can put my finger in my nose." You bet you can! Isn't it some sort of miracle that you can raise your hand when you decide you want to put your finger in your nose, and it gets there? Celebrate your wonder!

It all starts with you, and the great bridge that leads to everybody is *your* bridge. That's the important one. If I grow and grow, I can give you more of me. I learn so that I can teach you more. I strive for wisdom so that I can encourage your truth. I become more aware and sensitive so that I can better accept your sensitivity and awareness. And I struggle to understand my humanness so that I can better understand you when you reveal to me that you are only human, too. And I live in continual wonder of life so that I can allow you, too, to celebrate your life. What I do for me, I do for you. And what you do for you, you do for me, so it is never selfish. Everything you have ever learned, you have learned for everyone in your environment.

Get out of "you"—get into "us." It is the most beautiful way to see yourself and help others to see themselves. Power comes from that. So, first, bridges to yourself, but don't stop there. The next great span is bridges to others.

The Sixties were an incredible time. Everybody questioned everything, and teaching during the Sixties was one of the highlights of my career. My students didn't just sit there and write—they challenged everything I said. What a time to teach, and what a time to learn! The Sixties were basically characterized as a time of expression, of acting out, of dissent, of questioning. Now we are trying to look back at the Seventies and are wondering what has happened to the Seventies? Do you know what is beginning to emerge? The Seventies were a time of introspection. A quiet time. A time for people to go inside as we recognized that there were no more *external* trips to take. If we were really going to find answers, we would have to look inside. We have now had almost ten years of looking inside, and all it seems to have produced is a mass of egocentric individuals who don't seem to be able to relate again to the outside. Can it be that we've lost two decades?

The time to come out is now. The time to start building bridges to *others* is now. That's the second bridge. The salvation will be our working together for common ends, not bursting off into little provincialities and insisting, "I am right." One of my most significant discoveries in the last few years is that I don't have to be right all the time. Isn't that nice? That frees you to be right some of the time. And would you like to know something else I found out? I can be right, and you can be right. We both can be right. There are two rights! And then I discovered that there can be two hundred rights, that there really isn't a right or a wrong but an enormous gray area with all kinds of gradations. Dichotomies are distancing phenomena. Let's find out first what we have in common. There are no two of us alike in this room, still we have much in common, and it is in that commonness in which we can begin. If we can get in touch with that, we are on our way.

Today there isn't any place in the world—and that means the remotest places like the Vale of Kashmir or the Valley of Nepal or isolated villages in Tibet—where we cannot go in twenty-six hours. We are all neighbors. I can remember when, rain or shine, every Sunday, the Buscaglia clan used to go to Long Beach. Long Beach is now twenty-five minutes from the center of Los Angeles, but it used to take us three hours to get there from where we lived. Now, everything is so close.

A leaf can't fall anymore that doesn't affect every single one of us. There is no place to hide. We all affect one another. It is one great massive vibration going off in all directions. We had better start building those bridges or the crevasses are going to be so deep, we will never be able to span them.

There is a remote place called Chayah in central Thailand near the border of Malaysia. In the middle of a great body of water is a little island and on it a Buddhist monastery. They have no water and must bring it in from the mainland by boat and dump it into a big rainbarrel. My Buddhist teacher there was trying to explain to me about provincialism, and he told me a beautiful story. He said, "You work very hard all day, and you come back eagerly wanting a drink of this precious water that you know you can't waste. You open up the rain-barrel, reach in with your little scooper, and see an ant in the rainbarrel. You are furious! You say, 'How dare you be in my rainbarrel under my tree in my shade on my island—with my water!" And you squish the ant. Attached! Or you consider before you squish it, and you say, 'It is a very hot day, and this is the coolest place on the island. You're not hurting my water.' You scoop around the ant, and you drink." Unattached. And then he said, "There is also such a thing called 'non-attached.' Do you know what that is? The minute you open the rainbarrel and see the ant, you don't think about good, bad, right, wrong. You immediately feed the ant a lump of sugar." Love! We must begin to recognize that you are the only person who can feed me the sugar I need, and I am the only person who can do the same for you. We are so much less without each other.

The theme "Bridges to Tomorrow" is lovely, but I am little concerned about "tomorrow." I am very much concerned about now. My teacher used to say to me that most of us live an illusion. We live in yesterday; we worry about what happened yesterday. There isn't anything you can do about yesterday, and you have never grown up if you are still blaming anyone or anything that happened yesterday. Let yesterday go, for if you don't, it will hang around your neck like a dead albatross and drag you down. "My parents did it to me." Do you know what your parents did to you? They gave you what they knew. God bless them! They may not have been perfect. The sad part and maybe the reason you were disappointed is that you believed that they were, and they *let* you believe it. It is a wise parent who says to his child, "Look at me. I am crying. I am lonely. We don't know if this is going to work or not, but we want to talk it over with you." I remember times when Papa sat around the big table with all of his little bambini and said, "Look, kids, I've lost everything. We've got to work together to keep the Buscaglias going." What a nice privilege to "work together" to keep the Buscaglias going instead of my parents hiding in the back room and my dying of anxiety over something I could feel but not understand.

I remember going door to door selling magazines. I learned a lot that way. Doors were slammed in my face; people cussed me out. It was okay—all learning is good as long as you learn it. And I remember Mama saying, "It's all right, Tulio, we'll make it. We have a garden. I can make that marvelous torte every night." "Yuk!" we all said. Cabbage and bread and water. Does that fill you up! It expands in your stomach, and you never feel hungry. But being together, working together, was so beautiful—and we thought about the *now*. My mother, who was really a crazy lady, used to find something she could sell, and then we would come home expecting the bread and cabbage, and instead we would find a marvelous spread. My father would say, "Whatsa matter—you gone crazy?" She would reply, "No! The time we need joy is *now*." And we would sit down and gorge ourselves. "Yesterday," I have heard it said, "is a cancelled check, and tomorrow is just a promissory note. Only today is cash on hand." Spend it like crazy! This will never occur again. There is a world to spend it on.

I want to read you something that I love. I found it in the Journal of Humanistic Psychology. It was written by an 85-year-old man who learned that he was dying. He says, "If I had my life to live over again, I'd try to make more mistakes next time. I wouldn't try to be so perfect." We all have perfection fetishes. What difference does it make if you let people know you are imperfect? They can identify with you then. Nobody can identify with perfection.

He continues, "I would relax more. I'd limber up. I'd be sillier than I've been on this trip. In fact, I know very few things that I would take so seriously, I'd be crazier. I'd be less hygienic." Isn't that nice?

The 85-year-old man says, "I'd take more chances, I'd take more trips, I'd climb more mountains, I'd swim more rivers, I'd watch more sunsets, I'd go more places I've never been to. I'd eat more ice cream and fewer beans." We really revel in denying ourselves. It seems to be a self-punishment kind of thing. Certainly we can't do everything we want to, but occasionally we need to do something wild. You go to the gourmet section of the supermarket, and you see something you have always wanted, and you pull it off the shelf. It is marked $2.98 a jar, and you say, "Ohmigod," and you put it back and go buy beans. Just once say, "How nice," and buy six jars. You deserve it.

He goes on: "I'd have more actual troubles and fewer imaginary ones." Ninety percent of what we worry about never happens anyway, yet we go right on worrying about everything. That's why insurance companies in America are the wealthiest companies of all. They insure us against everything. Falling arches. Rising arches. He also says, "You see, I was one of those people who lived prophylactically and sensibly and sanely hour after hour and day after day. Oh, I've had my moments, and if I had it to do all over again, I'd have more of those moments. In fact, I'd try to have nothing but beautiful moments—moment by moment by moment." In case you don't know it, that's the stuff that life is made of. Only moments. Don't miss the now. "I've been one of those people who never went anywhere without a thermometer, a hot water bottle, a gargle, a raincoat, and a parachute. If I had it to do all over again, I'd travel lighter next time."

Buddha once made an incredible statement. He said, "The less you have, the less you have to worry about." Everyone says, "Oh, yes, that's so true." Yet we collect and we collect and we collect. We have things in our cupboards we haven't used in a thousand years. The dishes that Aunt Matilda brought over on the Mayflower—put them out! It is an insult to the person who made them to keep them locked in cupboards. Use them—that's what they were made for, too. Nothing is forever.

And finally, he says, "If I had it to do all over again, I'd start barefoot earlier in the spring and stay that way later in the fall. I'd ride more merry-go-rounds, I'd watch more sunrises, and I'd play with more children, if I had my life to live over again. But you see, I don't." Neither you nor I know what is beyond, but we do know what is here. This is God's gift to you, and how you use it is your gift to God.

Life is in your hands. You can select joy if you want or you can find despair everywhere you look. It is all yours. Why do some people always see beautiful skies and grass and lovely flowers and incredible human beings while others are hard-pressed to find anything or any place that is beautiful? Kazantzakis says, "You have your brush and colors. You paint paradise, and then in you go." It doesn't matter what colors you are using now. You can always decide on new ones.

A final point: I would like us to build some new bridges to madness. I am sick of sanity, especially our definition of it. When I looked up madness in the dictionary, I found the definition included "ecstasy" and "enthusiasm" and "laughter." (Look it up if you don't believe me.) It worries me that we are a society which is now depending on canned laughter. Somebody does some innocuous thing on TV, and everybody in the audience cracks up, and I am sitting there wondering, "Is there something wrong with me? I don't think that's funny." I can remember a houseful of laughter—gut-level laughter—with people rolling on the floor and beating on the carpets. I don't see that any more. Emily Post says that women in our culture do not laugh; they titter. Well, tough for Emily! Let *her* titter. *You* laugh! We know very little about ecstasy. We are constantly talking about "creating" enthusiasm. That's ludicrous.

My Buddhist teacher used the word—and listen to it and see if it doesn't strike you on a gut level—"rapture." Rapture! That is also your human right along with pain, despair, anxiety. You have a right as a human person to experience rapture before you die. Some of you have experienced great joy, great ecstasy, but rapture? Assagioli says in his work on psychosynthesis that many of our problems are based on the fact that we are locked into routine, never ending routine. You do the same thing the same way day after day, and consequently you are bored out of your mind. And the consequence of being bored is that you are usually boring. He says, "Break routine; break with the old ways." Think about it. Most of us live our lives exactly the same way day after day after day. We get out of bed on the same side of the bed. We walk into the bathroom and get the toothpaste and put it on the toothbrush and look at ourselves in the mirror and moan, "Oh God!" We get in the shower, and then we get out and drink our coffee, and then we go out the same door. Just one time crawl over your wife or husband. "Hey, what are you doing?" "I'm changing my life!" Or throw open the window and jump out and jog around the house seven times in your nightgown. "What are you doing, Sally?" You exclaim joyfully, "I'm jogging!" Walk in and say to that lovely lady, your wife, "Let's go out to breakfast this morning." She'll say, "But it isn't Sunday." And you can reply, "Yes, but let's do it anyway." You'll find out how magical that breakfast can be.

The final bridge: all of these bridges must be built in love. This was put most beautifully and succinctly by Thornton Wilder, who said, "There is a land of the living and land of the dead, and the bridge is love. The only survival and the only meaning."

I want to leave you with this: in India, every time you meet or say goodbye to somebody, you put your hands in front of you and say, "Namaste." That means, "I honor the place in you where the entire universe resides. I honor the place in you where, if you are at that place in you, and I am at that place in me, there is only one of us." Namaste.

The Art of Being Fully Human

I appreciate an introduction when the person introducing me knows how to pronounce Buscaglia. Like a Verdi opera. *I love* that name. Several years ago, I was asked to speak in Asia. Federal clearance was necessary because I would be going into Army and Navy camps. I filled out the forms in the Federal Building, and gave them to the clerk, who was to check it out and make sure that everything was okay. When he's ready, he calls your name over a microphone. I knew this was going to present a problem, because if you think of my full name, Felice Leonardo Buscaglia, it may be good for a Verdi aria, but it's not so good for Joe Smith. He had had no trouble with Sally Jones and James Brown and everything else, but I knew he'd reached my name when he picked up the paper, looked at it, and did a double take. Then he took a deep breath and started with my first name, and said, "Phyllis?"I swear I'll answer to anything but Phyllis! Not that I don't like the name Phyllis; it's lovely, but it doesn't suit me. Not quite.

I always am a little bit concerned as to where to begin, because I know that some of you have read my books, because you've written me wonderful letters or you've seen tapes of mine, and you know pretty much where my head is. And others of you—and it's right that it should be that way—have no idea who I am. And that's good too, because then we can get acquainted tonight. Perhaps one of the most beautiful moments in my life was when I spoke to a national conference of blind people. After it was over, a beautiful blind man came up and said, "Dr. Buscaglia, may I braille you?" Have you ever been brailled? It was like having a cool breeze or an electrical current running over my skin. So we can verbally braille, and if you want to do more, I'll stand down here and we can do more later on. You know that I'm a big Italian hugger. Mama used to say, "You can believe something when you touch it." So if you want to be believed, you know. . . .

What I'm going to be talking to you about tonight is a subject that is really dear to my heart, and that is the art—literally, the *art*—of being fully human. I don't know about you, but I really love the concept that I am a human being and have all the potential to be a human being.

I remember being terribly moved by something that I read in a book of Haim Ginott's. It's a very poignant thing and it's written by a school principal who gave this to Ginott. She said:

> I am a survivor of a concentration camp. My eyes saw what no person should witness. Gas chambers built by learned engineers. Children poisoned by educated physicians. Infants killed by trained nurses. Women and babies shot and killed by high school and college graduates. So I'm suspicious of education. My request is: help your students to be human. Your efforts must never produce learned monsters, skilled psychopaths, or educated Eichmanns. Reading and writing and spelling and history and arithmetic are only important if they serve to make our students human.

You know what occurred to me? We teach everything in the world to people, except the most essential thing. And that is life. Nobody teaches you about life. You're supposed to know about it. Nobody teaches you how to be a human being and what it means to be a human being, and the dignity that it means when you say, "I am a human being." Everyone assumes this is something you have, or you should have gotten by osmosis. Well, it's not working by osmosis!

I love to do talk shows because you encounter so many beautiful people. Everybody wants a definition. Isn't that interesting?

"Dr. Buscaglia, will you define love?" And I say, "Noooo! But if you follow me around I'll try to live it."

It's very difficult to define, because it's such an enormously broad concept. The more I live in joy and beauty, the greater a lover I become. Every day, I'm becoming a greater and greater and greater lover. And to define it would be to limit it. But at least along the way I kind of have an idea where I am. But I also know that if I put my hand out, you could give me new definitions, new strokes, new ideas, and together we could grow.

There are maybe two thousand people here tonight. There isn't one person who hasn't known loneliness. Isn't that wonderful? There isn't one person who hasn't known despair. Isn't that wonderful? There isn't one person who hasn't cried. But also, there aren't many who haven't laughed, who haven't known joy. And in all those ways, we can communicate. We're alike, because I've known it too, and we're all involved in the same struggle: to become fully human—which is the best thing we can become. And what a goal! What a wonderful goal.

To me, probably the most exciting thing in the world is the realization that I have the potential of being fully human. I can't be a God, but I *can* be a fully functioning human being! And what I'd like to do is talk to you about some of the things that I think are essential in order to become a fully functioning human being.

We must get back to the point again; and, this is going to shock a lot of people, and you're not going to like it, but I'm going to risk it. I feel this very strongly. We've got to risk again by saying that "I like me." You cannot give to anybody in this world what you do not have. And therefore you must concentrate on *getting*. You must become the most beautiful, sensitive, wondrous, magical, unique, fantastic person in the world to be able to have all of these things in order to give them away and share them. Think about it. If I don't have wisdom I can only teach you my ignorance. If I don't have joy I can only teach you despair. If I don't have freedom I can only put you in cages. But everything that I have I can give away. That's the only reason for having it. But I've got to have it first. And so I dedicate myself to becoming the best Leo the world has ever known.

Being the best Leo, I can love you as the best *you*. I will not have anybody playing "follow me." Because when you start following *my* way, it will lead you to *me* and you will get lost. The only way to follow is *your* way. You're that magic combination that will never be again, and I don't care who you are, how exalted you feel or how lonely you feel. Everyone of you is something unique and special. I wish we could tell this to children early so it wouldn't take them a *lifetime* to find out! You have a unique world to share.

People who have studied perception and sensation know that everyone sees the world in a different way. Yet, it's the same world. We don't observe a tree in the same way. Yet it's the same tree. Wouldn't it be wonderful if we could share that tree and see it in two different ways? Just the concept sends me in orbit. And yet I hear people constantly saying, "What have I to offer?" You know what you have to offer? A central piece of the crossword puzzle. Unless you assume the responsibility, that picture will never be completed. I'll never see your tree and I'm convinced that we still have misery, despair, agony, all of those things, because people didn't actualize themselves and share their worlds. Because if they had, our picture would have been clearer. You have something to paint on that tapestry, or weave, that's uniquely yours. Don't miss the opportunity. You *are* wondrous. You *are* magical. There is only *one* you.

The next time you pass a mirror, look in and say, "My goodness. You know, it's true! There's only one me!" Oh, if we could get into that! And the wonderful thing is, too, that it doesn't matter where we are in that "you." You're only just beginning, because do you know that no one has ever been able to find a limit to human potential, or to humanness? You are *unlimited possibilities*.

Erich Fromm says the pity in life today is that most of us die before we are fully born. Don't miss yourself! Elisabeth

Kübler-Ross tells us that the people who scream the loudest on their deathbeds are the people who have never lived. They've been observers of life, but not active participators. They've taken no risks. They stood on the sideline.

Everytime we put our hand out to someone, we run the risk of being slapped. But we also run the risk—fifty-fifty chance, which is better than you can get in Las Vegas—you also get a chance of somebody reaching out and touching you in love.

One of the most beautiful things I've ever seen happened in a park. There was a mama and a papa who had taken—actually taken the time from this mad, busy schedule of all these essential things to be done, to take their little child to the park. Their little kid was walking down to the lakeside. Papa saw this, and started to stop him. Mama, who must have been a very unique, lovely person, reached out and grabbed him. She said, "Let him go!" And down toddled this kid, just barely able to walk. This tale has a happy ending; the baby didn't drown. I'm sure Mama's heart was pounding hard. But all growth involves risk.

I'm one of those crazy people who loves to let everybody know that I see them. Heaven knows, so many of us are lonely because nobody sees us. We're sure we don't exist. And so I walk down the campus and I say, "Good morning. Hi, how are you?" The reaction is incredible. Some people say, "Hi." And then I get the opposite extreme of people who say, very angrily as if I invaded their privacy—and I probably did—"Do I know you?" And I say, "No, but wouldn't it be nice?" And sometimes they say, "No, it wouldn't."

And then I have a wonderful thing—if you don't think that I still get hurt—I have defense mechanisms that are outrageous to overcome my hurt. Freud would turn over in his grave. I walk away and I think, "Gee, what a pity that they didn't want to know me, cause I'm so nice. And so tomorrow, when I see them again, I'm going to say good morning *again* and give them another chance." Works beautifully, you know.

When I do see them again, I say, "Hi!" And if they say again, "Do I know you?" I say, "YES, I met you yesterday!"

Oh, learn to risk again. Go back to that point in childhood where the whole world was a gigantic, wondrous mystery that you had to understand. Get hooked on it. Say to yourself, "I want to know everything. I want to feel and touch and taste and understand everything, and there isn't time in life to do it all, so I've got to do it now." Value every moment as if it really is your last because it might very well be.

Lots of people look at death as if it's a real villain. I have come to the point, happily, where I've made a peace with death. I see death as a very positive force, because it tells me that I have a limited amount of time, and it plays no tricks. Death has told us that from the time we were born. It's never hidden itself away. If it's hidden, it's because we've hidden it. No one will get out of this world alive. But you know, there are actually some of us who believe we will? We act as if we have forever! "Oh, I'll do that *tomorrow*." "I've always wanted to climb a mountain. I'll do it tomorrow." You may not.

My students say, "When I get out of school, I'll be free to read." I say, "You will not! If you're not doing it *now*, you never *will* read."

Now's the time. Don't wait until tomorrow to tell somebody you love them. Do it *now*. Freak'em out. Get on the phone, long distance: "Hey, Mom? This is Felice. I know it's three in the morning but I just have something to tell you. I love you."

Now, if she doesn't die of a heart attack, it may be one of the most significant moments of her life. I'm always getting people who say, "Well, she knows that already." Maybe she does. But do *you* ever get tired of hearing it?

Say it now. There are lots of ways of saying it. Reach over and touch her. Squeeze. Tell him. Go home and wake up the kids. "*Hey! I Love You I Love You I Love—*."

"God, Mama's gone crazy!"

"You bet I have!"

So remember that it all starts with you, and you can't celebrate anybody else in this world until you celebrate yourself. With all your kookiness! Your forgetfulness! Even your ability to hurt.

One of the greatest attributes we have is this marvelous attribute of forgiveness. I forgive you for being less than perfect. I will demand that everybody else be perfect the day that I become perfect. So you're all safe! And so you celebrate yourself and your humanness with joy and with wonder and with magic. And then along with that, you celebrate *others*. Oh, the joy of my celebrating you!

Most of you who know my work know that I'm a leaf freak. And Fall is my favorite time of the year. Fall, to me, is complete magic. I *love* leaves. They say so much to me. And so when Fall comes and I am surrounded by sycamore trees that are deciduous, and when the leaves fall, I like to leave them there. In fact, I like to bring them in and put one on the desk of each of my students. I say, "Isn't it incredible! Isn't a leaf a miracle?" I start talking about sensation and perception, using a leaf as an example. Then all the people who knocked it off lean over and pick it up. (They didn't know it was part of lesson.) *Now* it's significant! But that old leaf was significant just on its own.

I remember a wonderful blind girl in the class. When we were sharing our feelings about leaves somebody said "Doesn't it look pretty?" and "Look at the little veins." While we were talking of what we saw, she said something that none of us had thought of. "Doesn't a dry leaf *smell* good?"

I like leaves and when they fall I prefer to leave them on the ground but I have very clean, neat neighbors. And it's clean-clean-clean-clean-clean-clean. Buscaglia's house (their perception) dirty-dirty-dirty-dirty-dirty. And then clean-clean-clean-clean-clean. You see? In fact, one of my neighbors has one of those machines that actually vacuums up leaves—Rrrraaaahhhrrr! And you see the leaves going AAAARRRRGHH! I can't watch. *My* leaves are safe.

Once I was having a seminar in my home, when my neighbors came—and they are beautiful wonderful people, they're just clean.

They knocked and I left the seminar for a minute and answered the door. They said, "Leo, we know that you travel on weekends and you work at the university all hours, and you haven't got time to clean up your leaves. We have this marvelous machine. We'll do it for you!" Now, you know, they really are loving neighbors if they'd do that for me. I said, "No, that's okay. I really didn't know that my leaves bothered you. I'll go out and clean them up." We talked a few minutes and then they left. I walked back to the room, and of course my students were incensed. "*Cop-out! You should have said, This is my house and I'll do what I—'*" I said, *shut up!*" (I'm a real nondirective counselor.) "Get out there and pick up those leaves and clean them all up. Put them in barrels, bring them in and dump them on my living room floor."

They didn't believe that. "You mean it seriously?" "*Yes, I mean it seriously!* Nobody can tell me yet what I can have on my living room floor." And so we dumped those wonderful things on my living room floor and we sat on the leaves and continued our seminar. And listen, sometimes I really need my neighbors. I'm glad they're there. Sometimes by giving up something of a lower order, we achieve something of a much higher order. I had my neighbors and they were happy, and I had my leaves and I was happy. And it was a very simple thing. Do you know that most divorces and most breakups in relationships happen over *stupid, insignificant, crazy things!* "I want a divorce. She squeezes the toothpaste tube in the middle! and it drives me crazy!" My God, buy two.

"He drops his clothes all over the house and I'm his maid!"

You're not his maid unless you want to be his maid! Leave it on the floor! Walk around it! "But what will the neighbors think?" Well, that will be their little problem if they come in and say, "What's this? Six coats on. . . ." "Oh, they're my husband's. Isn't he cute? He loves his coats on the floor. And I just leave them there. He has such a nice time sorting them out in the morning."

The next time you get really annoyed and angry, examine it. Usually it's crazy. If you sit and examine it, you get the giggles. You can say, "Isn't it great being a human being?"

What frightens me possibly more than anything else in our culture is our lack of humor. We take every thing so damn seriously. We've forgotten how to laugh. Think back, those of you who are my age and beyond, how much laughter there used to be at home. I don't hear much laughter anymore.

I remember my mother, who was really a remarkable lady—she was magnificently rotund. She was a b-i-g lady! She just loved eating. And that's a quality she passed on to me. But Madison Avenue tells us that we must be terribly slim to be attractive. It depends on where you are. Go to Italy and see who gets the most pinches. The more the merrier! But I remember, she used to get to laughing sometimes, so hard that she would get down on the floor and she would rock—all 180 pounds of her—and we'd be laughing with her.

But I don't hear much laughter anymore. We don't laugh. Things are not funny. We've forgotten how to be joyous, and worse than that, we've forgotten and we don't accept our own madness. Let's face it: each of us is a little cuckoo. *Oh, the joy of getting in touch with that cuckooness again!*

Live nutty. Just occasionally. Just once in a while. And see what happens. It brightens up the day.

Recently I was invited to speak to a thousand nuns in Wisconsin. A thousand nuns and Felice! Oh, Mama was in ecstasy up there, I'm sure: "Here's my little Felice talking to a thousand nuns!" Oh, what a beautiful, loving weekend we had. When they invited me they said, "We don't have any money, but this is our homecoming to our mother house and some of us haven't seen each other for ten years. It's going to be so nice, and we'd like you to come and have you share love with us."

I went there and everything I saw that I commented on, they did something about. It was Fall and Fall in Wisconsin is gorgeous. I thought the leaves were beautiful. They all went out and got leaves and gave me a great, big bag of leaves to take home with me. I commented on the largest pumpkin I had ever seen. Wisconsin pumpkins are freaks. ENORMOUS! They gave it to me. There was a sister there who made bread that was worthy of any gourmet table. I almost wept. You should see me at a good table. I do cry. People ask, "What's the matter, Buscaglia?" "Oh, this is so good!"

She gave me two loaves of bread. And then just before I got on the plane that evening, very late—it was a red-eye flight out of Chicago, they gave me six pounds of Wisconsin cheese. Nobody was on this flight except stewardesses, and *me* with my pumpkin, a bag of leaves and cheese. I carried them all on the plane.

After the "Coffee, tea, or milk?" routine, lights were dimmed. There's nothing really quite as wonderful as being hundreds of miles in the air in dim lights, very quiet, going from nowhere to nowhere, someplace suspended. And . . . . madness occurred to me. I went in the center section and I picked up all the arm rests and took my leaves and I put them in the seat. Then I took the pumpkin and put it in the middle of the seat—with the two loaves of bread on each side, scattered the cheese around and pressed the stewardess button!

Here came this tired girl, sort of sauntering back, expecting to serve coffee, tea, or milk. And I said, "Look!" And she said, "*Oh My God!*," lit up like a Christmas tree. I said "I want to share all these things. They were shared with me, and I want to share them with you and the other stewardesses if they want to."

She said, "Hold on," and went and got everybody plus two beautiful bottles of California wine and served them in real glass instead of those plastic things. That was the quickest trip back from Chicago any of us have ever had. And we set up a routine. We have an annual reunion in the fall. All because somebody decided to take what could have been mundane and turn it into a little bit of magic.

Because you are human, you do have magic. Get in touch with it. When you feel the insanity rising, don't push it down. Let it come out. *Just once*—and then let me know what happens!

And then I think if we're going to be human, we've got to recognize, for want of something better, a democratic character. That means the realization that there is nobody better or worse than we are. I think sometimes we tend to forget that everybody is human.

I always tell a story, because it was such a meaningful one for me. I was picked, to go to a "brain bank" in St. Louis with fifteen or twenty educators from across the United States. For three days we listened to learned papers. Good God! All that I can say is that if the future of education in America depended on those learned people, we are *doomed*! Halfway through those learned papers, I decided I'd had enough. The madness came up. And I said, "Excuse me, excuse me, excuse me," and I disappeared.

And I was walking along the river and I saw a little old man. No teeth—really what we would call dirty, because we're clean—you know, it's all relative—drinking a bottle of cheap wine, eating a piece of cheese, with a big grin on his face. I almost passed him by. He said, "Good morning, son." Anyone who calls me "son" is my buddy. So I sat down and we started rapping. We shared the wine, we shared the cheese, and we also shared philosophy. I said to this man "You know, you look so happy and contented and centered and peaceful. Do you have a secret to life?" He said, without a moment's hesitation, "Indeed, I do."

I said, "Would you share it with me?"

"Of course, son." He said, "If you want to live happy all of your life, always keep your mind *full* and your bowels *empty*." Now, there's wisdom! Nobody asked *him* to a brain bank! They should have!

You know, I have a strong feeling that this wonderful quality of humanness, with all of its wonder, is God's gift to you. And what you do with it is your gift to God. Don't satisfy yourself with anything less than offering God the perfect gift that you are. And have a blast doing it. Thank you.

Tomorrow's Children

I'm excited about your conference theme. I think you feel with me that it's kind of ludicrous and crazy to set aside *one* year as the Year of the Child. *Every* year should be a Year of the Child and it's about time that we recognize it. Maybe this will start the thing rolling, and we can move together recognizing that children desperately need us. The concept of the child, Tomorrow's Child—Lover or Loser, is what I'm here to talk about with you.

I'd like to start by reading a passage by Anthony Storr from his marvelous book called *The World of Children*. He says we are all children even if most of us have forgotten it. I think it would be nice if we could get back in touch with what it was like in the beginning of this process, when we were all first brailling the world. Seeing your first tree. Everyone of us had to go through the process of finding our first flower and rediscovering fire. It's a long process and we're still involved in it, or I hope we are. We're still brailling the world. It's not enough for us to see a tree, but we want to climb it, we want to smell it, we want to hug it, we want to taste it, we want to chew it, we want to truly *experience* it. And that's what gives life its marvel and its magic. But Storr says this:

> How ignominious it is to be a child. To be so small that you can be picked up, to be moved about at the whim of others. To be fed or not to be fed. To be cleaned or to be left dirty. Made happy or left to cry. It's surely so ultimate an indignity that it's not surprising that some of us never really recover from it. For it is surely one of the basic fears of personkind that we should be treated as things and not as persons. Manipulated, pushed around by impersonal forces, treated as of no account by the powerful and more superior. Each one of us may be a

> tiny atom in an enormous universe, but we need the illusion that we count—that our individuality demands attention. To be able to be totally disregarded as a person is a kind of death in life against which we are compelled to fight with all of our strength.

I think those of us who are in the helping professions know, perhaps more than anybody else, how hard it is to find that self, to maintain that self and to be able to stand up and say not "I am," but "I am becoming," for in reality, in so many ways, we are not even born yet. And still, as far as I know, there is no school for life and there are damn few models—people who can truly stand up and say, "I am becoming, I am. It's wonderful. Life is good, the world is beautiful."

There is a beautiful book that has always been one of my favorites, Dostoyevsky's *The Idiot.* I don't know how many of you have read it, but someday when you have a lot of time—it's a big fat tome, but it's worth it—pick it up and wade through it because it is magical. He writes about Prince Myshkin, who is kind of a misguided saint in a sinful world. It seems as if everything he touches in good, turns to pain and despair, and he can't understand it. He has epileptic seizures and every time he has epileptic seizures he gains enormous insight. The magic of Dostoyevsky's pen describes it this way:

> Suddenly in the midst of sadness, spiritual darkness and oppression, there seemed at moments a flash of light in his brain. And with extraordinary impetus, all of his vital forces suddenly began working at their highest tension. His mind and heart were flooded with extraordinary light. All of his uneasiness, all of his doubts, all of his anxieties were relieved at once. But at this moment these flashes were only the prelude of the final second with which the fit began.

But each time he has a seizure, insight occurs to him, and at one point, very close to the end of the novel, it all flashes in his mind and he screams out, "Oh God, why don't we tell the children?"

And, you know, I echo this, "Why don't we tell the children?" Why don't we tell them that they have a choice, that they can become lovers and they need not become losers. Because when you look around, there are an awful lot of losers. I don't know about you, but it scares me that there are over 26,000 successful suicides in the United States every year. The latest statistics show that crimes of violence have increased seven percent across the nation. What happened to people who used to be able to get married and stay that way, raise a family for something like 20, 30, 40 years, 50 years? What's the difference? Well perhaps the difference is that we've all been raised in walled gardens. We've been protected against life. We've not been allowed to see what life is all about—as if life is ugly and to be feared and therefore we have to be raised behind artificial walls in gardens full of flowers and wonder. It's not until adolescence that we climb eagerly over that wall and we find that we don't have the tools to survive the reality.

We don't want to suffer pain, so we take pills, we take drugs, we get stoned out of our minds, we get drunk. We're afraid to live, but we're even more afraid to die. We blame the past, *we love* to blame the past, and we love to blame everybody in the past, but we feel impotent about what to do about the present or the future. We're suspicious of others but most of all we're suspicious of ourselves. We've forgotten how to listen to our own voices. We're incongruent with what comes from us. We miss the present. We let it go. We don't know that we have choices and that we can select joy. We lack purpose and we don't really understand what life is all about. We never ask ourselves "what am I doing here?" Is your role to be here just to take up space?

I spent a lot of my time in Zen monasteries and Buddhist monasteries and ashrams in India to try to learn as many things as I could in as many cultures as I could. I was very fortunate to be able to learn that there are ways. But there was one thing that I saw in India that I have never seen anywhere else, and it happened sort of magically. When I arrived in Calcutta, I got off the train and had not gone 400 yards, when all at once, like perceptual overload, I saw every single thing there is to see about life! I saw misery, I saw despair, I saw children starving, I saw people with desperate looks, I saw joy, I saw rapture. Yes, I saw rapture. I saw flowers and dancing and beauty and death. In 400 yards—when it had taken me so many years of life to just begin to learn what life was all about.

And that's what I mean when I say that we deny children life. We wait until we're adults to teach them about death. We have children believe that life is indeed a rose garden. How disappointing when they find out it isn't. We allow children to believe that we're perfect and what a shattering experience it is when they find out that we're not. What's wrong with the concept of teaching humanity through being human?

But before we can teach children life, we've got to learn again how to simply talk with them. I would like to write a book called "How to Talk With Children," because all I can see that goes on among adults and children is we're always talking *at* them, we're always talking through them or beyond them. We're never communicating *with* them. In order to really communicate with the kids, we've got to practice deep knee bends. We've got to get down there so we're face-to-face with them. We've got to try to get into their world and stop telling them about ours. Listen to them. Ask them to tell us what they see and feel and hear, because, you may be surprised, they may teach you something. It may get you back in touch with some of the wonder that was you and which you've forgotten.

You know what I found in the last few years? I am more involved in *unlearning* than in learning. I'm having to unlearn all the garbage that people have laid upon me. And you're in the same process. And with each bit of garbage I discard, the freer I can become: and the freer I can become, the more I can become something for you. I still go around in schools all the time because, as I said, the most important thing for me in the world is to be a teacher. And what do I hear? I still hear teachers shouting, "We will not move from this classroom until the line is straight." Big deal. No learning can be going on, but that line had better damn well be straight. "Now Johnny, why did you do that?" For God's sakes it takes us a lifetime to answer that question! What's Johnny supposed to say? "I don't know." Has anyone ever asked you why *you* did something? What would be your answer? Unbelievable ways of noncommunication with children!

What *does* a child need to know? I'd like to share with you some of the things I think are essential for us to let the children know. And the first thing is, we must start early in letting children know about their wondrous gold mines of imagination that are strictly their own. We must convince them that in all the world they are the only "they." I think some of us have forgotten it.

One of the things about our society, I guess, is that we feel more comfortable if we can dump everybody into a mold. You must not be molded! Look at children's faces. I've never seen two that are anywhere near alike, and I like that. I like to think that they are that combination that will never again occur in the history of personkind. When you get in touch with that, you get a sense of pride. And as far as the meaning implied in this is concerned, do you think that they are here for nothing? All that uniqueness is theirs for nothing? You know, I like to see the world as a giant tapestry with each one of us having a responsibility to fill one little area, and if we don't assume that responsibility and actualize that responsibility, that tapestry will always be less than what it could have been and we'll all be worse for it. I don't want you to be *me*. Heaven knows one "me" is enough. And I don't like the concept of "Follow the Guru." If you want to lose you, follow me. When you follow me it leads you to me and you're going to get lost! My concept is "follow *you*," because when you follow you and you reach that essence in you, and I reach that essence in me, then someday we will become one, not be alienated from each other.

So we've got to teach children that they are unique in all the world. We've got to show them that they will always be the best them. And it's hard because very early we don't believe it. No one sees us or touches us.

We have to get children to understand that, not only do they have this incredible uniqueness, but they also have something that sometimes we forget about. They are also potentiality. They are mush more undiscovered than they are discovered. And there's the wonder of it. It doesn't matter where they are, they're only just beginning and the big magical trip of life is digging it all out and discovering the wonderful you.

I've only recently begun to understand what it meant when somebody said to me many years ago, "In my house there are many rooms." Because I used to think that my house was composed of a great big comfortable living room. And that was nice. It was well decorated and it was clean and it was pretty neat. And things were going on in that living room. I could entertain there, I could live there, I could do good things. But one day it occurred to me that everything in that room was something that somebody else had helped me put there. I'd had a thousand interior decorators decorating that room. But all in a sudden I also noticed there were many doors in that room. One day I really freaked out. I went over and opened one. And I saw a dank, dark, cobweb-filled room. It frightened me, and my impulse was to close the door again. Then, I recognized that that room was also in my house; and, therefore, it was my duty to clean it out, to refurnish it and to live in it. So I dived into that room, and it made all the difference. It's a wonderful airy room now, and I have at least *two* rooms to invite the people I love into. That room had seven more doors and I opened those seven doors. One led me to music, one led me to art, one led me to love, one led me to beauty, one led me to joy and now I've got a lot of rooms and every one of those rooms has seven doors. There is no end! No one has ever been able to find an end to rooms in their house. We can go on forever.

You know what really blows me out? We are the only living creatures that can think about thinking. We can use symbolic symbols to think about thinking. We can analyze, we can dream, we can create in our minds—that's what it means to be human and that's why it should give you a tremendous feeling of wonder and magic.

I think if I had a single wish in all this world it would be to give *you* back to *you*. Not in terms of egocentricity, but in terms of the fact that you know that you can make that person—you—the most wondrous, the most remarkable, the most open, the most beautiful, the most creative person in the world. Not to store it away, but to give it away because you can only give to others what you have. If you're ignorant you teach your ignorance; therefore, you must work at wisdom. If you're chained, you teach your prejudice and therefore you must work at your own personal freedom. It all comes from you. If I do anything for me, I do it for you. The closer I come to loving me, the more love I have to give to you. I think we need to tell children this very early.

Then I think we need to tell children that others are present also. Now that may sound kind of weird, but I only found out the other day a most amazing fact: there isn't any place on the face of the globe any more that we cannot get to—even the most remote places such as the Vale of Kashmir—in 23 hours. That makes us all neighbors. It used to be that people who were so far away, could be forgotten. And they were. They aren't that far anymore. There are no walls anymore. They're too easily climbed or bombed out.

Recently in a midwestern university, there was an interesting sociological experiment with the students concerning sharing and giving. They asked that each student bring a dime. They said, "There are people starving in India. There is a plague and they really need help. If you feel that you'd like to give to that, put the dime in an envelope and write on it, 'India.' That's pretty far away, India. There are some people in a local ghetto, a family, that really needs groceries to live now. If you want to help these people, it will be given to them anonymously. Put your dime in an envelope and put 'poor family.' Now, of course, we don't have a photocopier at the university and we need to get one for those of you who need to copy papers and manuscripts—and make it easily accessible. If you want to help buy a photocopier, put ten cents in the envelope and put 'Copier.' Eighty percent of that money went to a photocopy machine!

We've ceased caring. We've formed little tight nuclei. We say, "These are the things I must be concerned about. It's not my concern what goes on out there." I think you've arrived when you recognize that not a leaf falls without it in some way affecting you. There's no place to hide anymore! The boss yells at you. You go home and yell at your husband or wife. Your husband or wife smacks out at the kid. The kid kicks the dog that bites the cat that urinates on the rug. Where did it start! I need you and we better get back to group affiliation, to being able to give up a little bit in order to get. We've got to learn to trust again, believe again, and work together again.

It takes two to see one. You want to know who you are? Look at the eyes of the people around you who love you. They are the only people who will dare tell you that you've got dirt on your nose. Everybody else in the world is going to let you go around all day with dirt on your nose. The person who loves you is going to say, "Hey honey, there's dirt on your nose."

Then, I feel strongly that we've got to tell children about death, and stop protecting them and giving them concepts that we are immortal. We act as if we believe that we are. Freud said a lot of really nice things and one thing that he said was so many of our problems and our inability to live stem from the belief that we will never die. We think we have forever. If you think about it in the back of your mind, you always think it's the other person who dies, not you. Well I have news for you. We are *all* going to die! That is the most democratic thing that has ever happened. No matter who you are, how wealthy you are, how illustrious you are, how many degrees you have, how fouled up you've made your life, how beautiful you've made your life, you're going to die. But why fear it? You only fear death when you're not living. If you're involved in the process of life, you won't wail and scream. If you've treated people in your life beautifully while they were alive, you will not throw yourself over their caskets screaming, "Don't go, don't go!" For goodness sakes! We don't even let people die in dignity. We let them die guiltily by screaming, "Oh, please don't die."

What a weird concept we have of death. We don't want to take children to funerals. Some of you remember that we used to have open wakes and some of you were asked to go and look at Grandpa and look at Grandma and say "goodbye." Some of you had it explained that everything dies as flowers die in winter and then grow again. Death is a continuous beautiful process of *life*. Then when you've seen it, you don't fear it. Death is a good friend, an awfully good friend, because it tells us we don't have forever and that to live is now; therefore, you see how precious every minute is. We read it and say, "Oh, yes, that's so true." But do we live that way? How wonderful it is to be with the moment when you see a flower. When somebody is talking to you, for goodness sake, listen and don't look over a shoulder at what else is going on. Cocktail time! There's no greater insult. If you don't want to be with me, *don't* be with me! That's all right, I can adjust to that. But if you are going to be with me, will you *be with me*? You say "I am gong to look at the ocean." Do you look at the ocean? "Oh, isn't that a beautiful sunset." Do you mean it, do you see it, do you recognize it will never come again?

Death teaches us—if we want to hear—that the time is now. The time is now to pick up a telephone and call the person that you love. Death teaches us the joy of the moment. It teaches us we don't have forever. It teaches us that nothing is permanent. It teaches us to let go, there's nothing you can hang on to. And it tells us to give up expectations and let tomorrow tell its own story, because nobody knows if they'll get home tonight. To me that's a tremendous challenge. Death says "live now." Let's tell the children that.

The final thing I want to share with the children is that life is not only pain, misery and despair as heard on the seven o'clock news and read in the newspaper. Those are the things that make news. What we don't hear are the wondrous, enjoyable, great, fantastic things that are also happening. Somehow or other we've got to let children in on those wonderful things, too. In order to do that, what you've got to do is get in touch with your own joy and madness again. We're all crazy! And if you don't believe it, you're crazier than most. Boredom arises from routine. Joy, wonder, rapture, arise from surprise. Routine leads to boredom and if you are bored, you are *boring*. And you wonder why people don't want to be with you! We can choose. We have choice. You can choose how you want to live your life. You can select joy, freedom, creativity, surprise, or apathy and boredom. And you can make that selection right now!

This is something I really like and it brings everything together. It's written by Frederick Moffett of the Bureau of Instructional Supervision, New York Department of Education. He calls it "How A Child Learns."

> Thus a child learns, by wiggling skills through his fingers and his toes, into himself. By soaking up habits and attitudes of those around him, by pushing and pulling his own world. Thus a child learns, more through trial than error, more through pleasure than pain, more through experience than suggestion and telling, and more through suggestion than direction. And thus a child learns through affection, through love, through patience, through understanding, through belonging, through doing and through being. Day by day the child comes to know a little bit of what you know, a little bit more of what you think and understand. That which you dream and believe are in truth what is becoming that child. As you perceive dully or clearly, as you think fuzzily or sharply, as you believe foolishly or wisely, as you dream drably "—and I love this—" *or goldenly*, as you bear false witness or tell the truth, thus a child learns.

We need to tell children that they have a choice to become either lovers or losers. For to miss love is to miss life. Thornton Wilder says, "There is a land of the living and a land of the dead, and the bridge is love. The only survival and the only meaning."

Let's tell the children!

The Intimate You

I truly feel that if there is, in this world, *one* person whom we can touch totally, unabashedly and unashamedly, we will never die of loneliness. One person! I don't say fifty, a hundred, a thousand. It really doesn't matter who that person is, woman to woman, man to man, someone you can go to and lay it on the line with, who will listen. Someone you don't have to hide from. Someone to whom you can say "These are my feelings," and they say, "Good. It's all right." "This is me!" "That's O.K."

I often ask my classes, "How many of you have such a person?" I don't want you to answer, but just think about it! At home? In your family? Can you go to your husband? Can you go to your wife? Can you go to your next door neighbor? Can they come to you? There aren't many who know real intimacy. That's frightening.

But, we can select the joy of intimacy. Why not? Let me read you some of the reasons that people give for not choosing intimacy. (The amazing part is that I found myself in these answers just as you'll find yourself.) Listen to what they said:

"I'm not afraid of intimacy; I'm afraid to be hurt."

"I get bored with relationships right away. As soon as we know each other, and the newness vanishes, so does the excitement."

"People don't want intimacy, they just want sex."

"I'm afraid to let anyone know who I really am; if they really knew they'd be horrified."

"I don't believe in intimacy, I don't think it's possible. People are just too different."

"Intimacy always makes me feel insecure and jealous. The deeper I feel about someone, the deeper the insecurity and jealousy, so I'd rather be casual, and then I won't be hurt."

"It's funny," said another one, "but I only seem to fight with and hurt the people with whom I'm intimate." "Everytime I form an intimate relationship, I always feel cheated. I know there must be more, and so I go around looking for it and I ruin everything.

"We all have tremendous needs, and they're all different needs. Trying to fulfill someone else's needs adds to complications in my life. I have problems enough."

These are very human comments, and very honest. It's true that intimate relationships are a risk, and it's true that they will hurt, and it's true that they're going to make the greatest demands on you, and it's true that they're going to demand change, and it's true that they're going to bring out your deepest feelings and make you feel miserable sometimes. But as I said, it's also true that your only alternatives to intimacy are in despair and loneliness.

Our modern society doesn't reinforce intimacy. One out of every four marriages ends in divorce. In southern California, it's almost fifty-fifty between marriages and divorces. Good grief! One out of two will fail. Casual relationships, that start with great feelings of love and tenderness, last three months. When things become a little bit difficult or unpleasant, you can't stand it any more, so you leave. Then there are books such as the popular *Feel Free*. I want to read you what it says to us: "Feel free if a relationship becomes dull and sluggish, just to move out, and don't feel guilty, because lasting relationships between any two people are no longer possible." This author is a psychiatrist! So, if we get into an argument, if we disagree, say, "To hell with you. I'm not going to work anything out with you! Who wants the trouble? Why solve anything? It's easier to find another."

George Leonard says, "We can orbit the earth, we can touch the moon, but this society has not devised a way for two people to live together in harmony for seven straight days without wanting to strangle each other." They tell us that intimacy is out of date, but I say that *intimacy is absolutely essential or we are all going to go mad*. Go ahead and live in isolation, if you can. I believe that you can judge your level of mental health to the degree that you can form meaningful and lasting relationships. Not the *quantity* of these relationships, but the *quality* of the relationships.

There are many levels of intimacy. For example, I remember when I was doing my doctorate with so-called "washed-out schizophrenics," there was no contact at all. If you touched them, they'd shout "leave me alone!" They'd stand at windows for hours looking out, making contact with nothingness. And a step above that level is what we see as ritual relationships—a ritual interaction, as when you're walking down the street you say, "Oh, hi, Mary. How are you?" She says, "Fine." (She's dying of leprosy, but she says 'fine.') It comes out automatically. (You don't care how she is anyway!)—"How are you, Min?" She says, "Oh, my lumbago, it's killing me"—you don't want to hear it. What do you ask for? Wouldn't it be wonderful to say, "Hello, Mary" and look in her eye to show her you care? Don't ask unless you really want to know. Then if she tells, sit down, light a fire and listen.

A higher level, but pretty strange yet, is what I call "cocktail party talk," and that really is strange material. We talk about all the safe things that really don't matter. Have you ever gone to a cocktail party and said, "Let's get to the gut level. Let's talk about religion, politics, love. Is God dead?" You'll never be asked back!

And then a higher level still is what Berne calls "The Games People Play." That's a strange pastime, too. You go into the intimacy game to get the response you want. For instance, your husband hasn't been paying enough attention to you or vice versa, and so you come home and ask, "What's the matter, honey?" The answer, "Oh, nothing." And you say, "But there must be something. Look at you! You look like death warmed over." "It's nothing." "Then what are you trying to make a thing out of it for?" "*It's nothing*." "But honey there must be something." "No"—and on and on with the game.

But the highest level at which we're able to interact and have a relationship is what I am talking about today, and that is *real intimacy*. That is where we give and receive without exploitation. "I don't want to use you, I want to love you. I want to experience you. I want to know you. I want to smell you. I want to feel you. I want to grow with you. I want to dance with you, cry with you. I want to caress you." But as I said, it's going to take all the energies you have.

To strive for intimacy is a risk and may bring pain. But the only way you are ever going to see yourself and to grow is in an intimate relationship. In my book, *Love*, I said, "When I love you and you love me, we're like each other's mirror, and in reflecting in each other's mirror we see infinity." If I want to know about me I won't find it by living alone. I'm going to find it by your responses to me—every one of you, and if everybody is turned off by me maybe I should look at myself. How many people do we know who blame everybody but themselves? Society's against them, the secretary's against them, the kids are against them. Even God's against them. Well, you know, if that's true, couldn't it be that there's something about *them* that's turning people off? Maybe they should look at themselves? A wonderful way to look at yourself is the reflection in other people's response to you.

I think the second big thing about caring is commitment. It's the most beautiful combatant against loneliness. Isn't it nice to know that when you go home, there'll be somebody there to take you in? I don't know how many of you know the work of Joan Didion. She is a wondrous, sensitive writer whom almost nobody reads. Her latest book is called *A Book Of Common Prayer*—an incredible story. Her big thing is the liberated woman—not in the usual sense, but in the sense of "Let's knock off exploiting women; let's gain insight into the fact that they will not be exploited any more."

An earlier book of hers is *Play It Like It Lays*. She describes a beautiful Hollywood starlet who is used and abused by everybody. The director uses her, the producer uses her, the musicians use her and she's slowly going mad. She becomes, literally, a commodity, something to be used and discarded. She's dying of loneliness, but she can't find honesty. Every time she thinks she does, somebody cuts her down. She has a beautiful little statement that I'd like to read which I think helps to explain the gut-level loneliness which, if we are honest, all of us feel sometime:

> She would watch them in the supermarket and she knew all the signs. At seven o'clock on a Saturday evening, they would be standing in the checkout line reading the horoscopes and *Harper's Bazaar*. And in their carts would be a single lamb-chop and maybe two cans of cat food and the Sunday paper, the early edition with the comics wrapped around it. They would be very pretty sometimes, with their skirts the right length and their sunglasses the right tint, and maybe only a little vulnerability and tightness around the mouth. But there they were, one lamb-chop and two cans of cat food and the morning paper. To avoid giving off these signs, Maria shopped always for households: gallons of grapefruit juice, quarts of green chili salsa, dried lentils and alphabet noodles, rigatoni and canned yams, 20-pound boxes of laundry detergent. She knew all the signs of the lonely, and never bought a small tube of toothpaste and never dropped a lone magazine in her cart. The house in Beverly Hills overflowed with sugar, cornmuffin mix, frozen rolls and Spanish onions, and Maria ate cottage cheese.

How we need each other!

Another thing, too, about intimacy, is that it makes our world larger. I wish I had a drawing board here, because I'd love to show you this. I think it's a splendid thing to think about. Here's an "I" and "I" meet "You," and we stay together because we are attracted to each other and have certain commonalities and we share. These sharings become our "Us." As we continue to share together, we gain more and more "Us." "You" always remain "You," and "I" remain "I." We never disappear, but we develop the "Us" *together*, that is our common bond.

Woe be it unto you if you give yourself totally to another. You're lost forever. Maintain yourself as the others maintain themselves. Then you put "They" together and form "Us." Then work on that "Us," and that "Us" gets bigger and bigger while the "You" and the "I" gets bigger and bigger and form these enormous concentric circles that grow forever! Intimacy is that wonderful "Us." And if, by chance, you lose the special "Us"—you still have an "I" and loving memories to build with.

I work in a university where a lot of the wives are working their husbands' ways through school. I don't give advice often, but I give lots of alternatives, and I warn them, don't just sit in a dull, dreary office pounding a typewriter all day while your husband is in graduate school living it up with interesting new ideas of all kinds. You say, "Listen, Buster, relationships are a 50-50 proposition. Every Wednesday night I'm going out. You can help by getting the house clean."

You've got to keep growing. You've got to be bringing in newness every single day. Your main responsibility, along the way, is to yourself. Because if you don't feel that way, you can't bring anything to anybody else. You can only bring what you have. If you become alive by dancing through the world, swinging from the trees, doing kooky things, you become and stay exciting.

So it's the *sameness* that brings us close, but its newness that will keep us together. Be wise, be stimulating, be exciting, share new ideas, grow, develop. Don't ever be predictable!

When I was counseling parents, I had a couple who told this story, which was the honest-to-goodness truth. They had raised three children. They had worked their fingers to the bone, and their youngest daughter finally married. After the wedding was over, they went home and sat across from each other. He looked at his wife and said, "Who the hell are you?" That happens more often than we think! We're so busy making lives for others that we forget that the essential life is our own. Sit him down every now and then, do something wild, like eat gefilte fish by candlelight. If you don't like gefilte fish, try a McDonald's hamburger! But light a candle and put on romantic music! Open a bottle of wine and live it up! "That is *our* time. We don't even answer the telephone." Even if it's midnight—that's the nicest time anyway. We've forgotten how nice it is to watch the dawn come up.

Another thing that destroys intimacy is the lack of change. We're afraid of change. Intimacy needs change. It's changing, everything in it is in a state of change, and you can't expect others to remain the same; they're going to change too!

Also, intimacy cannot be *expected*. You can have *no* expectations in interaction with another. No one can always be or do what you would wish of them. Everything comes to you as a surprise, and if you think about it, every downer that you have is because someone didn't meet *your* expectations. Think about it! Every time you're down, it's because someone didn't call, or didn't remember your birthday. If they remember it, you dance around the table, do back flips, the splits! And if they don't remember, it's alright, too. It mainly requires that you be spontaneous in your approach to relationships. See what happens. Laugh yourself silly over what bothers other people. "He didn't remember my birthday, that sweet old guy. I'll buy *myself* a present, it's better anyway. I'll get exactly what I want." Predictability is a bore, if you want to be fascinating, be unpredictable. The only thing you can count on as far as I'm concerned is my unpredictability. You can never count on what I'm going to do or say. I change constantly, and I like it. When my students raise their hands and say, "That isn't what you said Tuesday." I say, "I know. I've grown since Tuesday. Do you expect me to be last Tuesday's Leo today?"

Show what you *feel* in relationships. If you feel like crying, cry your eyes out! When you feel like laughing, laugh your eyes out. Scream when you want to scream. Roll on the floor. Surprise everybody!

Please don't *wait* to communicate your feelings. I think one of the greatest destructive elements in relationships and intimacy is our inability to relate what we're feeling now. I always tell people, never have short arguments; always think of it as interminable. The trouble with arguments is that they are usually over before they solve anything, before we really know what we're arguing about. The longer you argue, the more you're going to get to the feelings, and so when they start walking out of the room, chase them! Say, "Wait! I don't understand. Keep talking!" Eventually you're going to find out what you're arguing about is pretty damn silly.

If we ever needed each other, we need each other now. The family is disintegrating, divorce rates are growing; relationships are casual and mostly meaningless. The suicide rate is doubling, especially among young people. Intimacy is not simple. It's a great challenge to our maturity. It's our greatest hope.

Choose Life

*T**o* me, the greatest thing we have is *life*. And where there is life—as the old adage goes—there is hope. So maybe, if we can get into *choosing* life, it won't be as difficult as we might imagine. And yet there are so many who don't choose it. Not too long ago one of my students came into the university. *He* was really despondent. He said, "You and your ideas about life. You make me sick. You say 'choose life.' Why the hell should I? Life chose *me*. I didn't *ask* to be born. I was made to come on this earth, and if I don't choose to live it, I don't see why it's my responsibility to choose it."

Thousands of people go to mental hospitals every year and relinquish their lives to doctors and therapists. Other people give it up and say, "You live my life *for* me," instead of taking this incredible gift and living it *fully*.

I don't know whether you are aware of it, but there's a growing phenomenon called "battered child syndrome," where we're beating up our children so miserably you can't imagine. Just recently in Los Angeles a little girl had her eyes gouged—things that are almost unbelievable. And there's another sickness arising that, to me, is almost incomprehensible, and that is, we are battering the aging. We're *beating* old people. Children are beating their aging mothers and fathers.

An interview was done of people 65 and over—thousands of them—and only 20 percent of these people said they were "happy." The rest called themselves "*victims*." Is that where we're headed? Is that the point of life? To live on to the point where we're going to be victimized in the end?

There are plenty of people going around talking about death, and despair, and misery. If you want that, you can get it everywhere. Read your paper. Turn on your TV sets. Or you can choose to say life is *good*, life is *beautiful*, let's *celebrate* it.

Have you ever thought about going to see what the dictionary says about a word like life? I'm going to read you what I found because it's glorious: "Life is the quality which distinguishes a vital and functioning being from a dead one." Now isn't that *glorious*? But it's not a lot of help, is it? There's another one, and I love this one. It says, "The period of usefulness of something." I thought, if usefulness is the determinant of our being alive or dead, then there are an awful lot of dead people running around the place. The one I love the best is the third definition: "To pass through or spend the duration." You know, most of us are really passing through and spending the duration. Not very many of us are really, in the real sense of the word, alive and living fully. The thing is, I'm certain that as long as you leave your life in the hands of other people, you'll never live. *You have to take the responsibility for choosing and defining your own life.*

I really believe most people are *afraid* of life. I don't know why it is. We're afraid to be what we are! We get marvelous, insane feelings and we don't act on them. You see someone really attractive and you think, "I'm going to tell her she's really beautiful." And *then* you think, "Oh, I couldn't do that." And then she goes all of her life not knowing she's beautiful! It's a shame because if we really don't live fully we keep other people from living fully!

We're afraid of living life, therefore, we don't experience, we don't see. We don't feel. We don't *risk*! We don't care! And therefore we don't live—because life means being actively involved. Life means getting your hands dirty. Life means jumping in the middle of it all. Life means falling flat on your face. Life means going beyond yourself—into the stars!

But you must decide yourself, for yourself. "What does life mean to me?" I'm convinced if we spent as much time—no, *one quarter* as much time each day thinking about life and living and loving as we do planning a meal, we'd be *incredible*!

But life has a wonderful way of solving this problem. It's always very fascinating to me because when life is not being lived, it *explodes* in us. It's like trying to hold the lid on when the steam is ready to blow. Something will happen, I'm *convinced* of it. You'll either turn to extremes of fear, pain, loneliness, paranoia, or apathy. All signs that you are not alive, you are not living! So if you're feeling any of these things, roll up your sleeves and say, "Let me live." The minute you start getting involved in life, *the steam lets off*, and you're safe. It isn't easy, but life lets us know that it must be led. How wonderful!

People come to me and say, "You seem to have things all together. If life is so great, how come we have death, pain, misery, and all these negative things? Why must children suffer? Why are there murders and rapes and wars? Why, why, why?"

I say, "How the hell am I supposed to know?" Greater men than I have been asking these questions for years. But you know what I've done? I have stopped asking the questions, and I've started living into the answers, and it's made all the difference.

Why death? *I* don't know why death. Why pain? I wish it weren't there, but I don't know "why pain." If I spent my life wanting answers about those things I would never live.

But I tell them I do know a little bit about life. There is such a thing called joy, because I've *felt* it. And there is such a thing as *marvelous madness* because I've lived it. And I know there is such a thing as loving because I have *loved*. And I know there is such a thing as *ecstasy* because I have known *ecstasy*. And I also know—because I have known people who have experienced it—that there is such a thing called *rapture*. Oh, I love that word "rapture"! *Reach for rapture!* I refuse to die until I learn what rapture is!

Anyway, one of the things I know is that you can give yourself these things. You can create these things. All of your life, you were *given* you. You *became* you. You learned to *be* you. And the wonderful thing—and as an educator, I can promise you this—anything that can be learned can be unlearned, and relearned in new ways. So if you want to be anything you want to be, you can *be* it—provided you're willing to get your fingers dirty, willing to suffer a little bit, willing to struggle a little bit, and willing to work at it a little bit because it doesn't come naturally. You've got to work at it. It's all there!

I like to think that the day you're born you're given the world as your birthday present. A *gorgeous box* wrapped with *incredible* ribbons! And some people don't even bother to open the ribbon, let alone open the box. And when they open the box they expect to see only beauty and wonder and ecstasy. They are surprised to find that life is also pain and despair. It's loneliness and confusion. It's all part of life. I don't know about you, but I don't want to pass life by. I want to know every single thing in that box. This little box is named Pain. Well, it's mine, too, and I'm going to open up pain and experience pain. And this little box is marked Loneliness. And you know what happens when I open that box marked Loneliness? *I experience loneliness*. And when you tell me, "I'm lonely," I can understand a little bit about *your* loneliness, and there we can come together and hold each other's lonely hands. I want to know *all* of those things. Because I *know* I can also *learn* rapture. If it's there, I will find it. I know that I have been able to turn pain into joy. And you can do it, too. I've been able to take anxiety and turn it into truth. And you can do it, too. There is nothing I can do that you can't do, too. I'm no super human. Everything that I can do, you can do, too. And some of you can do it a lot better. If you don't have it, it's not because you *don't* have it. It's because you're not working for it. It's *there*, and it's *yours*.

We can turn despair into hope, and that's magical. We can wipe away any tears and substitute smiles.

There are two big forces at work, external and internal. We have very little control over external forces such as tornados, earthquakes, floods, disasters, illness and pain.

What really matters is the *internal* force. How do I *respond* to those disasters? Over *that* I have complete control. Believe it or not. Several years ago there was a major earthquake in Los Angeles. It was just dawn. I heard this enormous "crack" and my living room collapsed. Down the hallway came a roar of dust. I really like to live, just like you, so my first response was, "Buscaglia, get the hell out of here!" Out the door I went, despondent, thinking "my pretty, wonderful house is gone and all those things I've accumulated—gone forever."

I got very *calm*, and I sat down on my back porch. The dust kept roaring through and we had little quakes all the time. I saw my neighbors across the fence and I said, "Hi!" They said, "Leo! Your house!!" I said, "I know. Something's wrong with my house, but I can't see it yet and I might as well wait."

Then we began to laugh. I had no utilities, but my neighbors had gas and were able to make coffee. We sat by the trees until the sun came up and then went in and looked at the damage. But, I could do nothing about it. To become hysterical was fine, but to get in touch with my own feelings and accept that—that was possible.

People always ask, "How did you really start to love life?" Well, I don't really know. How do you know when something starts? If you think I went to a mountaintop in Nepal and had a great vision, I'm sorry to disappoint you. It would be wonderful if I could tell you that, but it isn't true. I don't *know* when it started, but I have an idea that it started maybe with Tulio and Rosa, my two incredible parents. They were the craziest people in the world. Both of them. I just regret that they are no longer with us, because I would *love* to, share them with you. They were so insane. They lived on this strain of insanity that was just beautiful. I guess we all learned a little bit from them right off the bat about being crazy—that wonderful madness that you get in touch with, that keeps you going when everything else is so insanely sane!

Everyone says, "That Buscaglia is crazy." You should see my reputation at the university . . . "he's nuts." But that's wonderful because it gives me an enormous leeway for behavior. When you're considered nuts you can get away with damn near anything, otherwise they call the cops.

Papa died about five or six years ago. Every time I go to San Francisco I get a tremendous feeling of nostalgia because he *loved* that city. Mama and Papa would go to North Beach because, to them, that was a little bit of Italy. They'd eat pasta until they'd burst, talk Italian and get in touch with the culture again, and then return to the vast wasteland of Los Angeles.

It was a beautiful happening for us. They'd always bring all the *bambini* with them; they never went anywhere without them. They'd pile everybody in this little old Chevrolet. I remember we used to hang out the windows. Mama used to travel in comfort—she'd bring special chairs. We'd stop along the road where it said "Rest Area" and most people munch on sandwiches, peanuts or something. Not Mama—she'd cook gnocchi. We'd have a feast! Then we'd pile back into the car, with the stove and the refrigerator and the pasta maker. It used to take us *days* to get to San Francisco. I always thought it was 2,000 miles from Los Angeles.

I hope all of us are able to make peace with papas and mamas and brothers and sisters and loved ones before they die. Papa heard that he was to die of cancer. So I went to him and said, "Papa, I want to do something with you during that time. If you want me to, I want to be with you all the time during that period. Where do you want to go? Do you want to go back to Italy?

"Oh, no, no, no, no. This is my country now. But I'd like to go to San Francisco."

So we piled into the car and drove to San Francisco. For five glorious days we roamed the streets. We ate! Five meals a day! We did all kinds of things together.

You know what else he wanted to do? This will show you what a crazy man he was. He used to love the slot machines in Las Vegas, so he wanted to go and play the nickel machines—no big gambler but sit there and play the nickel machines. I told the hostess there, "You see that man sitting over there seriously playing that nickel machine? Don't ever let him run out of nickels." I gave her dollars, and she'd drop five dollars in—he'd say, "I'm winning! I'm winning all night!" Don't tell me he didn't know what was happening—he was too smart a man—but it was beautiful. He never had it so good!

Nevertheless, when he died, it was a very difficult thing for me, as it will be for you, to say good-bye to someone you dearly love. I remember returning from the funeral and really being wiped out. Just as I walked up to my porch I saw a big bouquet of flowers and a gigantic chocolate cake. Attached, there was a little note from a friend: "Leo, this is just to remind you there still are beautiful things and good things to eat."

You see, I couldn't keep Papa from dying when the time came, but the internal forces helped me to say "yes, it's all right."

My dad was the kind of person who gave everything away. Everything! He never had anything. The minute we'd get a little ahead and be able to buy shoes and things, he'd find some way to give his money away again. So we were constantly going from having to not having. But Mama was also able to cook wonderful things with so little. We had pan e choi—that's just bread and broth and cabbage. It is baked in the oven, and when put in the stomach, it *expands enormously* and you don't know you're hungry! So when things were bad, we always had pan e choi.

I remember my dad being really despondent. And by the way, they never hid life from us. They always let us know when they were despondent and unhappy and fearful. They never let us believe they were Rocks of Gibraltar. They always let us know they were human, and for that I'm grateful. They were not symbols of perfection; they were symbols of humanness!

I remember him sitting down and telling us that his partner had absconded with all their money and he didn't even know where our next meal was coming from.

Mama had the craziest habit—she loved to laugh. And that just struck her so funny. He was furious with her! She was laughing, tears were coming down her cheeks. You know what she did? We all went off and came home that evening and she had prepared a banquet such as we would have for a baptism, or a wedding: antipasto, pasta, veal, everything!

My father said, "My God, what's this."

She said, "I spent everything on this."

He said, "You are *crazy*!"

She said, "The time we need joy is *now*, not later. This is the time we need to be happy. Shut up and eat!"

Isn't that interesting?

We sat down. That was years ago—and I tell you I will never forget that dinner, Mama's Misery Dinner. And you know, we survived! Isn't that crazy? We survived. Look! I'm here! Papa lived to be 86.

So, certainly there are external forces, but what really matters is how you *personally* respond to those external forces. You can bring joy to despair. Believe it! Try it the next time!

There's one thing I'm certain of: misery loves company. Not only does it love it, it *demands* it! The miserable want you to be miserable, too. Boy, they're going to work at it, I'll tell you. "Don't you dare be happy." Well, they're not going to get *me* there. They might like company, and I'll be their company, but I'll be their *joyous* company, not their miserable company.

In order to do these things we've got a lot of choices to make. One of the major choices is "choose you."

Choose you.

Stop hating yourself. Stop running yourself down. Put your arms around yourself and say, "You know, you're all right! You may be losing your hair, but you're all I've got!"

When you make peace with your weakness, you've made it! They're not big, they're just a small part of you.

You've got to choose yourself. I'm sure the people who take their lives, who don't *live*, are basically those who have no feeling of self respect. I don't know when the last time was that anybody told you this, but I want to stress it: *You are a miracle*.

I'm always awed. All different faces . . . all so wondrous, all so beautiful. Eyes different, noses different, mouths different. So different are you that you can be identified by your fingerprints! If that doesn't tell you how unique you are!

Why were you made so unique? So that you could become like everybody else? I don't think so. I don't think that was God's intention. I think you were made unique because you have some unique statement to make. Dedicate your life to finding out what that statement is. Develop that statement, and share it with me, because in the process of sharing it with me, we will both become more. You have responsibility and a duty to becme all that you are. When you lose you, there is nothing left.

Maintain your dignity; maintain your integrity. Nobody can put you down except *you*. They may see you differently, but you *know* who you are, and you *be* that something, and with pride. "I am I"—remember Medea's statement at the end of that beautiful play, where they say, "Medea, what is left?" She says, "What is left? There is *me*!" That's a beautiful thing, because you are so much.

Each of us is a history. Isn't that amazing? We've done study after study—in one household with the same mother, the same father: one child can become a saint, the other can become a demon. Why? Doesn't that say something about the specialness of you, and the way you perceive things? All of you came tonight with a different world in mind. All of you came with a different history. Some of you had parents who were wonderful and loving and tender and kind. Others of you had abusive parents who tried but failed. Others had histories that were incomplete, with great gaps. Others had full and exciting histories. But you all came here tonight.

That is another big "why." How come? What commonality do we all have that brought us together tonight? I don't know, but I'm sure it's there. There's *something*. I like to think about it as magic. And what a wonder—think about that! You brought your special history. And you also have an emotional history that is uniquely yours. Some of you, right at this moment, are very lonely and in despair. Some of you, right at this moment, are very confused. Some of you are bitter. Some of you are joyous. Some of you are ecstatic. Some of you are bringing all kinds of wondrous vibrations. All of them are valid. All of them are good. All of them are beautiful. Embrace them all—they're all part of you. The mystery is that they brought us together. Let's not ask why.

We're a culture of people who analyze *everything*. Somebody says to you, "I love you," and you say, "Define your terms!" We've almost gotten to the point where we don't know how to experience fully again. Everything that comes at us goes through a strange, screening device, and by the time it gets to us, it isn't what *it* is, but what *we* want it to be, and therefore, we don't change. We don't grow, we don't mature. We go on doing the same things day after day after day . . . But you are a history. You are a unique history. You are a wondrous history! But, whatever that history is, it's gone and it's past. Love it and embrace it. Reinvent forgiveness. You are never going to be able to choose life until you learn to forgive! You forgive people who have done ill to you by *learning* to forgive them and saying, "It's all right." Because if you don't, then you carry those things on your back like dead albatrosses, and they *weigh you down*. When you learn to forgive, and when you learn grace again, you can cut those weights free, and all of those energies you use to keep those things in check can now be used to help you grow and become beautiful. So don't carry your past around like a dead albatross. *Let it go!* Learn from it and let it go.

You know, Eugene O'Neill said something lovely. He said,

> None of us can heal the things that life has done to us. They're done before we can realize what's being done, and they then make you do things all of your life until these things are

constantly coming between you and what you'd like to be. And in that way you seem to lose yourself forever.

So you are a past, but you are also a *future*. You know that. But who can judge what the future will be? Nobody can. So why be concerned with this future? The only people who become wealthy by being concerned with the future are insurance companies. They assure us. Heaven forbid! If anybody *doesn't* assure us, it's insurance companies. They put all kinds of strange ideas into our heads about having to protect ourselves from all these things so that we're worrying about worry.

But you are also a present. You're a "now." With will, intellect, desire, and rapture—you can become anything you want to be from this point on.

This may sound very, very naive to you, but I fully believe that if you were to decide to "be" tonight . . . let's say that you were to say tonight as you left, "I am going to find out what it means to be a lover of life," or "I'm going to find out what it means to be a lover, and starting tonight, I am going to behave as a lover. Whenever I start to say anything negative, I'm going to stick my fist in my mouth!" What would happen to you in the next three or four weeks would be outrageous. Incredible.

You *have* the power. You could do it. Nikos Kazantzakis says, "You have your brush, you have your colors, *you paint paradise*, then *in* you go." And if you want to paint hell, go ahead and paint it, but then don't blame me, and don't blame your parents, and don't blame society—and for goodness sakes, don't blame God . . . You take full responsibility for creating your own hell.

We're a past? Yes. We're a future? Yes. But the real thing that we must dedicate ourselves to, if we're going to *choose* life, is choosing life in the present! Right *now*! Because that's where it all matters. Because we are *also* a potential. But in order to develop this potential, we've got to rid ourselves of "self-defeating self." Paul Reps calls it "The paraphernalia of anti-self." And boy are we full of it! We've got to rid ourselves of "don'ts." We've got to rid ourselves of "nevers." We've got to rid ourselves of "can'ts." We've got to rid ourselves of "no's"—what a negative world! We've got to rid ourselves of "impossibles"—nothing's impossible. We've got to rid ourselves of "hopeless"—nothing's hopeless. These are words for *fools*, not intelligent people. Wipe them out of your vocabulary. Never say never! "Impossible? Of course it's possible."

The greatest dreams that have been accomplished by men and women have been called impossibilities—and somebody has *proved* the impossible was possible. People have been pronounced dying and stood up and said, "To hell with you. *I'm* not going to die."—and they don't. And they don't and they don't! Read Norman Cousins' *Anatomy of an Illness*. He was pronounced almost dead. They said he had a couple of months to live. Instead, the man's writing articles for *Saturday Review;* he's lecturing all over the world; he just wrote a book. He's teaching full time. He's active and wonderful—he refuses to die!

Say "yes" to life! "Yes" to wonder, to joy, to despair. "Yes" to pain, "yes" to what you don't understand. Try "yes." Try "always." Try "possible." Try "hopeful." Try "I *will*." And try "I can."

I'm convinced that your incompleteness is responsible for causing you your greatest suffering. Become all that you are. Embrace it. But that's not enough. You may say, "That sounds like an awful lot," but keep doing it because that's a life's work. Discovering new learning, new abilities, new creativity. You could live to be 500 and you could still be producing like crazy.

But if you want to change faster, more magically, you must change that "I" and broaden it to an "us." You must include me. I'm really very tired of the "I" and the "Me" generation and I think you are too.

But in order to take you into my life, I have to be able to give up a little of me. And that's good, because I gain so much more.

One of my greatest passions are trees and leaves. I'm a leaf freak, and I make no bones about it. When I go back east, where they come out in all their majestic glory, I go berserk. I remember I was visiting one of my students who lives in New England who wanted me to see these leaves in the Fall. Write down in your journals tonight, "I will not miss New England in the Fall under any circumstances. I will sneak away from work. I will give that to me as a gift. I will bring with me the people that I love. I will share this magic!"

So I'm driving along with my student, and I'm exclaiming, saying, "Oh! Stop the car! Oh my goodness! Look at that!"—I was going out of my mind! I couldn't stand it, I'd never seen anything like it! We miss that in Los Angeles. The leaves get dry and go "plop." Here were these trees with red leaves, gold leaves, blue leaves, purple leaves, brown leaves, magenta leaves, and black leaves—yes, black leaves—all on the same tree! Can you believe it? That's some sort of a miracle!

I turned to this *brilliant* student of mine, a graduate student—but don't let that fool you. One thing I learned many many years ago, and that's that education has no effect whatsoever. Some of the stupidest people I know have Ph.Ds. *I* have one. Anyway, I said to this brilliant student of mine, "How come?" He's living there, he's lived there all of his life. "How come this leaf chooses to be black and this leaf chooses to be yellow?"

He said, "I don't know. That's just the way it is."

I said, "It is *not* just the way it is! There's a good reason for it, and I want to know. You take me to the library right now!"

He said, "God, you haven't changed."

So we went to the library and looked it up, and you know, I found out it is *magic*. Now *I* know, and I'm not going to tell you.

But knowing the scientific reason for the change of colors doesn't make it any more or any less spiritual. It's still magic. It's still wonderful.

To choose life, we must be willing to risk again and love again. Can you think of anything more important? What do we work for? What do we strive for? What do we suffer for? What do we hope for? It's love. It's life. To miss it will always be your greatest loss.

But if you are willing to risk, to be hurt, to *suffer*, you will know love.

Van Gogh said a beautiful thing: "The best way to love life is to love many things." Isn't that nice? The best way to love life is to love many things. If you want to know what kind of a lover you are, listen to how many times during the day you say, "I hate"—"I hate this," "Ooo, take that away, I hate it," "I hate those kind of people," "I hate these kinds of things"—rather than, "I love." You say you're a lover—how many times do you hear yourself say, "I *love* it"? "I *love* this," "I *love* flowers!" "I *love* children," on and on.

Another thing you've got to be able to deal with and select, is death. We've got to make our peace with death in order to choose life, because death is an incredibly good friend. It tells us that we don't have forever. And if you want life, you'd better live it now! Because if you wait, it may not be there.

A wonderful thing about Democratic Death is that nobody knows when it's coming. And so it's a challenge to you to live *every moment* as if death were sitting saying to you, "I'm here, I'm here! I'm here!" There's nothing more abhorrent to us in our culture than a concept of death. I have never seen a people more afraid of death than in the United States. You know why? *Because we don't live!* If we lived, we would not fear death.

If you lived every moment—every God-given moment—when your time came, you wouldn't be screaming and yelling. Ask people who are studying death who the people are who die happily. It's those people who attempted to know life.

Death is a challenge. It tells us not to waste time. It tells us to grow, it tells us to become! It tells us to tell each other right now that we love each other. It tells us to give ourselves away *now*! There's a beautiful book called *Il Gattopardo*—"The Leopard." It's about a Sicilian man who *lived* with passion! He believed that the most beautiful singular thing in the world was *la donna*—the woman. He lived all of his life admiring beauty, especially female beauty. He also worked to keep a family together, but he never lost sight of the magic, of the beauty of all women. There were no ugly women for him. He becomes very, very ill, and happens to be in northern Italy at the time. A southern Italian, from Sicily, would never *dream* of dying in northern Italy. He says, "Get me home. Get me home! I've got to go back to my house and die with my family!" So they take this old man onto a train, to travel down Italy. It's a beautiful trip as they describe his pain and his despair. He's going home, because he knows he's going to die. He just gets into Rome, and he hears all the hustle and bustle in the station. He opens the window curtain and looks out. He sees the most *incredible* lady, the most beautiful woman he has ever seen. She's *all* in brown, with an enormous brown hat on, with a great brown plume, and brown leather gloves up to here. She's the most elegant lady he's ever seen. He looks at her and says, "Madonna mia!" Even in his sick state. She turns and smiles at him, and the train moves out of the station. He can't get the vision of this woman out of his mind.

In the next chapter he's dying, and all of his family are around him. They're all weeping. He's getting the last rites, the door suddenly opens, and in walks the lady in brown. With all the elegance in the world, she walks right through the family to his bedside. She lifts her hand and gives him her beautiful brown-gloved hand. He looks at her and says, "It's *you.*"

Isn't that wonderful? There's nothing to fear from death. Nothing to fear. It's the biggest challenge that we have. If you remember that we don't live forever, you might turn to the person next to you and not wait, and say, "you're great. Thank you for being you." You might just pick up the telephone and say, "Hey, Mama, you know lots of times we scream at each other, and everything, but I love you," and hang up.

So you see, life and living is a life's work. I remember reading that Kierkegaard said, "Life can only be understood in retrospect," backwards. You know that's wonderful, but *you've* got to live it *forwards*. So we may not be able to understand it, but I'm not sure that it's necessary to understand it. But it *is* necessary to *live* it. Dive in the boxes, open them all up. Say, "They're all mine. It's my prerogative, I have a right to them." You're God's gift to you.

I want to close with a beautiful little thing I found by Joan Atwater, from a book called *The Simple Life*. It's very lovely and very short, and it sort of ties this all together. She said:

> Our lives are overburdened, and living often seems to us a terrible complicated affair. The problems of the world are so incredibly complex and we see that there are no simple answers. The complexity always leaves us with a feeling of helplessness and powerlessness. And still, amazingly enough, we go on, day by day, always half subconsciously yearning for something simpler, something more meaningful.
>
> So how we look for our lives and living becomes tremendously important. It's up to us to bring this authenticity, this simplicity, this directness, this unburdened clarity into our looking. If such a thing as living life fully interests you—*(isn't that a nice way to put it? If living life fully interests you—)* then it's up to you to learn about it and live it.

Certainly we can talk together, and we can work together, and we can learn together, but in the end, each one must define his or her individual life. For it is your life alone, nobody else's. And there's no other way.

Choose Life!

Teach Life

I want to tell you an interesting thing that happened. Some of you know that during Valentine's Day I somehow become a national hero. It's really a wonderful thing to be associated with love, so I'm not complaining. But I get calls from all over the country asking for time for talk shows and newspaper interviews. Magazine people interview me. For one day a year I become a hero. It makes me sorry, though, that we have to set aside a day to remind everybody to love each other. It's sort of like setting aside Mother's Day. Every day should be Mother's Day. Every day should be Sister's Day, Brother's Day, Grandma's Day, Uncle Louie's Day. I don't know why we have to set aside these times, but I guess it's good occasionally to be reminded.

I get a big kick out of watching people's responses to Valentine's Day. We have a big shopping center near my house, and I went there to buy cards for some of my secretaries, and friends. I wanted them to be really special, and I was spending a lot of time. But I was also watching human behavior.

I saw a man come charging in to this beautiful stand that was full of little red hearts, and all kinds of smiling things, and signs that said "Love." He started searching through the cards as if he were going crazy. And he kept saying, "Damn it!" He was buying a heart for his wife. While he was going through he said, "Isn't this a hang-up! What do we have to do this for?"

And I said, "Well why do you do it?"

He said, "What do you mean, *why* do I do it? If I don't do it she'll *kill* me."

A few minutes later a very young lady came in and I smiled at her, and she smiled at me. I said, "Happy Valentine's Day." And she said, "You know what I'm doing here? You won't believe it, but my boss sent me here to buy a valentine for his wife." And she said, "Boy, I tell you if my husband sent another woman to buy a card for me I'd *kill* 'im." Here we were standing among hearts and love tokens and we heard about two planned murders in just five minutes! And all in a sudden it occurred to me why I go around talking about "choose love" and "choose life."

You know that besides all my running all over the country and all the crazy things I do, I'm basically a teacher, and I'm happy to be that more than anything else in the world. I have learned a long, long time ago that nobody has ever taught anything to anybody. That's an ego trip. I could be the wisest man in the world and tell you all I know, but if you don't want to know it you do not learn it. I know that, because I'm constantly yelling and screaming at my students, and I know that they have the power to look enthralled. They look at me like, "Oh, man, are you interesting." But nothing's happening. It's going in, it's getting down on the paper, but I know that they're often thinking about, "Now what'll I wear tonight?" To just toss out information is one thing, but learning is a decision that *you* make. I can't make it for you. Bandura at Stanford, who's doing all the wonderful research now in learning, is telling us again and again, we learn from *modeling*. We don't learn from being *told*. We learn from watching, observing, picking it up and trying it out. That's the way we learn. It's a volitional discovery process. It bothers me that we are demanding that our kids learn love, learn responsibility, learn joy of life, and we don't offer them too many models. We have people screaming over hearts and sending secretaries out to buy their wives valentines.

On commercial television there is an ad that really bothers me. It's a commercial about remembering your parents. It's a service where all you have to do is call in and they pick a gift and send it to your parents wherever they are. Then they show these two lovely old people. The doorbell rings, and they run to the door and pick up this gift that's been picked by some creep! That's not a *gift*. Better you keep it!

What do you think about statistics like these? In a recent mental health survey, only 20 percent of those people in America who were interviewed said that they enjoyed life and were happy. Twenty percent! One out of every seven of us is going to require psychotherapeutic help before we get to the age of 40. One out of every three marriages will end in divorce. And they say that before the year 2000 it's going to be one out of every other one—one out of every two. I just learned a statistic that really blew me out. Sixty million Valium prescriptions are given every year in the United States.

When we are this kind of model, what do we expect the people in our environment, especially the children that we're working with, to pick up?

People are always saying, "Oh, but Buscaglia, you are so lucky, growing up in that home you had." I smile when they say that. It's true. I was lucky. I had an incredible, wonderful Papa and an insane Mama. She was outrageous! She always brought joy and music and beauty and understanding into our home. Papa was very serious.

I was learning from them all the time. I didn't know that this woman was so amazing. No one ever stopped to tell me those things. But I learned. I learned pride. We were very, very poor. Some of you understand that. And that isn't everything. All of the money that we have cannot buy what I learned. But it was not all joy and pride and good.

I remember, I was a really skinny little boy, and Physical Education was my nightmare of the day. I was so uncoordinated I never learned how to throw a ball. I had real skinny spindly legs and long gangly arms. Big eyes, that's all you could see. And I would get in P.E. class in those shorts that were three sizes too big because Mama was smart—"You'll outgrow them, so get the big ones." So there I was in these great, big things which were hanging down around my knees. Just two eyeballs lost in a gymsuit. And so I'm standing there in line with all of these guys, and here's the big, macho guy over here. And he is going to be the team leader. And the other big macho guy over there, is going to be the other team leader. And they start choosing, remember that? "I pick *you*," big guy walks out there. "I pick *you.*" And the line is dwindling. And you begin to pray, and you say, "Dear God, make somebody pick *me*. Don't let me be *last*." Every time, last. I remember there was me and a beautiful, incredible, fat Jewish boy. The Dago and the Jew. Always the last two. These guys would be swinging and knocking balls all over the place, and I'd get up there with the bat, and say my little prayer: "Just once, God, let me connect *right out of the field*." Never. God had better things to be concerned about.

But what was I learning from these models? I was learning that I was inadequate, that I couldn't do those things other boys did. I was almost seventeen years old before somebody said to me, "You *can* throw a ball. What's the matter with you? It's an easy skill. Let me show you how to do it." And I wondered why they didn't do that back then. So many years of agony and despair, abhorring my body. I had a neat body. It was just skinny. Now I have a neat body. It's just fat. I love it. But we are taught every day without knowing that it's happening. I work with kids all the time. You know that that's my life. And again and again I hear, "I can't do that. I'm dumb." And I say, "Who told you you're dumb?" "My teacher." "My father."

Ooohh. I'd like to get hold of them. I'd like to introduce them to my favorite teacher of all time, whom I always write about. If you ever find her anywhere, tell me. I'll fly to Nepal to give her a hug. Marvelous Miss Hunt. For her, nobody was ever dumb. Everyone had a uniqueness that was totally theirs, and she knew it. She weighed three hundred pounds! All unique. All caring, all loving. All encompassing. Oh, when Miss Hunt hugged you and you disappeared in her . . . You would learn anything for her. *Anytime!* What a model!

And so every day we are modeling for our children. The question I keep asking is, what kind of a model are we? How can we demand that children become lovers when they don't see too many of them? How can we demand that they be responsible and caring and concerned, when they have no models for concern and caring and love? What they see and learn is what they're going to practice. It's what we're going to get. So I would love to talk to you about some of the things that we may want to model. And in order to do that, we must say, "I want to be the best model. I want to model life."

I'm so amazed when I read statistics such as only twenty per cent of the population in America would choose life. So many people say to me again and again, "I didn't ask to be born." What a pity, when there's so much. I can't ever take anything for granted. I'd go crazy. I love so intensively because there's so much to know and to see and to do and to taste and to chew—especially to chew!

I'll show you how naive I really am. Has it ever occurred to you? Aren't you amazed that carrots taste like carrots and radishes taste like radishes? And that if we mix them together, and make some kind of a goulash, we can get a third taste? I'm astounded by things like that.

I was in Albany recently, and I had come from 83 degrees into minus-fifteen. And everyone kept saying, "Oh, you poor thing." I said, "What are you talking about? Look, it's snowing and there's ice on the ground, and I don't see this all the time. I want to celebrate the weather." Then they were convinced, it's that kooky Buscaglia again.

One of the first things that we must teach children—and we can't teach it unless we believe it ourselves—is that each of you is a "holy" thing. I'm awed when I look at an audience or meet people, the gold mine of you. The very fact that I look at you and see all these incredible faces, sparkling eyes and red hair and yellow hair and brown hair and no hair. To say that there are no two of you alike, is awesome. We need to tell this to children early before they lose their individuality.

Why do we protect children from life? It's no wonder that we become afraid to live. We're not told what life really is. We're not told that life is joy and wonder and magic and even rapture, if you can get involved enough. We're not told that life is also pain, misery, despair, unhappiness and tears. I don't know about you, but I don't want to miss *any* of it. I want to embrace life, and I want to find out what it's all about. I wouldn't want to go through life without knowing what it is to cry. That's why I have lachrymal ducts. If I wasn't meant to cry, I wouldn't have them. It's all right to cry a little bit. I always find that tears clear my eyes.

I love the work of Martin Buber, and especially his concept of "I" and "thou." He says each of us is a Thou, and when we're interacting with each other, we must interact as if we are holy things, because indeed we are special. So when I'm interacting with you, you are a Thou. He says so often we interact with each other on the basis of I and It. Don't you feel angry sometimes about being treated so often like an "it"? I am never reticent to shout out, scream it, "I'm not an it! I'm *me*. I'm Felice Leonardo Buscaglia. One of a kind! Don't look *through* me. I have *dignity*." As long as we deal with people as "I" and "Thou," says Buber, we have *dialogue*. When we treat people as "I" and "*it*," it becomes a *monologue*. I don't want to talk to myself. I want to talk with *you*. And I want you to talk with me. We have dignity. And children have to learn that, and they have to learn it *early*.

They also have to learn that they don't find themselves by looking outside of themselves. They have to look *inside*. It's not an easy trip, the trip of finding your uniqueness to share with others, because all of your life you're told by others who you are. Has it ever occurred to you that you are not really you? Most of you are what people have told you you are. And maybe some of you have been wise enough to get hooked on the fact that others meant well, but what they say you are may not be congruent with what you *really* are, because you feel uncomfortable with the role that's thrown on you. And so you smash it. You say, "I'm going to try to find who *I* am," and if you do it's going to be your biggest challenge. There's going to be no peace, but it's also proof positive you will never be bored. Self-discovery is like all discovery. It's never easy, but you can't count on others for insight.

I love the Sufi story about the Mullah who was out in the street on his hands and knees, searching the ground. A friend came by and said "Mullah, what are you doing in the street on your hands and knees?"

He said, "I'm hunting for my house key. I lost my house key."

The friend said, "Oh, show me about where you lost it and I'll get down on my hands and knees and help you."

He said, "Oh, I lost it in the house."

The friend asked, "Then what the hell are you doing out here looking for it?"

The Mullah replied, "Oh, it's *lighter* here."

Most of us look for ourselves out here in the light. You're not going to find it there. You're going to have to get down on your hands and knees inside, where it's sometimes dark and spooky, and discover all those wonderful things about you. You are far more unactualized than you are actualized. And you can go on forever and forever. Einstein decried the fact at the point of death that so little of him had been realized.

It's true of all of us. We don't have to be Einstein. But knowing that you're limitless is your greatest challenge. Find out all of that wonder of you, and develop it, and stand up proudly and continue to search. And don't be afraid to fail. It's all right. You don't have to be perfect.

Somebody was very nice before I came out here, and said, "Be careful, there's a cable there. And there are two steps, and you're likely to trip." And I said, "Wouldn't that be fun, if I walked out before these thousands of people in all my glory, and fell flat on my—? Then if there was anybody in the audience who thought I was something special, they'd find out differently." I'm just very happy to be a human person like me, learning.

Then I think we need to teach children the importance of others, and that they cannot grow in this world without taking in others. The more worlds they take in, these unique worlds, the more they can become. We need to teach them to trust others again, because we're all frightened to death of each other. We're building higher and higher walls, stronger and stronger locks. Tear down the walls! Every day I see how we're distrusting and it hurts.

We've got to learn to trust again, to believe again. Of course it's a risk, but everything's a risk. We need to begin to go beyond just "being" again. We've got to get in touch with being *human,* and there's a difference. There's a wonderful story that Buddhists tell about an ant in a rain barrel, and the different attitudes about this ant. They say the first person goes in, looks in the rain barrel and sees an ant. He says to the ant, "What are you doing in my rain barrel?" And he goes "squish." No ant. *Selfishness.* The next person comes, looks in, sees the ant there, and says, "You know, it's a hot day here, even for ants. You're not hurting anything. Go ahead and sit in my rain barrel." *Tolerance.* And the third person comes and doesn't think about being tolerant or angry. He sees the ant in the rain barrel and spontaneously feeds it a handful of sugar. That's *love.* When you get to the point where you don't have to analyze it any more, you've got it made. The spontaneous reaction. Somebody's on the road and they need me. I stop. Somebody needs to get on the freeway, I let them go. Someone's crying, and I say, "Can I help?" Somebody said to me in an interview, "But what about when you go to people and say something to them and they tell you to mind your own business?" And you're likely to get that. Well, you don't love in order to be loved in *return.* You *love* to *love.* You do it because it's natural to reach in and give this ant some sugar. What have you lost? So many people who have potential are afraid to let you see what they are. So much beauty is lost because we're afraid.

I also think it's important to tell children about the continuity of life. We live in a stratified society. Little children are kept together. Adolescents are kept together. Young marrieds are together. And if you remain single you lose your best friends. Old people, for goodness sakes, are kept together. And where does a kid learn that life is a trip? That it's continuity?

I was so lucky as a child, because my house was always full of people—grandmas and grandpas, and children who had been newly born, and pregnant ladies, and newly-marrieds. I could tell you stories about that. All in the same house! And we learned early that life is a continual process and not stratified. We saw old people and we knew that some day we would be old too. We saw people dying and we began to appreciate life. But when you don't see it you don't know that it's there, and you're scared to death of it. Most of us are horrified about death. We don't know how to die or live with dignity. If you have lived with dignity, you'll die with dignity. You don't have to worry about it.

One of the most fascinating letters I got in the last year was from a woman who was dying and only had three or four months to live. And every other word was "I" and "me." But I could sense that she was a very feeling and beautiful person. She just didn't know how to handle death. I took a gamble, and I answered her and said, "You know, instead of sitting around waiting to die, take full advantage of these few days or few months that you still have and *live*! See what happens if you *do* something. Go to Children's Hospital. In Children's Hospital there is a ward of little children who are also dying. So visit with the children."

Thank goodness she did. The wonder of wonders is that the children taught *her* how to die. The minute she walked in, little kids went up to her and said, "Are you gonna die, too?" No adult was ever daring enough to say such a thing to her. She was not only *dying*, but she was dying of *loneliness*. I don't know why, but she said, "Yes I am." A child said, "Are you afraid?" She said, "Yes." "Why are you afraid? You're gonna go see God." Isn't that interesting? So many of us say that when we die we're going to go see God, and yet we scream and yell in horror when death comes. That's a very interesting dynamic that's worthy of study.

One little girl said, "Will you bring your doll?" The woman is still alive and she's still working, and I don't think she's too worried about when death will come. There's still something to do. There is still time. Age has nothing to do with becoming senile.

It's feeling that you have no more options that makes you senile. As long as you have life you can live right through to death. But children have to have some knowledge of this. They have to *see* it. We hide them from funerals. We don't let them see bodies. We don't give them answers when they say "What happened to my dog?" "What happened to Grandma?" "She went away on a trip." Little kids are going to learn what you teach them. They pick up the attitude of their parents. If their parents are scared to death, so are they. And that's no pun intended.

Then another thing that's essential, and that is that children learn that they have choice. They will only believe that they have choice if you give them alternatives in their lives. Those people that commit suicide, for instance, are those people who have the narrowest aspect of life, they have no choices. Every year at the University, during final examinations, people attempt suicide. There are always beautiful young ladies and young men who slit their wrists because they are afraid to fail. Can you believe having so little self-concept that you're willing to give up your life for an exam? I always say to my students, for goodness sakes, what other things can you do? Certainly, suicide is a viable alternative—but what else could you do? Be creative!

People are always saying that one of the reasons we like to accumulate and amass wealth is because it gives us greater alternatives. That's insane! The highest rate of suicides is among the wealthy. If you don't have the alternatives *now*, you can have all the money in the world and still not have alternatives.

I also remember when we were little, the big thing we did every week, and we always anticipated it, was to get into an old Chevrolet. Can you imagine such a big family in a Chevrolet? The top of it was loaded down with all kinds of wonder because Mama, in all of her splendor, loved to be comfortable. We would go to Long Beach. It would take us almost two hours to get there. We sang all the way. We'd do all the operas. Mama was a singer. She taught us. So one time we'd sing *La Boheme*. The next time we'd do *La Traviata*. This crazy family, with an umbrella, some chairs and boxes. Mama was never satisfied with sandwiches. We cooked spaghetti at the beach. Can you believe it? Antipasto. People would watch us in awe! We'd arrive at the beach and it would take us about two hours to get everything off. Mama would check the wind. "Now put the umbrella here, and put the chair right there out of the wind, facing the sun." We'd get all set, then jump in the ocean and get wet, dry off and change. Oh, I remember that wondrous time. We were so financially poor. We didn't have *anything*. And all these people around us, who had *so much*, were looking at us and wondering, "Who are those freaks?" But we had alternatives to poverty. We had choices, or so we believed in our naive way. But what difference does it make if you're naive and stupid if you're living and alive? I don't think we were so stupid. We were alive and it was fun.

I remember we wanted to take Papa to Hawaii before he died. We knew he was going to die. And we found out that there was a fare on an airplane that was really cheap. They called them "no frills" sections. It was one of those fares where they don't even *look* at you, let alone *feed* you. They just stashed you in the back of the plane. We didn't care. It was all right. We went through the First Class, and we went down to the back. You were allowed to buy your own box lunch. *You* remember that! Don't be so sophisticated. You didn't always have all that you have. Papa said, "So what? We'll cook our own dinner!" I shall always remember what we had because it was so outrageous. We sat there, my sister and I and my niece and so on—we had a whole row—and Papa. And he opened up a box. He had done rosemary garlic chicken. First Class was salivating eighty rows away! I remember the stewardess kept coming back saying, "What do you have there?" He had marinated, garlic mushrooms. Oh, it was such a *special* dinner. Nobody ate as good on that flight. And we shared with everybody. Someone would turn around and look at us. We'd say, "Have a piece of chicken." You *have* choice. You can select joy over despair. You can select happiness over tears. You can select action over apathy. You can select growth over stagnation. You can select you. And you can select life. And it's time that people tell you you're not at the mercy of forces greater than yourself. You, indeed, are the *greatest* force for *you*. Now, you can't do it for *me*, but you can do it for *you*.

People say, "Oh, Buscaglia, you are so naive! You say people can select Joy." Try it. The next time you're in a situation where you can find yourself screaming at someone, try smiling. It's amazing. Some of you have heard me talk about the man at the airport who was screaming at everybody that he had to get out of that airport even though there was a blizzard and it was impossible. Also, there was a little woman who collected all the children and relieved the stranded mothers to go have something to eat. That's the kind of choice *you* can make. And I said, "Why do you make the screaming choice that only reflects on you and gives you bleeding ulcers, instead of making other people happy?" A man I met later said he had never thought about that before, amazingly enough. After he heard this he was in Chicago, the same place where my experience happened. That's a wonderful place to have experiences. It's bound to happen if you go through Chicago enough times. He said he arrived in a blizzard and they told him that they would have to take him to where he was going by bus, there was no possible way of getting out of the airport that night. There were two women on the flight in wheelchairs. They didn't even know each other. There was one on one side and one on the other side. He said, "I thought of Buscaglia who seemed to say to me 'Well, don't just sit there, do something!'" (That was really Mama speaking.)—He said he walked over to each of these two women and he said, "Are you going where I'm going?"

They said, "Yes."

And he said, "What about your luggage?"

And they said, "Well, we can't get out of the wheelchairs and there's no attendant to—"

He said, "I'll take care of you." He went over and got their bags and put them on the bus and helped them on. He said, "I never had such a good time in my life! It was a beautiful, joyous experience." A choice!

Let's talk about risk, because risk is so nice. Once you begin to become hooked on risk, your whole life changes. But change and growth take place only when you're willing to risk and experiment with your own life. You're never sure of anything. Everything's a risk. I remember many years ago I sold everything that I had—much against everybody's advice. I wanted to go around the world. I wanted to hear a crystal-clear temple bell in Nepal. I wanted to sit in a rice paddy in Thailand and talk to people, or at least hug them. And I did. I sold my insurance policy, my house, my car, everything I owned. And I went. People said, "Oh my goodness. You gave up your secure job. You're never going to find another job. You're going to starve when you come home." I came home with about ten cents. I didn't starve, I learned. So much more important were the things that I learned. I learned about attitudes. In Bangkok they say *mah-pen-lai.* I heard people say, "*mah-pen-lai*" all over the place. I wondered, "What's this *mah-pen-lai* stuff?" Finally, when I got acquainted with some Thai people, I said, "There's a phrase I keep hearing in the marketplace, in the airport, in the museums, on the canals, on the rivers, *mah-pen-lai*—what does it mean?" They sort of smiled, and said, "It means 'it's all right, it doesn't matter.'" All in a sudden it dawned on me. My goodness! No wonder they're called the land of smiles, if so many people can say, "It's all right, it doesn't matter." And then I thought about our culture where *everything matters*. "What do you mean, it doesn't matter?! If you think it doesn't matter, it's because you're frivolous!" It *doesn't* matter. The world will go on without you. Ninety percent of what we worry about doesn't happen anyway. And we worry and we worry and we worry. And then we worry about worrying!

Every time I speak, I risk. I always go to people with open arms, saying "You know me." I don't say, "How doo you doo?" Goodness, I'm one of those crazy people who risked hugging the Dean. No one hugs the Dean! The Dean sits behind a desk that's a mile long and two miles wide. And you sit on the other side and you say, "Yes Dean, yes Dean, yes Dean." That's what you do with a Dean. You don't *hug* him. Well, I was sitting there one day and he was saying all kinds of really nice things. And I thought, "What a sweetie. I'll bet he'd love to be hugged." So I just got up and I said, "Dean, that's beautiful!" And I charged at him, sitting in a swivel chaïr. He goes "Aaagh!" So I throw my arms around him and I hug him—much to the horror of my colleagues. "My God, Leo's crazier than we thought!" Well, you know, I'm always consistent, and every time I saw the dean after that, I'd say, "Hi, Dean," and I'd hug him. And I knew he liked it because later on he started cuddling! No one's too big for a hug. Everybody wants a hug. Everybody needs a hug. It changes your metabolism. Risk!

I want to read you this:

"To laugh is to risk appearing the fool." Well, so what? Fools have a lot of fun.

"To weep is to risk being called sentimental." Of course I'm sentimental. I love it! Tears can help.

"To reach out to another is to risk involvement." Who's *risking* involvement? I *want* to be involved.

"To expose feelings is to risk showing your true self." What else do I have to show?

"To place your ideas and your dreams before the crowd is to risk being called naive." Oh, I'm called worse things than that.

"To love is to risk not being loved in return." I don't love to be loved in return.

"To live is to risk dying." I'm ready for it. Don't you dare shed one tear if you hear that Buscaglia blew up in the air or dropped dead. He did it with enthusiasm.

"To hope is to risk despair, and to try is to risk failure." But risks *must* be taken, because the greatest risk in life is to risk *nothing*. The person who risks nothing, does nothing, has nothing, is nothing, and becomes nothing. He may avoid suffering and sorrow, but he simply cannot learn and feel and change and grow and love and live. Chained by his certitudes, he's a slave. He's forefeited his freedom. Only the person who *risks* is truly free. Try it and see what happens.

Speaking of Love

We only have an hour, so let's get going. Isn't it incredible that this lecture is going to go up in satellites?* You and me, together. And the first thing before we go into satellite, now that you've seen my new jacket, is that I'm going to take it off.

A short time ago one of my neighbors told me of a little church near my home where beautiful, spiritual things occurred, and he wanted me to go and experience it. So I said I'd love to, and we went there. No sooner did we open the door of the church, when everybody reached out for me. They took my hand and they petted my shoulder and they felt my hair. Right at the door! And *then* they brought us in. There was a lot of singing and a lot of moving around and dancing—a real celebration. But the high point came when the minister stood up and said, "Friends, Brother Jonathan is going to give the sermon today, and his subject is going to be faith." Little Brother Jonathan stood up. He was about 5'4". He stood before everybody for a minute, folded his hands, and said, "Faith, faith, faith, faith, faith, faith." Then he sat down! The minister stood up with a big smile on his face and said, "Thank you Brother Jonathan for that beautiful lecture on faith." I thought, some day I'm going to wise up and when I go to talk to people as I am tonight, about love, I'm going to fold my hands and I'm going to say, "Love, love, LOVE, LOVE, LOVE, love, love," and *then I'm gonna go home!* It'll be the most beautiful evening we've had. But I'm not that secure yet, I'm going to spend an *hour* telling you what this man said in a minute.

I'm really concerned about the fact that we all need and crave love and so little of it is seen around. I took a course in play therapy.

**This lecture was broadcast to PBS stations by satellite.*

This was for little children; because as adults, we can use language for therapy, and we can talk our way into health. But with children, the natural way is to play with them. You bring children into a room and give them all the little things they can act out on, and you say, "Let's see, let's talk, let's be together, let's share." And you do it in action. I was given a little emotionally ill girl. It was the first time I had ever worked with a child that young. She was five years old. She did all kinds of incredible things. Thank goodness we're finding out that even little infants in cribs know what's going on. Now we're talking big things like "infant stimulation." Good mamas knew that years ago when they held their children and loved them and rocked them and bounced them and threw them across the room instead of leaving them there for fear of spoiling them.

But anyway, Lelani was going through a lot of things, and for several days, she was doing something that really was bothering me. She was getting pieces of clay and she was rolling them up into little snowmen. And then, After she had them all built, she'd go POW! And she'd say, "Mommy!" And then she'd do another one, and she'd go, POW! And she'd say, "Daddy!" She'd go through her whole family, banging them away. And then she'd want *me* to do it! And so, being a very terrible child therapist—really awful, you know, because I was so involved with these kids, and I was supposed to be there just reflecting: "Oh. Lelani smashed her mother." I just couldn't do that. I felt a sort of involvement, and I said, "Lelani, how come you're smashing all the people you love?" She looked at me sort of indignantly, like "you jerk," and she said, "because those are the people that are always hurting me."

Five years old! And then, again being a very bad therapist, I said, "But I love you and I don't hurt you." And she said, "That's 'cause you're crazy." Five years old and she'd already learned that love can be painful. Five years old, and she'd already learned that if you love unconditionally, you must be crazy.

And since then I've done a lot of adult talk shows and we're not too far away from that, even now. The phone rings, and I say, "Hi." And this person says, "Hey Buscaglia, where is this thing called love? I live in a little apartment house on Melrose and I'm all alone. And I don't have the guts or the knowledge about how to break out. Where is it?"

So it doesn't bother me, then, to go someplace and say, "Let's talk about love." I don't care. And if you think I'm crazy, that's wonderful, because when you think I'm crazy, that gives me lots of leeway for behavior. And we accept and forgive people who are crazy. But I want to share some not-so-crazy statistics about love that concern me, and I hope they concern you.

Do you know that there are about 26,000 suicides in the United States per year? Especially for someone like me who thinks the greatest loss in the world is loss of human potential, I want to scream and say, "Hey, *wait a minute!* Don't you know that there are other alternatives?" And do you know that many of those suicides are people who are over the age of 65? Maybe that tells us a little bit about the way we treat people who are old, and how we feel about them, and how we're a society that detests anything old. We don't want it around. We tear it down. We send it away so we don't have to look at it, instead of bringing it in and realizing that old can be beautiful and that those people who have lost a sense of history are going to have to relieve it themselves. One of these days, *you're* going to be there, and unless we do something about it right now, you're going to be stashed away someplace, too. It also bothers me that though the highest suicide rate is above 65 years old, the highest rising rate is among adolescents. Thirteen and fourteen and fifteen-year-old kids who don't even know yet what life is about and who have never been told how wonderful and magical and spiritual and exciting it can be. And they end it all. It's finished for them. There isn't a second chance!

Did you know that one out of every seven people in the United States is going to need some form of psychotherapy before they reach the age of forty? One, two, three, four, five, six, seven—you! One, two, three, four, five, six, seven—you! It doesn't have to be. It isn't necessary! You have all the resources in you to heal yourself, which is what you're going to have to do anyway. You might as well start on that process right now.

Don't miss love. It's an incredible gift. I love to think that the day you're born, you're given the world as your birthday present. It frightens me that so few people even bother to open up the ribbon! *Rip it open! Tear off the top!* It's just *full* of love and magic and life and joy and wonder and pain and tears. All of the things that are your gifts for being human. Not only the really happy things—"I want to be happy all the time"—no, there's a lot of pain in there, a lot of tears. A lot of magic, a lot of wonder, a lot of confusion. But that's what it means. That's what life *is*. And all so *exciting*. Get into that box and you'll never be bored.

I see people who are always saying, "I'm a lover, I'm a lover, I'm a lover. I really believe in love. I act the part." And then they shout at the waitress, *Where's the water?!*" I will believe your love when you show it to me in action. When you can understand that everybody is teaching everybody to love at every moment. And when you ask yourself, "Am I the best teacher," and if your answer is "Yes"—great. Go around—listen to how many times a day you say, "I love," instead of, "I hate." Isn't it interesting that children, as they learn the process of language, always learn the word "no" years before they learn the word "yes"? Ask linguists where they hear it. Maybe if they heard more of "I love, I love, I love," they'd say it sooner and more often.

I've been concerned for such a long time about love that I looked at hundreds of textbooks in psychology and sociology, looking among professionals who really should be the people concerned about this to see what they said. You know, it wasn't even indexed? That's how much we think about love. When I wrote my book, *Love*, it was really funny, because my publisher said, "Oh, Leo, you're going to have to change the name, because I'm sure that someone has used that name before." I said, "Why don't you send it in and see what happens?" So we sent it in and I got the "copyright" for Love! There are books called *Love and Hate, Love and Desire, Love and Fear, The Joy and Power of Love*, but no one ever thought of a book called simply *Love*. L-O-V-E. Such a good word. Such a limitless word. Such a limitless concept.

Who is the loving person? The loving person is the person who loves him or herself. I say this so often, and people say, "Oh, yes, you're so right," but they just *don't do it!* You will never be able to love anybody else until you love yourself. Wiesel, the wonderful Jewish writer, wrote a beautiful thing in a book called *Souls on Fire*. He said:

> When we die and we go to heaven, and we meet our Maker, our Maker is not going to say to us, why didn't you become a messiah? Why didn't you discover the cure for such and such? The only thing we're going to be asked at that precious moment is why didn't you become *you*?

That is your prime responsibility, because if it were not, why is it that you are so incredibly unique? Everybody is different. Everybody has something to give that nobody else in the world has. Isn't that enough for you to become enthusiastic about yourself? And also, to say to yourself, "My goodness, I've got to find out what that is."

I tell that to my students, and they say, "Me? I don't have anything useful." Well, if you believe it and you listen to everyone else, they may convince you that that's true. I don't understand why people are always putting us down instead of encouraging us to become, because when you do become, you will give me a world that I couldn't have any other way. I'm probably in the *Guinness Book of Records* for hugging. Do you know that there are no two people that even hug alike? You have the gentle hugger who sort of floats in your arms. You have the jock hugger who goes rrrhhhooowww. You have the back-slapper that goes Bam! Bam! Bam! You have the tender lover that just disappears in you and then wiggles. Don't tell me that it ever gets boring to hug!

But one of the most difficult things you're going to have to do—it should be the simplest—is to *be you*, to find out who you are and what you have to share. And then dedicate yourself to the process of developing it so that you can give it away to everybody else, because that's the only reason in the world for having anything. The wonderful thing about the self is that it isn't anything that's concrete. The thing that you'll leave behind is something that's not tangible. That's what's so wonderful. It's a great spiritual something. That's what you are. And if you develop that, you'll leave that to everyone you touch. And *they'll* be more. But it's going to be a battle.

Under the guise of love oftentimes comes the greatest violation of the person, because our love is always given within conditions. "I will love you if you bring back good grades." "I will love you if you're nice and you meet my standards." I like to think there's at least *one* person in this world who will just say to you, "I will love you,"—you know, that's what families should be. Robert Frost said, "Home is the place that when you go there they always take you in." And they don't say, "I told you so. You shouldn't have done that." But rather, Mama and Papa go out and get the bandages and say, "Sit down. I'm gonna put 'em on . . . try again." One person! That isn't asking too much. Be that to somebody. And when it's offered to you, accept it, because it's just as hard to take it as it is to give it. Some of us find it far more difficult to take than to give.

So, the hardest battle you're ever going to fight is the battle to be just *you*. You're going to have to fight it for the rest of your life in a world where people feel more comfortable if you can be there for their convenience. But if you give "you" up, there's nothing left. But if we can get our stuff together we can become all that we are. And only then can you say, "I am. I am becoming. I am a lover, because I give you all that I am with no smoke screens. I give myself free." What a nice thing to be able to say. Don't miss it. Don't miss *you*. Somewhere along the line, encounter yourself. Shake hands and say, "Hi. Where the hell have you been all these years?! Well, now that we're together, we can go on our way." And you're going to find that there is no end to you. Your potential is limitless. We've never been able to find a limitation to human potential. You can learn to touch like you've never touched before. Look like you've never looked before. Hear like you've never heard before. Feel like you've never felt before! Do "you" like you've never done before! And after you've done it, you realize you're nowhere. You've got more and more and more and more, all to develop and give away. How fantastic! So that when you're asked when you get to that gate, "Have you been you? Have you become you?" you say, "Yes!"

I was on an airplane recently. I travel a lot, and I really love airports. Some people hate them. I hate getting *to* airports, but I love airports, because I learn more about human behavior in airports than any place in the world. Watch people! Don't be bored. Don't keep looking at what flight's leaving. Watch all the stuff that's going on in that place, the dynamics of life happening.

When I got on the plane, I sat next to a kid who looked like he had everything. He was going to a university in Colorado. He started to talk. Every other word was "I" and "me." "I don't like this," and "schools are for the birds," and "professors stink," and "the world is awful," "America—" Finally, being a good nondirective counselor, I said, "Shut up! Do you realize how many times in the last 500 miles or so you have said, 'me,' and 'I'? What about *us* and *we*?" After a long pause, he said, "Who are you?"

Contrasted with that is my experience last year at O'Hare Airport when it was completely snowed in, and I mean *completely snowed in* for two full days and nights. I was one of those people who was there. In fact, I'll tell you something. Ours was the last plane allowed to land. And then it was announced that not only were we stuck with no flights going out, but we couldn't leave the airport, because there was such a blizzard. We were stuck at the airport. But they told us all the food was free. And the bars were open. Well that was heaven! But there were still people who went around screaming at stewardesses, "*Get me out of this airport! I've gotta be in Cincinnati*!" And I could see their faces, "Boy, would I love to get you back to Cincinnati!"

Contrasted with these people who were screaming and demanding to get out of there right now, was a wondrous woman. She went around to the mothers that were travelling with children: "Let me have your kids. I've always wanted to be a kindergarten teacher and I'm going to start a kindergarten. I tell a wicked story—and while I do this, you go and have a drink and get something to eat."

And you should have seen this woman in that airport with all these kids around her, telling them stories. It was the same situation, the same blizzard. What was the difference between the guy who was screaming and the woman who set up a kindergarten? A choice, that's what it was. An incredible, wondrous, magical, personal choice. I recognize you. And I want to help you, because my joy comes in that, too. Not only that. You know. There could be a lot of harm in giving, giving, giving, giving. Some of you know that. Sometimes the greatest gift you can give is by holding it back. But in this case, how beautiful. To give. To share. Because you have it! And you made the decision that as of now, I'm going to give all that I have to give, and make life easier for *you*.

I was one of those lucky people who was able to see the Dalai Lama of Tibet when he came through, and I wish you all could have experienced this man. Talk about, faith, faith faith! He came on the stage and he looked at the Shrine Auditorium full of people, and we just all sort of melted in his warmth. And if there's a man who has a right to be bitter, if there is such a thing as having a right to be bitter, he has. You know what he said? He said, "Our greatest duty and our main duty is to help others." And then he smiled a little bit, and he said, "and please, if you can't help them, would you please not hurt them?"

You know, if each one of us tonight said to ourselves, well, it's just not in me to go out and help people. I can't do it. But I promise myself that I'm never going to hurt anybody, at least not volitionally. *My goodness, what a wondrous place this would be!* Every time you hear evil conjuring up in your mouth, stick your fist in it! In a little while, it'll become second nature to shove an invisible fist in. And then you won't have to anymore. That's the response you get by being positive—because positiveness begets positiveness.

We hear that and we laugh about it—but everybody loves a lover. We think they're a little bit crazy, but we like them around. So it's wonderful to be able to reach out, because when you reach out and you take in, you get a really positive mirror. It's the only real way we have of seeing ourselves and growing from it!

When we become two and then three and then four, do you realize how much more we get? When I take you in my life, I now have four arms instead of two. Two heads. Four legs. Two possibilities of joy. Sure, two possibilities of tears, but I can be there while you cry and you can be there while I cry, because nobody should ever cry alone.

And nobody should ever die alone. Do you know that in Los Angeles we have a service where you can hire someone for $7.50 an hour to sit with you while you're dying, so you don't have to die alone. That's repulsive! If you reach the point of death and you don't have *one* person who's going to hang on to your hand, review your life. No one should die alone. And if you want these people in, you're going to have to reach out for them and going to have to risk. Learn again to trust!

I love the story of a guy going up a road—it's a very narrow road going up in the mountains, only two lanes—and he gets up to a place where there's a very, very precarious curve. And just as he's about to turn, a woman comes zipping around in her car, and she sees him and she sticks her head out the window and she yells, "*Pig*!" And he says, "Why you—." And he screams back at her, "*Sow, Sow!*" Then he turns the corner and hits a pig!

We don't believe people who want to do good anymore! Just try to get on an L. A. freeway sometime. I'm sitting there in my car and I see these people with these determined expressions: "*Death to you, Buscaglia! Rarrh, Rarrh, Rarrh!*" And it's so funny, because when I slow down to allow someone to enter the freeway from the ramp, which I love to do as I'm never in that much of a hurry, I say, "Come on." You know they don't believe me? I almost get clobbered because they're saying, "Me, me!?" "In! In! In! Yes!" It makes their day. Someone allowed them on the freeway.

But we really become human at the point of reaching out and risking and trusting to bring people in. I've told this story before, and I've even written about it. But it's such a great story that it gives me a joy just to talk about it. There are many things in my classes that I call voluntarily mandatory. Many of you know about a lot of them. One that's very voluntarily mandatory is that everybody do something for somebody else. Sometimes they actually say to you, "What do you mean, do something for somebody? What's there to do?" I get very close to strangulation. I contain myself. I say, "What's there to do!?"

One of these kids came to me. His name was Joel. And he's become notorious because I tell this story so much. He loves it, and I have his permission to tell it. But he actually said to me, "What's there to do?" and I said, "Joel, come here." Not far from USC there was a convalescent home. I brought him in there. Everybody should go—if you want to see your future, go to a convalescent home. I brought him inside and here were a lot of aged people lying around in beds in old cotton gowns staring at the ceiling. Senility doesn't come from old age. It comes from not being loved and not feeling useful. As long as you are useful, you'll never be *old!* Don't depend on others. You do it yourself. You stay active. You *find* things to do! And meaningful things. Then you say when you get to be 170, "Buscaglia was right."

Anyway, we walked in, and he looked around, and he said, "What'll I do here? I don't know anything about gerontology." I said, "Good! You see that lady over there? You go over and say hello."

"That's all?" "That's all."

She must have been sent by God. He went over and he said to her, "Uh, hello." She looked at him sort of suspiciously for a minute and she said, "Are you a relative?" He said, "No, I'm not." She said, "Good! I hate my relatives! Sit down, son."

And he sat down and they started to talk. Oh my goodness, the things she told him! Like I said, when we ignore our sense of history, we're doomed to repeat everything over again.

This woman had known so many wondrous things about life, about love, about pain, about suffering. Even about approaching death, with which she had to make some kind of peace. But no one cared about listening! He started going once a week and pretty soon that day began to be known as "Joel's Day." He would come and all the old people would gather.

You know what this wonderful woman did? She asked her daughter to bring her a lovely dressing gown. And there she was propped up in her bed one day for Joel in a beautiful satin dressing gown with a very low neckline. She'd had her hair done again, which she hadn't done in ages. Why have your hair done if nobody sees you? The people in that home don't look at you. They *do* to you. I don't want to be done to. Don't do me any favors. Better you should look at me and say, "How are you, Buscaglia?" and mean it, than *do* for me.

Wonderful things began to happen on Joel's day. And probably the greatest triumphant moment in my educational career came one day when without knowing it, I walked out on campus and there was Joel, like the Pied Piper, with about 30 little old people following him, hobbling to a football game!

What's there to do? Look around you. What's there to do? There's a lonely person next to you to touch. There's a hassled saleslady that needs you to tell her that she's great. What's there to do? It isn't monumental. It's *teeny* little things that make the difference. Small things, side, by side, by side.

I'm going to read you something that Elisabeth Kübler-Ross wrote in her last book called *Death: The Final Stage of Growth*. She says:

> What is important is to realize that whether we understand fully who we are or what will happen when we die, it's our purpose to grow as human beings, to look within ourselves, to find and build upon that source of peace and understanding and strength that is our individual self. And *then* [and the accent is mine] to reach out to others with love and acceptance and patient guidance in the hope of what we may become together.

I can't do it alone. It takes two to see one. Four see one even clearer. And everybody in this audience together see even *clearer*. If we really put our love energies to work, we could make Sacramento levitate. The first city in the world to rise up in satellite without the use of anything else except human power!

There's that crazy Buscaglia again, saying these nutty things. I believe it! And then another thing we need to do as lovers is to free ourselves from words. The tyranny of words. Words are traps. You've learned and gotten caught in these traps before you were old enough to really write your own dictionary. So people told you whom you should hate, whom you should love, what was important, why it was important, all the words. And you believed it. And you're still dealing with it.

You know, a word conjures up all kinds of things in you. You think it's just an intellectual exercise? What nonsense! Every time you *hear* a word, you hear a dictionary definition, but you also *feel* something within you. Think about it. *Communist. Catholic. Jew*. You see? *Black man. Hispanic*. And whatever feeling that conjures up to you that's still there, that gnawing something that you learned *years* ago and *never redefined*, is where those words are mentioned. And too often they're full of hate, prejudice and destruction, because you've never bothered to redefine them.

I learned that very early in life because my parents, were Italian immigrants. They came to this country with *nothing!* Absolutely nothing. They settled in Los Angeles and raised their family. And for a long time we didn't even know where our meals were coming from. They worked, both of them worked and worked and worked, night and day. It was wonderful to watch. They taught us about work, and they taught us about responsibility. We didn't sit around. We all had something to *do*. We were a real part of a family.

But we didn't speak English. We were the "Dagos" in the neighborhood, and we were going to make the property values go down. I remember going to school, hardly speaking English, but I spoke fluent Italian. I had learned seven operas. But I went to school, and kids called me Dago and Wop. I remember going home and saying to my dad, "Papa, what's a Wop?" What's a Dago?" "Never mind, Felice. Never mind. Doesn't mean anything. Names can't harm you." But you know, the names *did*. They hurt, because people didn't want me around. And you know what else it did? I was tested by these learned educators. And they decided that, because I couldn't speak English, I was mentally retarded. Another nice label! So they put me in a classroom with mentally retarded children—best education I ever had! I remember very few teachers, but I remember *that* teacher. She was a great, enormous Brunnhilde type. You know, 92" 36" 97". Oh, and talk about a lover! She didn't care that I was a Dago! She used to come and lean over me. I used to remember disappearing in her. The warmth of it all. She hugged me, she felt me, she saw me, and boy, did I produce for her! I wrote all kinds of things, and finally they decided they'd made a grave error. And they moved me out into boredom—they called it "regular" education.

But what was sad is that our neighbors never came to visit us. Here my mother and dad came from a beautiful little village at the base of the Swiss Italian Alps where everybody loved everybody, and if Felice got sick, you made chicken soup and you went to church and lit candles and prayed, and when Felice got well, there was a big festa for everybody. There was no existential problem about "do I exist." Hell, here we don't even know who our neighbors are and we could care less! We go thirty miles across town to friends. We don't even say hello to the people next door to us. It's strange.

But you know, these people missed a lot by labeling me, and by labeling my family. They missed the fact that Mama was a beautiful witch doctor. She had a cure for everything. It was garlic! And you know what she used to do? She used to line us all up when we went to school in the morning and put it in a little pouch, and tie it around our necks. I used to say, "Mama, don't do that, it *stinks*!" And she used to say, "*shut up!*" She was the first nondirective counselor. I went to school with garlic and

I never was sick a day. I used to get special certificates for having 100 percent attendance. Of course I have my theory: no one ever got that close to me! But now I'm very sophisticated. No garlic but colds, malaria, *everything*! She also used to make a thing called *polenta* when you caught colds. She would boil it, spread it on cheesecloth and put some olive oil over the top of it and slap it down on our chests. Because she loved us. She also sang all the time. She loved opera. And she used to sing—one day we were "Carmen," the next day we were "Traviata." All this magical music, all this joy, all this laughter, all this food! We were so many that we used to have to put those wooden horses and put boards on top to seat all the people around the tables.

Oh, and Papa had a wonderful technique about education. Just gorgeous. He never let anyone leave the table until we had told something *new* that we had learned that day. We thought that was *horrible*. And when my sisters and I were washing our hands in the bathroom, I'd say, "What did you learn?" My sisters would say, "Nothing!" And I'd say, "We'd better learn something!" And then we'd sit down at the table, and eat marvelous meals where odors were enough to make the neighbors flip! Then Papa would sit back and pour his glass of wine. He'd curl his little mustache—he has a beautiful little curl on his mustache—and he'd say, "Felice, what did you learn today?" We had memorized something out of the encyclopedia and we'd say, "The population of Nepal is three million, four—" and he would say, "Huh?" And as a kid, I'd think, what a cuckoo man! And I'd say to my friends, "Do you have to tell your father something new?" They'd say "I don't even *see* my father!" And then Papa would look down the table and say to Mama, "Rosa. Did you know that?" And she'd say, "Hell I don't even know where Nepal is!" So we'd get the encyclopedia. We'd find out where it was. It was so much fun. And all of us always had something to share. And even now, when Felice works a hundred hours a day, and he crawls in his sack, he lies back and he hears Papa say, "Felice, what did you learn today?" And if Felice can't find something, I hear Papa's voice saying, "Encyclopedia." I learn something, and then I can sleep.

Life is not a trip in itself. It's not a goal. It's a process. You get there step by step by step by step. And if every step is wondrous, and every step is magical, that's what life will be. And you'll never be one of those people who reach the point of death without ever having lived. Because you've never missed a thing. Don't look over other people's shoulders. Look in their eyes. Don't talk *at* your children. Take their faces in your hands and talk *to* them. Don't make love to a body, make love to a person. And do it now. Because that moment doesn't last forever. It's fast disappearing, and it'll never come again. And most of us spend our lives crying over past moments. Too late! But there are still a million more to come.

One of my colleagues had a massive heart attack. He was around 52 years old. His wife called their daughter, who lived in Arizona, to come at once. She was 22. She rented a car at the L.A. International Airport and drove on the Los Angeles freeway, and was in a violent accident in which she was instantly killed. She was 22 and she's *dead*! He has recuperated. You never know. It's a great, wondrous mystery, and the only thing we know that we have for sure is what is right here right now. Don't miss it. To use it all up is love.

I'd just like to end with something that I'm still working on, but it's something I call "A Start."

> Each day I promise myself not to try to solve all of my life problems at once. Nor shall I expect you to do so.
>
> Take it easy, you can't be the perfect lover tomorrow. But maybe next week. . . .
>
> Starting each day I shall try to learn something new about me and about you and about the world I live in, so that I may continue to experience all things as if they have been newly born.

You're never the same person. After tonight you're different. And when you walk through those leaves, leaving tonight, you're going to be different. And tomorrow morning after breakfast, you're going to be different. Even if it only means you're a little bit fatter.

> Starting each day I shall remember to communicate my joy as well as my despair so that we can know each other better. Starting each day I shall remind myself to really listen to you and to try to hear your point of view, and discover the least threatening way of giving you mine, remembering that we're both growing and changing in a hundred different ways. Starting each day I shall remind myself that I am a human being and not demand perfection of you until I am perfect.

(So you're safe.)

> Starting each day I shall strive to be more aware of the beautiful things in our world.

I know there's ugliness. But there is also beauty. And don't let them tell you any differently. I'll look at the flowers. I'll look at the birds. I'll look at the children. I'll feel the cool breezes. I'll eat good food, and love it. And I'll share these things with you. One of the greatest compliments is to say to somebody, "Look at that sunset."

> Starting each day I shall remind myself to reach out and touch you gently, with my fingers. Because I don't want to miss feeling you. Starting each day I shall dedicate myself again to the process of being a lover, and then see what happens.

You know, I'm really convinced that if you were to define love, the only word big enough to engulf it all would be "life." Love is life in all of its aspects. And if you miss love, you miss life. Please don't.

Together with Leo Buscaglia

I'd like to talk to you about a concept that means a great deal to me, and that is the concept of togetherness. I really am concerned about how separated we all are. Everybody seems to be involved in what Schweitzer talked about so many years ago when he said we're all so much together in crowds and yet all of us are dying of loneliness. It's as if we don't know how to reach out to each other any more, to hold each other, to call to each other, to build bridges. And so I'd like to talk about togetherness, you and I, and some crazy ideas I have about building some of those bridges so that we can get a little bit closer.

I think it's personified, that separateness, loneliness, and despair, by what happened to me recently while I was traveling across country. So many things happen on airplanes. I just love airplanes. You meet old friends you've never seen, you make new friends because people know they may never see you again; it's like true confessions. They tell you about their wives and their husbands. I'm a real people person as you know, and I love to hear about wives, husbands, children, triumph, tears—all the wonderful things that make us human.

In a 747 jet another man and I were lucky to have the area with just two seats. At least *I* thought it was very lucky. He was at the window and as I walked to him I said, "Hello," which I always do, thinking we could start things going. If you're going to be together for five hours, you might as well say "hello," even though some people won't answer. I said, "Hello," and he said, "Oh, damn, I thought this seat next to me was going to be left empty so I could stretch out." And I said, "Oh I promise you that as soon as we get in the air, if there's an empty seat, I'll take it and let you have this one."

I sat next to him and got the seat belt tightened and a woman came on with a little baby. I couldn't help thinking, "Isn't it lucky to have airplane travel for women who have to travel with babies?" I think of Mama when she had little Vincenzo in her arms traveling across the country when she first came from Italy. It took seven days! And here this woman would make it to New York in just about five or six hours. I was thinking this positive thing when he said, "Oh, damn. Look, there's a woman with a baby. The baby is going to squawk all the way to New York." That was number two. We hadn't even taken off yet! Number three occurred when the stewardess announced that there was a "no-smoking section" and he said, "Smokers should be shot!" I said, "All of them? I know some very nice smokers. I don't happen to be one, but I wouldn't want them all to be shot." Then we received the menu. Isn't it amazing that you can fly across the country and only feed you, but they give you a menu with a choice of three entrees? That's phenomenal! He looked at everything and said, "Oh God, they never have anything good on these damn planes." Imagine, we still hadn't taken off yet. And then the stewardess got up and started pointing to the two exits in the rear, two exits in the front, you know how they do? They *have* to do that. He said, "Look at those stupid dames. You know, they don't do anything. They're only there to meet wealthy men. They don't work, they're just glorified waitresses." On and on he went. It was amazing me—all of this before the plane even left the ground.

When we were in the air (I couldn't move; I was stuck there; but I was determined he would be a lover before we arrived in New York), he turned to me and said, "What do you do?" I replied, "I'm a professor at a university." He said, "What do you teach?" And I said, "Courses in counseling and in loving people and relationships." He said, "Thank God, there's someone else who feels about people the way I do." Everybody thinks they are lovers! Before we got to New York I found out his wife had left him and he defined his children as "thankless bums." Isn't that amazing?

Reach out. Learn to reach out. Listen to yourself and hear how many times you say, "I am a lover." My question is, how many times a day do you hear yourself say, "I love," as opposed to "I hate, I hate, I hate." Very interesting phenomenon. I am sick of this kind of an approach to life, that's so centered on "I" and "me." I'm tired of hearing people say "I" and "me." I would love to hear people using "us" and "we" for a change. Isn't that nice? "us" and "we"? "I" is important, but my goodness, the strength that comes from "us" and "we"! You and I together are much stronger than you or I alone, and I like to think that when we get together, I'm not only giving, I'm getting. I will now have four arms, two of yours and two of mine, two heads—that means we've got all kinds of new creative ideas—and two different worlds, your world and my world. And so I want you to come in.

I have learned some very interesting things that I believe are a result of people getting trapped in the concept of "I" and "me." This is from a book called, *On An Average Day In America.* Get this: On an average day in America, 9,077 babies are born, and that's wonderful; 1,282 are illegitimate and not wanted. About 2,740 kids run away from home on an average day in America. About 1,986 couples divorce on an average day in America. An estimated 69 beautiful, incredible people will commit suicide on an average day in America. Someone is raped every 8 minutes, murdered every 27 minutes and robbed every 76 seconds. A burglar strikes every 10 seconds, a car is stolen every 33 seconds, and the average relationship in America today lasts three months. Now if that doesn't freak you out! And that's the world we're creating for ourselves! That's the world of I and me. Well, I don't want to be a part of that world, I want to create a different kind of world—and we can do it together. That's the wondrous thing.

I really have nothing to sell; I have a lot to share. And I'm positive that if we could relate, you could give me some ideas of how we can reverse this trend by recognizing that we can't survive alone and that aloneness and ego involvement leads to death and destruction.

Also we're learning a great deal about learning. I'm a teacher and I've been a teacher all my life and I love being a teacher, but I've only just recently found out that I teach nothing to no one. That's an ego trip if you believe that you can teach anything to anybody. All that I can be, at best, is an excited, wondrous, magical facilitator of knowledge. I can lay it out, but if you don't want to eat it, I can do nothing about it. But I also find that if I can make it attractive and exciting, that maybe a few people get hooked and wonder, "What is that kook talking about? Maybe if he's so crazy about life, maybe life is worth living." When I dance in the leaves, and I do it often, I find that other people get enough courage to go and dance in their leaves, too. And that's good. If I can teach someone to dance in the leaves, I'll run the risk of being called crazy. I love being called crazy because, as I said before, when you're called crazy it gives you a lot of leeway for behavior. You can do damn near anything and everybody says, "Oh, that's crazy Buscaglia dancing in the leaves." And I'm having a ball and all the sane ones are bored to death.

You see, what we really need, the behavior modifiers tell us, are good *models*. We need models of love, people who can show us. Those of you who know my book *Love* know that I dedicated it to my parents, Tulio and Rosa Buscaglia, because they didn't teach me to love, they *showed* me how to love. And they had no idea about behavior modification. But people like Bandura at Stanford are showing us that the best way to teach is by modeling. Without telling anybody anything, without teaching anybody anything, you *be* what you want your children to be and watch them grow.

Many of you know that I grew up in a wonderful, great big, fantastic, loving Italian family and grew healthy and happy and wonderful on bagna calda and pasta fasule and polenta and all those marvelous dishes. But I also learned a lot of other things from these models, most of which was taught without my knowing. One thing they taught me is that we need to be touched and we need to be loved. And so I've been touching and loving all my life and I've been having a ball, touching and loving. It's been so nice and I didn't know that in "the outside world" you don't touch and you don't love—not without reservations. The first note I ever received from a teacher in America was a note written to Mama. You can imagine how sensitive this lady was if she wrote the following to a poor Italian immigrant woman who could barely speak English. "Dear Mrs. Buscaglia. Your son Felice is too *tactile*." Can you believe that? I brought the note home to my mama who looked and said, "Hey what's this a-tactile? Felice, if you did something wrong, I'll smack your head in." I said, "I don't know what tactile is Mama, honest. I don't know what I did." So we went to the dictionary, which we did a lot of, and flipped to the word "tactile." It says, to feel, to touch. Mama says, "So what's wrong with that? That's a-nice. You gotta crazy teacher." I have never had an existential problem as to whether I exist or not. If I can touch you and you can touch me, I exist. So many people are dying of loneliness because they are not touched.

Also, they taught me how to share. We had a tiny house and a big family and boy, do you learn to share! Now we have enormous houses; everybody could get lost. Then we had lots of people and one toilet. Oh, do I remember! That was the center of the house. Everybody was in and out of the toilet all the time and the minute you'd get in there and sit down and relax for 30 seconds, "Get out of there, it's my turn." So you learned to give and you learned to share, you learned to get out and you learned to speed up and you learned to use the same sink and sleep in the same rooms. It's a wonderful thing to learn. I'm convinced that the family that goes to the toilet together, stays together. But now we have a toilet for Mary and a toilet for Sally and a toilet for Papa and a dressing room for Mama. That's too bad—we don't need all that space. It's so funny, but we build enormous houses and we work our fingers to the bone and we say it's for our children. But if you think about it, we bring them into these beautiful houses with lovely furniture and we don't let them live in them. "Don't touch this!" "Don't touch that!" "You're going to break that." For goodness sakes, who's the house for, the neighbors? Not in our house! The house was there for us to live in.

So I learned to share and I learned a wonderful sense of responsibility from Mama, who was a rugged lady. When she said something, it went. This always amused me when I got into the university and I studied theories of counseling and all this permissive stuff. Mama was the most magnificent nondirective, permissive counselor. She'd say, "Shut up!" We always knew what that meant. It was a beautiful kind of interaction with the family. Not too amazing, none of us have ever had a mental problem.

I remember as a kid, I wanted to go to Paris. She said, "Felice, you're too young for traveling." "But, Mama, I want to go." At that time, Jean Paul Sartre and Simone de Beauvoir were all involved in the wonderful concept of existentialism; and Felice wanted to go there because he heard that everybody was in misery and he wanted to go there and be miserable, too. I wanted to try everything. Mama says, "OK, you go, but if you do, you're declaring yourself an adult and don't ask me for anything after that. You're an adult. You're free, go." Oh, was it fantastic! I didn't have a lot of money, but I had a little bit and I went there and I lived everybody's dream. I had a tiny apartment. I could see from my skylight all the rooftops of Paris. I sat at the feet of people like Sartre and de Beauvoir—didn't understand a damn word they said—loved every minute of it. Suffered! Oh, did I suffer! And it was wonderful, on Camembert cheese and French wine. Pretty soon there was no money. I had no real concept of money. I was sharing with everybody, I was the last of the big spenders. I always had the bottle of wine, everyone came to my place to share it. This had been the way I grew up, the modeling I had learned. At our house the postman would come and Papa would pour him a glass of wine. "Eh, poor man, he's working all day. He needs a good glass of wine." We would say, "Papa, don't give him wine!" It would kill us when the teacher came to visit and Papa offered her wine. "The teacher won't drink wine." Then we were shocked when the teacher drank wine. She was no kook. It was good wine! But I remember getting to the point where I really had very little money—almost none. I thought I'd just wire home, that's all. I went to the telegraph office in Paris, and, to save money, just wrote, "Starving. Felice." One word but significant. Twenty-four hours later I had a telegram from Mama and *it* said, "Starve! Mama." The moment of truth! At long last I was an adult. What was I going to do now?

I'm going to tell you what that taught me. It taught me about hunger, it taught me about how cold a place can be, not only physically, but when you don't have the bottles of wine to share, the people who called themselves your "friends" don't come around anymore. It taught me a lot and I never would have learned it if Mama had relented and sent me a check. And I stayed there and stayed there, just to show her I could do it. When I went home many months later, she said to me one evening, "That was the hardest thing I ever had to do, but if I hadn't done it, you would never have grown to be Felice." And it was true. So through modeling, they taught me so much about living and loving together.

I'm often asked to be on talk shows. It always interests me that every other call, if not every single call, has to do with loneliness. "What do I do? I was married, I had kids and now I'm alone. I'm in an old apartment house, by myself. What happened? I would love to make friends with my neighbors, but I'm scared to knock at the door." "I walk down the street and I see attractive people and I try smiling at them, but I'm scared." We're teaching everybody everything there is except what is essential, and that is how to live in joy, how to live in happiness, how to have a sense of personal worth and personal dignity.

Those things are taught, and they're learned. We need more people who teach that sort of thing by doing it, by risking, by saying hello, by sitting next to this man, by trying to show him that the stewardesses are people just like him, that this woman does have a baby and it's wonderful.

Recently on a talk show I heard a woman make an incredible statement. She said, "You know, I've spent the last 20 years trying to change my husband and I'm very disappointed in him. He's no longer the man I married." Isn't that marvelous?

I don't know how many of you know Rodney Dangerfield, but he says the craziest things. This is the zenith of what I'm talking about. He says, "We sleep in separate rooms, we have dinner apart, we take separate vacations, we're doing everything we can to keep our marriage together." Isn't that outrageous? And yet it's almost come to that.

Loving relationships, togetherness, away from "I" and "me" and to "us" and "we," is where the joy really lies. Eating a good dinner by yourself is fine, but sharing it with five or six people whom you love is heaven. Going in the park and looking at the trees by yourself can be lovely, but having someone on your arm who says "Look at the purple ones" while you're looking at the blue ones, and you don't miss the purple or the blue ones, is fantastic! Don't miss togetherness, because it's yours and it's available to you. Erich Fromm, who has written so many beautiful things about togetherness and love, said "The deepest need of man is to overcome his separateness. To leave the prison of his aloneness. The absolute failure to achieve this aim means insanity." And, he's a psychiatrist.

If you think about people who are mentally ill, they're the ones who have moved the farthest away from other people. The healthy ones dive right in the middle, no matter what it means. In love class we talked about risking and going out and I would say, "Why don't you do it?" "Oh, I'm afraid to be hurt." Good grief. What a crazy attitude. Being hurt occasionally can spice up your life. When you're crying, you're at least alive. Pain is better than nothing. We need to reach out, we need to bring in, we need not to be afraid. The biological sciences tell us this. I read something really interesting by Ashley Montague. He said, "Without interdependence, no living group of organisms could ever survive." Imagine—that's *all* forms of life! "And in so far as any group of organisms depart from their functioning, from their requirement of interdependence, to that extent does it then become malfunctional and inoperative." But, he adds, "Whenever organisms are interacting in a related manner, they are conferring *survival* benefits upon each other, giving each other *life*." So, I'm involved in the process of *giving life*. It's the most incredible gift and it's yours to take.

Since all of these things are *learned*, what are some of the things that can bring us together, some of the things we need to know about togetherness, about relationships, about caring, about love? The first is so essential, because we have a very crazy concept in our culture called romantic love. That's why so many of us are disappointed! We really still believe what they tell us in musical comedies, that we look across a crowded room and there we see those special eyeballs that have been waiting for 20 years. You are drawn together, you embrace and walk out into the sunset and never have a problem. What a shame! And what about that wonderful courtship, when you are on your best behavior, she is on her best behavior? She always looks glorious every time you go to the door. You are always (gallant). You even bring flowers and chocolates. You tell her how nice she looks and then you get married and the next day you say, "Who are you?" All of a sudden she appears in rollers. You say, "My God! I married someone from outer space!" "Wouldn't it be nice just once during courtship to answer the door and say, "Look, I wear rollers. So if that freaks you out, it's going to have to be." Why not? Presenting ourselves as we are, you recognize that if you are expecting a relationship to be a continual honeymoon of perfection you're going to be so disappointed.

But there are many kinds of honeymoons. I just love to talk to old people because they can tell you about the honeymoon transitions. Looking back, in order to learn. We don't do that, we're always looking ahead. But in looking back, they can tell you so many things. There was certainly a honeymoon of getting acquainted. Then there was a honeymoon of the first apartment and all that used furniture, maybe even boxes for bookcases, but in those times who the hell cared? You were so happy in that honeymoon. And then there was the honeymoon of the first kid coming. The honeymoon of watching everybody grow up, much to your amazement those 12, 15 years pass so fast and all of a sudden there you are, honeymoon after honeymoon after honeymoon. Elisabeth Kübler Ross tells us even that last honeymoon called "death" can be a glorious experience if we embrace it as we do all the other honeymoons, with no expectations. It's there, it's mine to experience and I want to know it when my time comes. I would like to live that way.

I don't want to harp on Mama and Papa, but since it's so close to me . . . do you know that my mother used to tell us the story that she had never seen my father until five days after they were married? It was an arranged marriage and in Italy when you arrange a marriage, the man comes over to the home and, of course, all the women there were waiting on the table, with him sitting at the table, but she would never dare look at him. She would ask her sisters, "What does he look like?" They'd say "Oooh, he's so handsome. You're really going to freak out on this one." She said she didn't dare look at him. At the wedding her eyes were always down, and that marvelous day about five days into the marriage where she actually turned around and faced him, she said, "I did good!" He already knew it. But isn't it amazing these two people who supposedly didn't go through this period of having to fall madly in love, managed to survive in a beautiful relationship that was constantly growing for over 55 years? If you had seen how close they were when they parted. You just had a feeling that death wasn't going to break them apart, there was some way that it would just be a transitional period and eventually they would be reunited, there's no question about it. So remember always, the most essential thing about a relationship is that one and one together always make two, and if you want to survive the relationship, you must always maintain who you are and continue to grow through change. You are two wonderful, magical individuals. You have your life, he has his life and you build bridges to each other; but you always maintain your integrity and your dignity because all relationships, no matter how magnificent they are, even if they last for 60 years, are temporary, and eventually you are going to be faced again with you. One of the saddest things is the person who has invested everything in a relationship and when the relationship ends they must ask, "What do I do now?"

If you love someone, your goal is to want them to be all that they are and you will encourage them every inch of the way. Everytime they do something that helps them to grow or learn something to help them to become more, you dance and celebrate the occasion. You're not growing apart, you are growing together, but hand in hand, not melting one into the other. You are a unique person, it's impossible to melt into somebody else.

Some of you know the beautiful poem by Gibran about relationships. I'm just going to quote a couple of sentences. It's so lovely. He says, "Sing and dance together and be joyous, but let each one also be alone. Even as the strings of a lute are alone, though they quiver to the same music." Isn't that nice? Go to someone and say, "I want to quiver with you." "Give your hearts, but not into each other's keeping, for only the hand of Life can contain your hearts. Stand together and yet not too near together for the pillars of the temple, in order to hold the temple up, stand apart. The oak tree and the cypress do not grow in each other's shadow." Don't ever grow in anybody's shadow, you cannot *grow* in someone else's shadow. You find your own sunlight and you get as big and wonderful and as glorious as possible. And you share, telling them, "Let's communicate, let's talk, let's let it happen." But it doesn't happen in someone else's shadow. There you wilt, you forget who you are, you lose you and if you've lost you, you've lost the most essential thing you have. So you're one and one but you're two and you're together. You're an "I." He's an "I" and you are together an "us."

Secondly, I think loving relationships and togetherness are made in heaven, but it has to be *practiced* on earth, and sometimes that is very difficult. In fact, I know of nothing that is more difficult. I'm preparing a book now on loving relationships and I've done an enormous amount of research on what I consider to be the most dynamic aspect of human behavior—and I can't find much. If you want to learn about loving relationships, you're hard pressed to do it. Sure, loving relationships may bring pain. Coming together and having to give some of yourself up may bring pain. But you can also learn from pain. It really annoys me when, in our society, nobody wants any suffering at all. The minute you begin to suffer, you start popping pills or drowning yourself in alcohol, not knowing that some of the greatest learning can take place in a state of pain and despair. The difference is, you experience it and you don't *cling* to it. It's sick to *cling* to despair. You experience it and you *let it go*. There are great moments in all of our lives that were despairing. If you think back and you used them well, they helped you to grow and become a far greater person.

I mentioned earlier about how estranged we are from each other. In this culture we learn that the way to meet people is to stand erect and say, "How do you do?" Talk about a distancing phenomenon! If you're really lucky, somebody will give their hand and say "How do you do?" It's usually very quick. It's no wonder that though we all crave each other, we don't have each other, we don't touch each other. In our culture, at the age of five and six, a boy child is told "No more of this hugging nonsense, you're a *man* now and men don't do these things." I'm glad I was in a home where people said, "Who said?" Nobody in my house said, "How do you do?" When the door opened and someone arrived, everybody kissed. Everybody! Nobody was ignored, everybody was touched. What a wondrous experience to be touched in love. And there are many ways of touching. Do you know the wonder of walking into a room and having people happy because you are there? That's the greatest thing. Instead of an expression on their faces saying "Oh my God, there he is again," a joyous smile appears because you've walked in. An aura comes with you that lights up the whole house. Know that feeling? Don't miss it!

What amuses me, is that now we're finding out that scientifically touching does make a difference in our lives, physiologically and psychologically. There is a Doctor Bresler at the UCLA pain clinic. He isn't writing regular prescriptions any more, he's writing a prescription that says, "four hugs a day." People will say the man is crazy. "Oh no," he says, "hug once in the morning, once at lunch, once in the evening and once before bed and you'll get well." Dr. Harold Falk, senior psychiatrist at the Menninger Foundation, said this: "Hugging can lift depression, enabling the body's immunization system to become tuned up. Hugging breathes fresh life into tired bodies and makes you feel younger and more vibrant. In the home, hugging can strengthen relationships and significantly reduce tensions." Helen Colton in her book, *Joy of Touching*, said that the hemoglobin in the blood increases significantly when you are touched, fondled and hugged. Hemoglobin is that part of the blood that carries the vital supplies of oxygen to the heart and to the brain—and she says that if you want to be healthy, you must touch each other, you must love each other, you must hold each other. One of the saddest things in our culture is that we stress the sexual aspect of a relationship way out of proportion. What a pity, because in those things we are often missing the tenderness, the warmth. The kiss when it's not expected, the touch on the shoulder when you really need it most—that's "sensual" gratification. Jim Sanderson, a syndicated columnist who writes for the *L.A. Times*, recently had a letter I just loved. It came from a woman who just gave her name as Margaret. She was 71 years old. Her son came to see her one night and burst into the house without knocking. What nerve! He burst into the house and there was Margaret on the couch really having a blast with one of her boyfriends from the Senior Citizens. Do you know that this man was so horrified to see his mother kissing a man on the couch that he turned on his heels, said, "That's disgusting," and left. What an ass! So poor Margaret writes, "Did I do wrong?" And you know what Sanderson answered her? I've got to read this because it's so beautiful. He said,

> The best things in life, Margaret, go on forever. Every human being requires conversation and friendship. Why do we assume that the needs of older people stop there? The body may creak a little but there is no arteriosclerosis of emotions. Older people literally hunger for caring and affection and physical touching, just like anybody. Adult children and other family members seldom provide anything more than starvation rations—an occasional kiss. We know that sex is perfectly feasible at any age, given good health, but even when this does not seem appropriate for various reasons, why should there not be a little latter day romance, a little love, a little innocent contact, a stolen kiss, a gentle massage, a caress on the cheek, one hand fondling another? Many women of your age, Margaret, often feel strange and alarming stirrings within themselves, feelings that may not have surfaced for years. This is the life force coming to your rescue to remind you that you are a male or a female, not just an all-purpose senior citizen. Rejoice in this, Margaret, you've had enough bad news.

You never cease needing to be recognized in a hundred different ways. Relationships and togetherness must be lived in the *present*. You have to live *now*, you have to enjoy it *now*, you have to do for people *now*. One of the saddest things I heard in the last year was a colleague of mine whose wife died suddenly, very young. Because death is an amazingly democratic thing, it never tells you when it's going to come. We just all know, believe it or not, someday it will come to *us*. And by living every moment you are ready for it. The only people who scream and yell at the moment of death are those people who have never lived at all. If you live now, when death comes you say, "C'mon, who's afraid of you?" But my colleague told me his wife had always wanted a red satin dress. He said, "I always thought that was really stupid and in bad taste." Then he said to me, with tears in his eyes, "Do you think it would be all right if I buried her in a red satin dress?" I felt like doing a Mama and saying, "Stupido!"

If your wife wants a red satin dress, get it now! Don't wait to decorate her casket with roses. Come in one day while she's sitting there alive and inundate her in roses. Throw them at her. We're always putting things off for tomorrow, especially, with people whom we love. Who cares what "people will say"? In reality they don't really care. "It's foolish for me to tell her I love her. She knows it." Are you sure? And do you ever get tired of having somebody say, "I love you?" Do you ever get tired of picking up your coffee cup and finding a little note underneath it that says, "You're incredible"? Do you ever tire of getting a card, not when it's your birthday or Valentine's Day, but a card that says, "My life is so much richer because you're in it"? The time to buy the dress is *now*. The time to give the flowers is *now*. The time to make the phone call is *now*. The time to write the note is *now*. The time to reach over and touch is *now*. The time to say "You're important to me, sometimes I seem to forget, but I don't. My life would be pretty empty without you," with no strings attached, is *now*. Losing a loved one is a hard way to learn that love is lived in the now. It's a hard way to learn that you buy the dress now, or write the note now. But *we* have another chance. That husband *doesn't*.

Loving relationships depend upon open, honest, beautiful communication. Never have a short argument. Never! The worst kind of argument in the world is when you walk in and say, "What's the matter honey?" "Nothing." "Oh, c'mon, there's something." "No, there's nothing." I've found a wonderful way to make the next argument a forever argument; you say "Oh, I'm so glad, it really seemed to me like there was something, and I'm glad to know that there is nothing. Bye." Next time you say, "What's the matter?" they're going to tell you. We don't listen to ourselves and the things that we say.

We need to listen to the way we say things because we've learned them from others. It's like teachers who say to kids, "I'm waiting for Sally!" It's no wonder Sally says, "Wait you old. . . ." But we say things that are just as obnoxious. You hear yourself saying, for instance, "The trouble with you is. . . ." Usually the trouble with me is *you*. "One of these days, you'll be sorry." Oh, *no* I won't. "If I've told you once, I've told you a thousand times." Then what the hell are you telling at me *again* for? "I've given you the best years of my life." If these are the best years, what do I have to look forward to? "Do as you please, it's your life." Well, you know, if it is, will you let ME *live* it?

Togetherness. From "I" and "me" to "us" and "we." Your relationships will be as vital and alive as *you* are. If you're dead, your relationship is dead. And if your relationships are boring and inadequate, it's because *you* are boring and inadequate. Liven yourself up! Be aware that the world and the people in it are not created solely for *you*. Try making *someone else* comfortable. Assume that people are good until you *actually* and *specifically* learn differently. And even then, know that they have potential for change and that you can help them out. Practice using and thinking "us" and "we" rather than "I" and "me." Love *many* things intensely because the measure of you as a lover is how deeply you love how much. Remember that all things *change*, especially human relationships, and to maintain them, *we* must change with them. Make the change in growth. Make sure that you're constantly growing *together* but *separately*. Seek *healthy* people in your life who still remember how to laugh, how to love and how to cry. Remember that misery doesn't only love company, it *demands* it. Have none of it.

And lastly, I heard the Dalai Lama of Tibet last year. One of the things that he said was so poignant. He said, "We live very close together. So, our prime purpose in life is to *help* others." Then he sort of smiled and said, "And if you can't *help* them at least don't *hurt* them." If each of us promised ourselves that in terms of our human relationships and our togetherness, we were dedicated to the process of helping each other to grow, and that if we couldn't do that, we were at least not going to hurt each other, what a magical thing that would be. An Italian poet, Quasimodo, who won the Nobel prize for poetry, wrote a little poem that says: "Each of us stands alone in this vast world, momentarily bathed in a ray of sunlight. And suddenly it's night." The poem is called "Ed e' Subito Sera"—And Suddenly It's Night. If you stand together with me, we can share the sunlight, and believe me, the night won't seem so frightening.

The Paraphernalia of Anti-Self: The Self-Defeating You

Tonight I would like to talk to you about something really important to me. I'm constantly meeting people and working with people—and I'm becoming so very concerned, because the people I meet are afraid to show their wonder and to show their beauty. They are in constant doubt about being beautiful and being wonderful. If there is to be any hope for us as lovers we've got to make sure to express this love and this caring, to bring it out in the open and not be afraid. So I would like to talk to those people who aren't sure yet and are a little bit reticent about being all that they are. I've called the talk, "The Paraphernalia of Anti-Self: The Self-Defeating You," and I give it to you with love.

It's amazing—you may not realize it, but so much of what you are *not* is because you are literally standing in your own way of becoming. And what I'm pleading with you about is, get the hell out of your way! Fly, life and love is all available to you! And all you have to do is take the responsibility and grasp it. But so many people don't trust themselves. They don't believe in themselves. They don't even *like* themselves. I was in the office recently—many of you know that I have a lot of things in my classes that are voluntarily mandatory. And one of the things that is voluntarily mandatory is that everybody comes to visit me. Now that isn't asking too much, but I get frightened people that come in all trembling. I had a lovely girl that sat across from me, and I said, "Tell me about yourself. We're going to be together for sixteen weeks in classes, and I don't want you to be a stranger. You tell me about you and then I'll take over and tell you about me."

And she said, "I don't have anything to say."

I said, "What do you mean? Tell me about all your wonder."

She said, "Wonder?!" And then there was a long pause, and she said, "Well, I'm too short."

You know, that had never occurred to me until she told me. And then I thought, well, I'll counteract with something good. I said, "Yes, but you're a darn good student. Do you know that you got an 'A' in your midterm?"

And she said, "Sheer luck."

How do you like that? I said, "But you know that you're unique in all the world—"

"Not me! I'm not unique." She said, "Stop the baloney! I know I'm not very good looking, and not a lot of people seek me out. And I'm lonely a lot of the time."

It occurred to me that if she really believes that she's short and ugly and stupid and has nothing to contribute, why would anybody seek her out? Oh! Did I work on that one. When she walked out, she was four inches taller and if I ever see her lean over again, there's going to be hell to pay.

Jack Paar says a wonderful thing. He says, "My life seems like one long obstacle course, with me as the chief obstacle."

Isn't that great? And I want to read something to you that I love and will start this all out. It's called "Locked In." It's by a man named Gustavson. He says this:

> All my life I lived in a coconut.

Isn't that a great place to live?

> It was cramped and it was dark, especially in the morning when I had to shave. But what pained me most was that I had no way to get in touch with the outside world. If no one out there happened to find the coconut and crack it open, then I was doomed to lead my whole life in a coconut. And maybe even die there.
>
> I died in that coconut. A couple of years later they found me shrunk and crumbled inside. 'What a shame,' they said. 'If

only we'd found it earlier, then maybe we could have saved him. Maybe there are more locked in like him.'

And they went around and they cracked all the other coconuts within reach. But it was no use. It was meaningless. It was a waste of time. A person who chooses to live in a coconut, such a nut is one in a million. But you know, I couldn't tell them that I have a brother-in-law who lives in an acorn.

Let's not live in coconuts. Let's not live in acorns. There is a world to be appreciated. There are fantastic things to be seen and to be felt and to be desired and to be aimed toward and to be achieved. You are an incredible gift, and you're yours! You were never meant to spend your life in an acorn or in a coconut. That would be the greatest sin, to experience less than what you are.

I love *Souls on Fire*, a book by Weisel, in which there is a beautiful statement. It says that when you die and go to meet your maker, you're not going to be asked why you didn't become a messiah or find a cure for cancer. All you're going to be asked is, why didn't you become you? Why didn't you become *all* that you are?

So stop this paraphernalia of anti-self. How often have you heard yourself say, "I'm nothing." Well, you're nothing if you *think* you're nothing.

Mama would get me aside every night and say, "Felice, some day you're gonna be a *big* man." You know, I'd look at her and I'd say, "Am I?" She'd say, "Wait and see." She did that to *all* my brothers and sisters. Sometimes I get really sad, because in a supermarket I hear mama with her little kid talking to her neighbor, saying, "This is the *dumb* one." She'll say, "Now, his sister, boy, she is the genius."

As if the little kid were deaf! It's a self-fulfilling prophecy. He hears, and what is he hearing? That he's stupid. You become what you believe you are. I always heard at home, "What do you mean, you *can't*—go out and do it!" Somehow or other I found a way to do it. And I'm doing it still! Sometimes people show me schedules, and I think, I can't. At the end of the day, I've done it! It's done. What do you mean you *can't*?

"I *won't*." That's a dead end street, "I won't." If we wanted to get the back of Papa's hand, we said, "I won't." You won't?! POW!

I love the word "Yes." Have you ever thought how beautiful that word is? Sometimes I ask people, "What is the most beautiful word in the English language?" To me, it's "yes." It's even a continuant. It goes on forever. Yesssssssss.

"No" is the end of the line. When you say "no," that shuts the windows, shuts the doors, and you're in your coconut. And if you can't stand "yes," if that scares you too much, try "maybe." At least there's a chance, there's an opportunity! But "I won't?" That's sad. And then I hear, "That's the way it is, and there's nothing that can be done about it." You know, that *isn't* the way it is. And there's always something that *can* be done about it. Just get in there and try.

Oh, I hate this one. "I'm too *old* for that." How often have you heard that I'm too old to go to the park and dance in the leaves? Try it once and see how young you are! We have a big thing about age. I will never tell anybody how old I am. I think it's a hangup. It's sick! Because the minute we attach an age to you, you're supposed to behave like something. If you're sixty years old, you don't dance in the park. Who said? And reporters are always asking, "Buscaglia, how old are you?" I say, "In some ways I am not even born yet. And in other ways, I'm an adolescent and I'm struggling, and I'm rebelling, and I'm really raising hell. And in other ways, I'm a sage, I'm 190 years old. So how can you ask me? What do years have to do with my age?" And when you hear yourself saying, "I'm too old for that," you're also closing doors. You're never too old for anything! Because age is in your head, nowhere else.

I really love this self-defeating idea: "It's a dog-eat-dog world." I don't know about you, but I've never known a dog to eat another dog. Like them? Yes. Eat them? No.

And then this one: "I've been hurt before, and I'm never going to trust again." What's a little hurt? You can learn from pain.

What a silly world we live in, where you believe that everything has to be on a high, joyous level all the time. It kills me. We learn that from the media. We turn on our television set and we see people giddy over cornflakes. They're absolutely freaking out! I saw an ad the other day that I couldn't believe. There was a woman—and I think it's degrading to womankind—she was going out of her mind over a new product called "A Thousand Flushes." Here she was in her toilet saying, "Oh, I love this product!" and "My life is complete!" Good God, if your joy depends on "A Thousand Flushes," you're sick!

But we're all asking the question, if these people are so ecstatic over such simple things as a toilet cleaner, what's the matter with me? I should be happy all the time, too. There's nothing wrong with a little pain. I've learned so many wonderful things over the years in painful situations. In fact, sometimes it takes death to teach us about life; it takes misery to teach us about joy. So embrace it when it comes. Say it's a part of life. Put your arms around it. Experience it! Learn to feel it again. Don't deny it. Maybe it does hurt. Say it's okay to hurt. Scream, yell, gnash the walls. Experience the pain. Cry. Bang on the table! Be angry! Let it come out. And then *forget* it. Otherwise you're going to store it up forever. And you know what happens when you store up pain? It takes its toll from *you*. You're the one who gets the ulcers and the migraine headaches.

So where do we get these self-defeating ideas, these ideas that limit us, the ideas that make us lonely? The ideas that keep us bored? The ideas that kill spontaneity and surprise? They're anti-life. They're anti-growth and they're anti-change. So let's knock it off. And where do we learn them?

Sometimes we learn them from the people we love the most. We learn from our family. If you're going to learn personal growth and dignity, there is no better place to start than in your own home. Sometimes we show the least amount of loving to the people we love the most. We'll compliment people in the office, but we'll never compliment our own children, our own wives, our own husbands. Never let a day go by without seeing something good in the people who surround you. And tell them! Maybe it's going to be difficult that day. You've got to really search. But find *something* good and say, "That was really good." "That was well done."

I'm always telling teachers it's impossible for children to deal with a concept that out of fifty, they got forty-nine wrong. Why not tell them, "Johnny, you got *one* right!" Bravo! "Tomorrow we're going to make it *two*!" Remember that Grandma used to say, "You catch many more flies with honey than you do with vinegar." So why do we concentrate on the vinegar all the time? What you *should* be. What you *should* do. And always under the guise, "I'm telling you this because I love you." This constant criticism is for your own good. So would compliments be! If you love me, say something nice. Okay, I'm a creep. Okay, I'm stupid. But isn't there *something* about me that's *nice*? Think about it. It's a very funny dynamic and yet it's so real. Those people whom we should be reinforcing the most because we love them so much are often the people we tell the least. And that's a pity. So in your homes is where you begin to set this atmosphere of personal dignity. Recently I received a letter from a woman who was with me in elementary school. She had seen me on a TV show. That's the wonderful thing about being on television, all your old friends pop up. She wrote me and she started her letter by saying "There could only be one kook like you." And, "even as a kid you were crazy and now I can see it in you as an adult. And there's only one for sure who has a name like Felice Leonardo Buscaglia. You know what I remember about you, Felice?" And she conjured up something out of the past that I didn't remember anymore. She said, "I remember once everybody surrounding you and making fun of you, because you were in your sister's coat. It was winter and you were wearing your sister's coat."

Suddenly that memory came to me and I remembered how poor we were. And I remember that it was a very cold day, and

Mama took my sister's coat. It had a little fur collar, and it buttoned on the wrong side. She put it on me. I said, "Mama I don't want . . ." You know, my mother, I told you was a wonderful nondirective counselor.

"Shut up!" she said. "You'll be grateful that you have something to keep you warm. What about the people who don't even have a coat to keep them warm? Who cares if it's your sister's coat? If you wear it with pride, you will look good."

Well, it didn't work. But I'd forgotten. In retrospect, the thing that's so wonderful is not the coat or the pain and the being made fun of—"You're in a girls's coat."—you know, that kind of stuff. The thing that I remember is Mama saying, "If you wear it with pride . . ." and "There are some people who don't have a coat to wear." That's learning something vital and positive for life, you see. And that's what we need to do, because we're made, mostly, by the people who surround us. We make each other every day. I'm constantly telling this to people. They say, "Oh, loving is so difficult. I say, "Don't you know how easy it is? Loving is simple. It's we who are complex." Loving means offering the hassled waitress a "Thank you. That was great." I ate recently in a real greasy spoon in Arizona. It was one of those places that you walk in and the odor is enough. Even the rats have deserted. But the food was really good. I had ordered pork chops, and somebody said, "You're crazy. You're gonna die! Nobody eats pork chops in a place like this."

I said, "But they smell so good!" And someone down at the end was having them, and he had an enormous dish! These pork chops were huge! And so I ordered the pork chops, and they were magnificent. After it was over, I said to the waitress, "You know, I'd really like to meet the chef." And she said, "Was there something wrong?"

I said, "No, I want to tell this guy how beautiful it was."

She said, "Oh, my God. No one's ever done that." And we walked back, and he was back there sweating. He was a big man.

And he said, "Whatsa matter?"

I said, "Nothing. Those pork chops were just fantastic and those potatoes! They were really wonderful. I've eaten at some of the best restaurants in the world, and they were as good."

He looked at me like, "God, this man's out of his mind." And then do you know what he said, (because it was so awkward for him to receive a compliment)—he said, "Would you like another?" Isn't that beautiful? That's love. That's all it means. It means sharing joy with people. When you see something beautiful, it means going over and telling them. When you see someone lovely, say to them, "You're lovely." And then back away! Because it's going to scare the hell out of them.

One of the funniest experiences I've ever had—maybe I've even told this to some of you—but it occurs to me now and it's such a beautiful kind of example. I saw this lovely girl on campus. She had golden hair and it was billowing in the sun. It looked so special. I passed her by and it flashed on me: What beautiful hair that girl has. And then as I walked by I thought, I should tell her. So I spun around and I charged back toward her. And she could sort of feel me, you know how you can do. She turned around like "AAAACK!" And I said, "Don't be scared. All I want to do is tell you that you have the most beautiful hair with the sun on it, it's a real trip. I just *really* liked it. Thank you very much."

And then I moved away, because I know about the psychological premise of approach-avoidance. You know, the further you get from the feared object? So I moved slowly away, and as I got further and further away, it began to dawn on her that someone had paid her a compliment. And she started to smile. And by the time I got to the university entrance, she even waved and said, "Thank you." It seemed to me that as she walked away, she stood ever taller, bringing her closer to the sun.

What's so difficult about that? We have those opportunities every single day of our lives, and we don't take them. We start with those people around us. We teach them self respect and we make sure that everybody leaves with their beautiful compliment that day. People say, "Oh, but Buscaglia, that's artificial." It doesn't have to be artificial when you really see it. Don't tell me the people around you don't deserve an occasional compliment. What's artificial about that?

I remember that Mama loved to have her food praised. And we'd all say, "Oh, Mama, this is wonderful!"

And she'd say, "I know, I know, you don't have to tell me." But boy, if we didn't. . . .

And it never hurts anybody to be told that they are loved, to say to somebody, "I love you." People say—especially this is true of men—"Oh, she knows I love her. I don't have to tell her I love her." Oh really? When she's gone, then maybe you'll wonder why. It's a simple thing to say, "I love you." And if you can't say it, write it. If you can't write it, dance it. But say it! And say it *many* times. One never tires of it. One may say, "Oh, never mind telling me that. I know . . ." But it's so nice to hear.

Besides in our homes, we also learn self-defeating ideas in schools. I can tell you that and you can tell me that. I recently talked to a little boy, and the dialogue went like this:

"I can't do that."

And I said, "How do you know?"

He said, "Cause I'm dumb."

I said, "How do you know you're dumb?"

"Cause the teacher told me I was."

Well what hope is there when teachers are going to tell you that you're dumb? It seems to me that we've got to start somewhere by saying, "You have the potential. There's something there. We'll find it together."

Our culture is constantly teaching us to be suspicious. Not to trust. Not to believe. To be afraid of everything! What we're doing is we're building higher and higher and higher walls to protect us from each other! I don't ever want to be protected from *you*. I want to just dive right in the middle of you. I want to experience you. I don't want to be protected from you. I'll trust. And if there are one or two of you who smack me along the way, that's okay. But I don't want to miss you. Never. That scares me most. But our culture keeps telling us these things. "The person next to you can't be trusted." We don't even know our neighbors. And that's a shame. Because what are we doing? We're telling our children also that they must not trust. And we're becoming more and more separated from each other. It's time we start to build little bridges.

Many many years ago I decided I wanted to see what the rest of the world was like. And so I sold everything. All the things that people think are essential. My car, my clothes, everything to make money so that I could go to Asia and see the other half of the world about which I knew nothing. Did people cry there? Did they hug each other there? Were they like me? I needed to know this. I really had an insatiable desire to go out and sit in a little buri somewhere in Indonesia. I wanted to climb a mountaintop in Nepal. And so even though everyone said I was crazy and when I came back there would be no job, and I would be without work, and so on and so forth, I said, "So? I'll survive." And I did. See?

I wandered around places like Bali. I remember arriving in Bali. Talk about beautiful cultural messages that were sent out! I wasn't in my little house more than two hours when at least seven or eight people dropped in. They brought me presents: A piece of batik, flowers to make my place prettier. Gifts! I had nothing to give them. And of course, being from our culture, I felt that we have to give a gift for a gift, never assuming that the gift is enough. I gave them my underwear, and my T-shirts. When I think back, I think, "What a kook you were. Giving these beautiful people in Indonesian batiks, T-shirts!" They also told me that every evening around six or seven o'clock, the whole village went down to the river where everybody bathed together. That was the communal time. Grandma and Grandpa, and the little babies. Everybody was in the river bathing. Do you know the only person that had a problem with that? *ME!* I was sitting there embarrassed. *Your sister's coming in the pool?* They looked at me like, what's the matter with you? Why not?

Also, I remember, it was Christmas Eve. And most of them had never heard the Christmas story. I thought it would be nice to tell them. I said, "This Christmas Eve."

And they said, "What's Christmas Eve?"

So I told them the Christmas story. When you are in a non-Christian country, and you're telling that story, it's ever more special. They listened intently, and they loved it. They thought, "Isn't that magnificent!" But there was one thing they could not understand, and isn't this interesting? "What do you mean they wouldn't let Mary in the inn?"

"Well, you know, there was no *room* at the inn."

"So what does that have to do with it? How much room does a woman take? There's *always* room at the inn."

Try explaining that sometime. She had to give birth in a manger. Really, the last thing that one of the kids said to me as they put me on the bus to go back to Djakarta was, "I still don't understand why you didn't let her in."

There are people who don't know their neighbors. They've been living there for twelve years. Someone comes to the door, and we're afraid to answer the door. What's happening to us? The sad part about it is that once we get these addictions and these beliefs, then everything that we learn that's new, we filter through those beliefs of suspicion and fear and we don't change. They keep us from becoming all that we are. All I'm saying is drop them, because if not, then your world is going to be very limited, full of suspicion and ugliness.

I remember when I was an adolescent, because I was bilingual, I was taking American tourists through Italy. That was the way I could visit my relatives and get it paid for. So I was wandering through places like Venice. That was so beautiful! Don't miss it. I would take them to favorite places, not just the Grand Canal, but little back canals. There's a beautiful little island in Venice that you get to by Vaporetto. Don't take the gondola. It's too expensive. The little Vaporetto is like a seagoing bus and it goes chug-chug-chugging to the island. I used to bring them there, and they'd wander through very uncomfortably, and they'd look around. Do you know what one of them said to me? "What Venice needs is a good *paint* job." Do you know what the Italians call that Island? The Italians call it the Island of the Rainbows. The paint is all faded. It's becoming pastel. It's chipping off the walls. But it reflects in the water in purple and yellow and green. They were not ready to see beauty. All they could see was that what Venice needed was a good paint job.

In southern Italy there's a place called Positano that has a big staircase. They call it Scalinatella. Isn't that beautiful? Big long staircase! There were thousands of stairs, which I always loved to take them down. It was so beautiful. They'd come clomping down. Then half way down they'd say, "What the hell's wrong with these people? What they need is a good escalator." We must be careful that we don't carry our addictions and preconceptions with us and see nothing but ugliness. We're filtering through our ugliness and we're not seeing what *is*. We're seeing what *we're* projecting there. So everywhere we look, we're suspicious. We're fearful. We're afraid. And what are we doing? We're keeping ourselves from beauty and life. Stop working against yourself. Let's get away from this frozen self. Remember that you are a holy thing.

You are God's gift. So give birth to yourself. Allow you out. Get rid of all those self-defeating ideas, self-defeating ideas about others that keep you and me from coming together. Learn to trust again. Learn to forgive. Learn to believe that I am more like you than different.

I don't know where you put me, but believe me, I'm nowhere else than where you are. I'm just as confused. I'm just as lonely.

I'm just as despairing. I cry as often. I have no more answers than you do. I've just stopped asking the questions. I'm just involved in the process. I'm not even asking for answers anymore. I just think it's a wonderful thing that I am. And people write me letters, and they say, why death? Why pain? Why must children die? Why must we be despairing, etc? I write back and say "How the hell should I know?" Greater people than I have been asking those questions for centuries. I don't know why. But I do remember that many, many years ago, somebody said that sometimes we get so involved in the questions that we don't live the answers. I'm very actively engaged in life. I want to experience everything! I want to know everything. Everything that life is, I want to experience. I'm not afraid of you. Because I know that down beyond that veneer that you've created (that is the self-defeating veneer) lies a person just like me, who is questioning, who is fearful, who is alone, who is lonely, who is joyous, who wants to live, who wants to know themselves before they die.

But we go around pretending that we have it all together, that we are so secure, that we don't need when it would be so much easier to be able to say, "I'm vulnerable, I make mistakes. I'm imperfect. I'm afraid. In other words, I'm a human being. And that's my greatest asset. That's really all I want to be."

Someone shared this with me a few years back, and I really like it. It's called, "Don't Be Fooled by Me." And this is what it says:

> I want you to know how important you are to me, how you can be the creator of the person that is in me if you choose to. You alone can break down the wall behind which I tremble. You alone can see behind my mask. You alone can release me from my shadow world of panic and uncertainty and loneliness. So please don't pass me by. I know it will not be easy for you. A conviction of worthlessness builds strong walls. And the nearer that you approach me, the blinder I may strike back. You see, I am to be fighting against the very thing I need the most.

Isn't that amazing?

> But I am told that love is stronger than walls, and in this, lies my only hope. So beat down those walls with your firm but gentle hands, for the child in me is very sensitive and can't grow behind walls. So don't give up. I need you.

We're more alike than we are different. All of us feel that. We need to have those bridges built between you and me, because we need each other. And the real you of you can only really grow with all of the bridges intact of me, of someone else, of the person next to you. All of us feeling the same thing. And give up this business of not trusting each other. It's a gamble, of course. But everything is a gamble! The other night I was leaving my office, and there was a woman in the parking structure. There have been some terrible things that have happened in this parking structure. She was playing with a tire. I saw it, and so I dropped my briefcase in the car and I went over and I said, "Can I help?" It was as if someone was going to hit her! She said, "No, no, I can do it alone, thank you."

I said, "I'd really like to help you."

"No. Thank you. No!" I thought, goodness, what kind of a world is it where someone comes up and says "May I help you?" and it horrifies you?

We need to get away from those self-defeating ideas about our not being wise enough to know what is best for us. Learn again to listen to your own voices and to trust yourself. Nobody knows better than you what is right for *you*. Papa used to always say, "If you don't lead your life, Felice, someone will lead it for you." And that's true. If you're constantly not believing that you have the ability to be the perfect you, someone else is going to take over, and then you're really going to get lost. Don't play "follow the guru." Oh my goodness, are we ever in the scene of, "If I follow what this person says, they're going to make me well." You know if you follow that person what's going to happen? You're going to become them. And only they can be what they are. You're going to get *you* lost. Teachers, gurus, can be guides, but only *you* can take the trip. They can only give you alternatives.

And mistrust someone who says, "This is *the* way." There are *many* ways. And yours is as valid as mine, provided that they all lead to goodness, to gentleness, to beauty, to joy, to growth and not to destruction. Listen to yourself, trust yourself. There are so many columns that you write to about what to do about so and so. How does this person know what to tell *you*? They're fun to read, aren't they? And you think, "Listen to that advice!" Every time somebody writes to me and says, "What shall I do?" I say, "Listen to yourself. The answers for you are in *you*. Because you are already the perfect you. And I don't know what that is. But if you get in touch with it, *you* will." Know that you know and listen to what you know. Then act upon it.

Learn to trust your own voices. Learn to hear again. Learn to believe. Try it out! You'll never know until you do. And then when you do, you know that you're congruent with you and what you're doing is right for you. It's not what Emily Post has told you to do or Ann Landers. She's fun. It's like reading "Peanuts." But how sad to relinquish yourself to "Peanuts." In fact, I think I'd be much better off to relinquish myself to "Peanuts." "Peanuts" gives some pretty good advice. Be suspicious of people who say they have the answers for you. Nobody has the answers for you. Be delighted that they have the answers for them. But take over full responsibility for your own life, and find out what happens. The wonderful thing about doing that is that you not only release yourself and become free, but you allow everybody else to be free, because then you are responsible for all you do, for the actions that you take. And don't be afraid to fail. We live in this society of perfectionism. Forget it!

I always talk about Julia Child. I really like her attitude. *She*'s someone I would write to. I watch her because she does such wonderful things: "Tonight we're going to make a souffle." And she beats this and she whisks that, and she throws things on the floor. She wipes her face in her napkin and she does all these wonderful human things. Then she takes this souffle and throws it in the oven, and talks to you a while. Then says, "Now there's one ready." When she opens it up, it caves in. You know what she does? She doesn't kill herself. She doesn't commit Hari-Kari with her butcher knife. She says, "Well, you can't win 'em all. Bon apetite!" I love it! That's the way we have to lead our lives. You can't win 'em all. You know, "Bon apetite. Sit down!"

But I know people who are still flagellating themselves over mistakes that they made twenty years ago. "I should have done this," and "I should have done that." Well, it's tough that you didn't. But who knows what surprises there are in tomorrow? Learn to say "Bon apetite." Sit down and oink out on today! Life is a picnic. And you can make some mistakes. Nobody said you were perfect. It might even be more interesting. You burned the dinner, so you go *out*.

And then these crazy, self-defeating ideas about age! You know, I commented earlier how sad it is that we're in a society that really puts age in such a strange place. Like all in a sudden, when you get to be a certain magical age, then you're not good for anything anymore. Don't let it happen! Don't believe it. You want to wear a red sequined dress at 87 and dye your hair purple? And wear roller skates? Do it! You know, I hate the titles like "senior citizen." It's better to be called man, better to be called woman, because that's what you are. We've forgotten that people like Galileo, for instance, wrote his last book when he was 74. Michelangelo was 71 when he was appointed supervisor of the Sistine Chapel, believe it or not. Grandma Moses didn't even do her first painting till she was 71. I love that story of Duke Ellington. He was passed over by the Pulitzer Prize Advisory Committee at 66, and he said—and I love this—"Well, God didn't want me to be too famous too young." Isn't that great? He died at 75. Pablo Casals played a concert at the White House when he was 85 years old. Susan B. Anthony, that wonderful lady, was president of the Suffragettes until she was 80 years old, and was going down the street banging her drum. She was arrested at age 52 for voting. She went into the booth and said, "I wanna vote. What do you mean, a woman can't vote?" She was given a new experience—jail!

There's so much you can do. I love the idea that George Bernard Shaw fractured his leg at 96. And you know how he did it? He fell out of a tree that he was pruning. So knock it off!

You can make the decision tonight to drop these crazy, self-defeating ideas, and to be all that God intended you to be, which is the least thing you can do for God. How dare you die without becoming all that you are! And you can do it by making the *decision* to do it. It's as easy as that. That's the way change occurs, and change is always possible. It kills me to hear another self-defeating idea: "You can't teach an old dog new tricks." I've taught a lot of tricks to old dogs. But you have a choice. Life is a choice and it's *yours* to make. You can live it happily or you can live it sadly. You can be giddy. You can be ever so serious. But take full responsibility for the choice you make.

If you're bored, if you're afraid, if you don't like the scene that you're in, get the hell out! Who says you need to be there? As long as your heart and your mind are working and your spirit is high, you can go into any scene you want. You can choose your own. Create a new one. Starting tomorrow, it's going to be different. And then *make it so*, because it only happens in actions. To talk about something is only the beginning. Insight is only half the solution. The rest of it is getting out and *doing* it.

Choose the way of life. Choose the way of love. Choose the way of caring. Choose the way of hope. Choose the way of belief in tomorrow. Choose the way of trusting. Choose the way of goodness. It's up to you. It's your choice. You can also choose despair. You can also choose misery. You can also choose making life uncomfortable for other people. You can also choose bigotry. But what for? It doesn't make sense. It's only self-flagellation. But I warn you that if you decide to take full responsibility for your life, it's not going to be easy, and you're going to have to learn to risk again. Risk—the key to change.

I want to read you this: "To laugh is to risk appearing the fool." So what? I often say that people look upon Buscaglia as being some sort of a nut. Crazy, he is! But I'm having a blast while the sane person is dying of boredom.

"To weep is to risk appearing sentimental." I'm not afraid to cry. I cry all the time. I cry in joy, I cry in despair. Sometimes I read my students' papers and I cry all over them. I cry when I see people happy. I cry when I see people loving each other. I don't care if I appear sentimental. That's tough. I like it. It cleans my eyeballs.

"To reach out to others is to risk getting involved." What else in life is more important than becoming involved? I don't want to stand on an island by myself. The very fact that you and I are together means that we were meant to be that way. Let's find ways of making it a joyous occasion.

"To show your feeling is to risk exposing your humanity." Well, I'm glad to expose my humanity. There would be a lot worse things to expose than my humanity.

"To place your ideas and dreams before the crowd is to risk their loss." That's all right. You can't win 'em all. And you cannot be loved by everybody. There's always going to be someone who says, "He's a jerk. Come on, Mabel, we've heard enough of this. Let's go home." And you know, that's good and that's valid. You can't be loved by everybody, that's for sure.

I always tell, and I write about it, and many of you have heard this a thousand times, but I love it so much. In Love class one night when a girl said, "I know why I'm so despairing all the time. It's because I want to be loved by everybody, and that's a human impossibility. I could be the most delectable, the most delicious, the most wondrous peach in the world, and I could offer it to everybody. But there are people who are allergic to peaches. Then they may want me to be a banana." And so often we become a banana for other people who want peaches. What a messy fruit salad. Isn't it all right to say to them, "I am so sorry I cannot be a banana. I would love to be a banana if I could for you, but I'm a *peach*." And you know what? If you wait long enough, you'll find a peach lover. And then you can live your life as a peach, and you don't have to live your life as a banana. All the lost energy it takes to be a banana, when you're a peach!

"To love is to risk not being loved in return." And that's all right too. You love to *love*, not to get something back, or it isn't love.

"To hope is to risk pain." And, "To try is to risk failure. But risk must be taken, because the greatest hazard in life is to risk *nothing*. The person who risks nothing does nothing, has nothing, and is nothing. He may avoid suffering and sorrow, but he simply cannot learn, feel, change, grow, live, or love. Chained by his certitudes or his addictions, he's a slave. He has forfeited his greatest trait, and that is his individual freedom. Only the person who risks is free."

To keep you hidden, to lose you because of self-defeating ideas is to die. Don't let that happen. Your greatest responsibility is to become everything that you are, not only for your benefit, but for mine.

Acknowledgments

The author is grateful to the following publishers who gave permission to reprint excerpts from selected materials:

Sorokin, PA: *The Ways of Power and Love*. Chicago. Henry Regnery Co. 1967. © Copyright 1954 by The Beacon Press.

Laing, RD: *The Politics of Experience*. New York . Ballantine Books, 1976. © Copyright, Penguin Books.

Castenada, C: *Teachings According to Don Juan*. New York, Ballantine Books, Inc, 1978. © Copyright. 1975 by The University of California Press. Used by permission of Viking Penguin Inc.

Miller, A: *After the Fall*. New York, Viking Books. © Copyright 1964 by Arthur Miller. Used by permission.

St Exupéry, A de: *The Little Prince*. New York. Harcourt Brace Jovanovitch. Inc, 1971. © Copyright by Harcourt Brace Jovanovitch, Inc. Used by permission.

Hammerskjold, D: *Markings*. New York, Alfred A Knopf. Inc, 1964. © Copyright by Alfred A. Knopf, Inc. Used by permission.

Tzu, L: *The Way*. New York. Bobbs Merrill Co. Inc. 1962. Used by permission.

Dostoyevsky, FM: *The Idiot*. New York, New American Library, 1935. © Copyright by New American Library. Used by permission.

Weisel, E: *Souls on Fire: Portraits and Legends of Hasidic Masters*. New York, Random House, Inc, 1973. Copyright by Random House, Inc. Used by permission.

Kubler-Ross, E: *Death: The Final Stage of Growth*. Englewood Cliffs. NJ, Prentice-Hall. 1975.

If you enjoyed this book,

You might like to read more by Leo Buscaglia . . .

Loving Each Other
The classic guide on how to build loving relationships;
4 million copies sold

Love
The findings of Buscaglia's extraordinary
university course on love